To Katherine, Aidan and Emily
for all your love and support.

contents

	Preface		pg. IX
	Intro	**The Hawthorne Hotshots**	pg. XIII
1	David Marks on . . .	**"Surfin' U.S.A."**	pg. 1
2	Dennis Diken on . . .	**"Shut Down"**	pg. 9
3	John Sebastian on . . .	**"Surfer Girl"**	pg. 13
4	Alice Cooper on . . .	**"In My Room"**	pg. 17
5	Hal Blaine on . . .	**"Fun, Fun, Fun"**	pg. 23
6	Roger McGuinn on . . .	**"Don't Worry Baby"**	pg. 28
7	Daniel Lanois on . . .	**"I Get Around"**	pg. 34
8	Alan Boyd on . . .	**"Kiss Me, Baby"**	pg. 39
9	Jon Stebbins on . . .	**"Do You Wanna Dance?"**	pg. 44
10	Alan Jardine on . . .	**"Help Me, Rhonda"**	pg. 48
11	Peter Bagge on . . .	**"I'm Bugged at My Ol' Man"**	pg. 55

12	James Mercer on . . .	"Girl Don't Tell Me"	pg. 62
13	Carol Kaye on . . .	"California Girls"	pg. 66
14	David M. Beard on . . .	"The Little Girl I Once Knew"	pg. 71
15	Dean Torrence on . . .	"Barbara Ann"	pg. 76
16	Scott Totten on . . .	"Sloop John B"	pg. 84
17	Tony Asher on . . .	"I Just Wasn't Made for These Times"	pg. 89
18	Jim Fusilli on . . .	"Caroline, No"	pg. 97
19	Sean O'Hagan on . . .	"Let's Go Away for Awhile"	pg. 102
20	Zooey Deschanel on . . .	"Wouldn't It Be Nice"	pg. 108
21	Lyle Lovett on . . .	"God Only Knows"	pg. 113
22	Al Kooper on . . .	"Here Today"	pg. 119
23	Jace Lasek on . . .	"Good Vibrations"	pg. 123
24	Robert Schneider on . . .	"Heroes and Villains"	pg. 129
25	Carnie Wilson on . . .	"Our Prayer"	pg. 139
26	Mark Linett on . . .	"Surf's Up"	pg. 143
27	Matthew Sweet on . . .	"Wonderful"	pg. 149
28	Danny Hutton on . . .	"Darlin'"	pg. 153
29	Stephen Kalinich on . . .	"Little Bird"	pg. 159
30	Ira Kaplan on . . .	"Meant for You"	pg. 164
31	Mike Kowalski on . . .	"Do It Again"	pg. 168
32	Gregg Jakobson on . . .	"Forever"	pg. 174
33	Scott McCaughey on . . .	"This Whole World"	pg. 181
34	Adam Marsland on . . .	"Long Promised Road"	pg. 186
35	Cameron Crowe on . . .	"Feel Flows"	pg. 191
36	David Leaf on . . .	"'Til I Die"	pg. 195
37	Bruce Johnston on . . .	"Disney Girls (1957)"	pg. 200
38	Blondie Chaplin on . . .	"Sail on Sailor"	pg. 206
39	Jim Guercio on . . .	"Good Timin'"	pg. 215

40	Earle Mankey on . . .	**"It's OK"**	pg. 222
41	Peter Ames Carlin on . . .	**"Johnny Carson"**	pg. 229
42	Billy Hinsche on . . .	**"Farewell My Friend"**	pg. 235
43	Randy Bachman on . . .	**"Keepin' the Summer Alive"**	pg. 242
44	Steve Levine on . . .	**"Getcha Back"**	pg. 248
45	Russ Titelman on . . .	**"Love and Mercy"**	pg. 255
46	Mike Love on . . .	**"Kokomo"**	pg. 261
47	Don Was on . . .	**"Still I Dream of It"**	pg. 268
48	Darian Sahanaja on . . .	**"Mrs. O'Leary's Cow"**	pg. 275
49	Scott Bennett on . . .	**"Midnight's Another Day"**	pg. 283
50	Brian Wilson on . . .	**"Rhapsody in Blue"**	pg. 289
	Endnotes		pg. 297
	Acknowledgments		pg. 306
	Index		pg. 309

PReFaCe

The Beach Boys have assumed the title of "America's band," and why not? Their success on the *Billboard* charts puts them ahead of all challengers: 36 top 40 singles, including four number ones; 23 top 40 albums, including two number ones. They've sold a purported 100 million–plus records and played before countless fans worldwide — including nearly 2,000,000 in just one day. *Rolling Stone* ranked them the twelfth greatest artists of all time. They were inducted into the Rock and Roll Hall of Fame in 1988 alongside The Beatles, Motown founder Berry Gordy Jr.,

The Supremes, The Drifters and Bob Dylan, and received a Grammy Lifetime Achievement Award in 2001.

As the band's surviving members marked their 50th anniversary with the international Celebration tour and a new album, its past was one well worth honoring. But it's not just history: the music remains as fresh and heartfelt, innocent and sophisticated, as it did when it first came over the airwaves. And the group's impact on popular culture transcends the beautiful sounds it created. The Beach Boys' songs have enhanced the reputation of their home state of California as the playground of the young, helping forge an image that continues to hold sway around the world.

The group first cast its spell on me when I was seven, around the time I witnessed Bruce Jenner's gold-medal decathlon performance at the 1976 Summer Olympics in my hometown of Montreal. I had no musical favorites, but that changed when my 15-year-old cousin Tracy slipped a pair of headphones over my ears and put on an 8-track tape of *Best of The Beach Boys Vol. 2*. I was captivated. The melodies, the harmonies — the *emotion* — in that music hooked me, and from then on every time I came over to my cousins' house I would play "Don't Worry Baby," "California Girls," "Help Me, Rhonda" and "I Get Around" in a seemingly endless loop.

My family didn't own an 8-track player, but I then realized what our record player was for. I convinced my parents to buy me The Beach Boys' *20 Greatest Hits* LP I saw advertised on TV, featuring those songs I loved and 16 more from their initial 1962–1965 creative spurt. Then I got *Good Vibrations — Best of The Beach Boys*, which focused on the more esoteric ensuing years. I couldn't get a handle on the intricacies of "Surf's Up" and "Heroes and Villains," but I loved most of the other songs. Then there was *Beach Boys '69* (a.k.a. *Live in London*), which documented the excitement of the band's concerts.

And soon I would get a chance to see them for myself. They were coming to the Montreal Forum on July 12, 1979, and all I knew was I had to go! My mother wasn't keen about me going to my first rock concert, but Tracy agreed to take me and assured my mom she would hold my nose if any errant marijuana smoke wafted in our direction. What I remember most about that show was Brian Wilson, who sat at the piano at the side of the stage, very much in his own world, more interested in smoking cigarettes than playing. I had seen stories on TV about Brian and his return to the band after a self-imposed retreat, but couldn't really understand the fuss. I didn't care who had written all those great songs; I only cared who sang them! I still had a lot to learn about The Beach Boys.

My education began soon afterwards. As a thank-you for my parents' having bought her ticket, Tracy gave me David Leaf's 1978 Brian biography *The Beach Boys and the California Myth*. It was way over my head, but I held onto it and revisited it frequently over the years. To me and most of the world,

The Beach Boys sang about surfing, cars and the girls on the beach. But Leaf discussed at length their introspective and acclaimed *Pet Sounds* album, and even more fascinating were the chapters about its aborted follow-up *Smile*. My fanaticism was further fueled.

And over the years it remained solid. I grabbed every band-related record, magazine article, book and video I could find. But I do recall that when I was in CEGEP (the Quebec equivalent of junior college in the U.S.) I kept my fondness for the group under wraps. It just seemed so *uncool* to like them. One day I brought some Beach Boys records to school for a friend who had asked to borrow them, and I freaked out when he pulled them out of the opaque bag I'd put them in. I didn't want anybody to see. But that self-consciousness quickly passed, and with a Brian Wilson comeback in 1988 — another one, this time as a solo artist — and the later rediscovery of the group's back catalog on CD, many others got hip to The Beach Boys.

I always had wanted to write a book about the group, and after a decade as an entertainment journalist in Toronto, I finally decided to do it. Aptly enough, the idea came to me on the beach. Mind you, not in Del Mar or Manhattan Beach or any of the legendary locations name-checked in "Surfin' U.S.A.," but on the significantly chillier shores of Lake Huron. The band's forthcoming 50th anniversary provided a perfect opportunity for reflection, and I figured what better way to mark the occasion than have 50 people discuss a Beach Boys song that's somehow meaningful to them. In this book, band members — except, sadly, Brian's younger brothers Dennis and Carl, both long gone — and key collaborators provide eyewitness accounts of the band's evolution and the creation of its most memorable records. The Beach Boys' contemporaries recall the music's initial impact, while modern-day artists explain its continuing influence. Finally, fellow authors reveal how a song inspired them to explore The Beach Boys' saga.

I conducted the interviews from September 25, 2009, to July 18, 2011. They were done expressly for this book, except for my Brian interview, which was for an August 25, 2010, feature in Canadian newsweekly *Maclean's*. Most of the interviews were conducted over the phone, while Peter Bagge, Scott McCaughey and Cameron Crowe communicated via e-mail. I spoke in person with Darian Sahanaja prior to a Brian show at Milwaukee's Pabst Theater on October 24, 2009, where I was introduced to Brian.

The number of people who have played a role in The Beach Boys' story, plus the musicians and writers they have touched, quickly runs into the hundreds, so, inevitably, only a fraction are included. That is not to diminish the significance of those who are not. There are some missing voices that should be noted. Not accounted for is official member Ricky Fataar, who drummed, composed and produced for the band from 1972 to 1974, but who did not respond to multiple interview requests. Brian's first wife Marilyn Wilson-Rutherford, singer in Brian-produced girl groups The Honeys and Spring, and Van Dyke Parks, Brian's *Smile* collaborator, replied in the sweetest way possible that they are largely stepping away from Beach Boys Q&As.

Each of those who did participate brings his or her unique point of view, the aim being to provide a broad and balanced perspective on the band. Using a light hand, I tried to guide which songs each would discuss, in an effort to include the most praised, popular and representative cuts of the group's career. Sometimes, the match of song to interviewee is obvious as he or she was directly involved in its creation or, as an outside artist, has covered the tune. Whatever the case, I wanted each interviewee to choose a track based on a strong connection. As a result, there are a disproportionately high number of selections from *Pet Sounds*, the *Smile* era and even *Surf's Up*, yet nothing from the worthy *Carl and the Passions — "So Tough."*

I have included one cut from Dennis' *Pacific Ocean Blue* solo album, which garnered ecstatic reviews in 1977 and when rereleased in 2008, and five from Brian's solo career, which is where the story goes in terms of significant studio work from 1988 to 2012, with The Beach Boys' anniversary reunion album pending. And while 50 may sound like a lot of songs, missing are such favorites as "Little Deuce Coupe," "Be True to Your School," "The Warmth of the Sun," "When I Grow Up (To Be a Man)," "Dance, Dance, Dance," "Wild Honey," "Friends," "I Can Hear Music," "Break Away," "Cotton Fields," "Add Some Music to Your Day" and many more, which speaks to the depth of the band's catalog. There will be no shortage of material left to dissect on the group's centenary.

THE HAWTHORNE HOTSHOTS
INTRO

The 50th anniversary celebrates events that began in 1961, when Brian (then 19), his brothers Dennis (16) and Carl (14), their cousin Mike Love (20) and Brian's school chum Alan Jardine (19) formed a band called The Pendletones, named after the plaid Pendleton shirts they favored.

Music was in the Wilsons' blood. Their father, Murry Gage Wilson, was a small-time songwriter whose peak was the performance of his composition "Two-Step, Side-Step" on Lawrence Welk's radio show. Murry was born on July 2, 1917, in the railway town of Hutchinson, Kansas, and at age four moved to California with his mother and siblings (who eventually numbered six). As recounted in Timothy White's *The Nearest Faraway Place*, there they met up with their father, William Coral "Buddy" Wilson, a master plumber swept up in the notion of the Golden State as Promised Land. The family got off to a humbling start there, however, living in a tent on the beach in Cardiff, but things quickly looked up thanks to an oil boom in Huntington Beach, where Buddy laid pipe. They soon moved to a small apartment in Pasadena, and then into their own house. By 1929, they had settled in Inglewood. But while Buddy may have improved his family's lot economically, he also terrorized them with drunken, violent outbursts. These were temporarily forgotten during family sing-alongs.[1]

Murry married Audree Korthof in 1938 and the young couple moved to south Los Angeles. First child Brian was born on June 20, 1942. Like his father, Murry possessed a stormy personality that contrasted with Audree's cheerful disposition, but they shared a love for music. They would sing duets, he at the piano and she at the organ, as he dreamed of writing the hit that would put them on Easy Street. For the time being, however, they had to be content with a bungalow at 3701 W. 119th Street, a couple of miles south and west in Hawthorne, where Murry moved the family after Dennis was born on December 4, 1944. Baby brother Carl rounded out the family with his arrival on December 21, 1946. Hawthorne was touted early in the century as "the town between the city and the sea," situated as it is just three miles from the Pacific Ocean and a 30-minute ride from Los Angeles on the Redondo Electric Car Line.[2] Like Murry, many of its 15,000 residents had come from America's Dust Bowl towns looking for a sunnier future.

But for Murry, Hawthorne only brought hardship. In 1945, while working at the Goodyear Tire & Rubber plant, an acid-dipped pole flew into his left eye, damaging it irreparably, and subsequently he had to wear a glass replacement. He soon quit Goodyear, then worked five years as a foreman at AiResearch, an aeronautics manufacturing company, followed by a post with brother Doug at a heavy-machinery leasing business.[3] Itching to get out on his own, he borrowed money to launch the ABLE (Always Better Lasting Equipment) Machinery Company, which imported British lathes.

If Murry's secret dreams of songwriting fame and fortune had yet to pan out, Brian showed tremendous potential from an unnaturally early age. Murry would brag that his son could hum the entire "Marines' Hymn" before his first birthday, and one year later Brian was already enraptured by George Gershwin's "Rhapsody in Blue." His formal musical education consisted of little more than six weeks of accordion lessons and a couple of high school and college classes. The radio proved a better teacher, and hearing the sophisticated, jazzy vocal harmonies of The Four Freshmen provided a musical awakening. He would spend hours dissecting their records and then distributing the harmony parts to Murry, Audree and Carl. Dennis wasn't interested. Brian then became obsessed with playing the piano. According to a story in David Leaf's book, Brian learned about musical arranging from a record entitled *The Instruments of the Orchestra*.[4]

Murry expected much from his gifted son and would come down hard on him verbally and physically. It is popularly believed that a childhood blow inflicted by Murry was the cause of near-total deafness in Brian's right ear. (Other theories are that it was caused by a punch from a neighborhood boy or that it was a congenital defect.) Murry's abusive behavior towards his boys would send Audree to the bottle or to the kitchen, where she would serve up lovingly heaping meals. Brian was afraid of his father and carried that anxiety everywhere, but his childhood wasn't all gloom. He had a prankish sense of humor and played lots of sports, for which his tall build was well suited. He played centerfield for his varsity baseball team and quarterback for the Hawthorne High Cougars. Murry would stand on the sidelines and criticize his performance,[5] while Brian did his best to win his father's approval. Like his mother, he just wanted to make everybody happy.

Dennis was the lone wolf, the wild middle-child. He didn't care for the family meals or vocal sessions. With a cocky expression and blond crew cut, he liked to play with fire — figuratively and literally. He received the brunt of Murry's beatings, but as much as he tried to distance himself from his father, he displayed the same volatility. If he wasn't off fighting some other guy in the neighborhood, he was trying to seduce one of the girls. He found an escape in surfing. He loved the thrill of the sport and the whole beach culture — not least of all the honeys.

Baby brother Carl was good-natured. He was Audree's favorite, which seemed to forever irk Brian. Carl was more grounded than his brothers, but not without his vices, which included overeating, smoking and truancy. Nonetheless, he was spared much of Murry's wrath. He was the next to follow a musical path, getting his first guitar when he was 12. He would jam with David Marks (born August 22, 1948), who lived across the street and was two years his junior. Together they took lessons from John Maus, later known as John Walker of pop group The Walker Brothers. Carl loved Little Richard, Chuck Berry and Johnny Otis, and when he played these R&B artists for Brian, it knocked his older brother's socks off. Brian then decided he was going to fuse his jazz influences with rock 'n' roll.

More than seven miles north in View Park, Murry's younger sister Emily "Glee" Wilson Love, her husband, Milton, and their six children lived in an impressive house at Mt. Vernon Drive and Fairway Boulevard. Milton had made a small fortune in the family sheet-metal business. Music was similarly prevalent in the Love household. Glee was an opera enthusiast and at Yuletide gatherings she taught Christmas carols to her children and the Wilson boys.[6] Oldest son Mike (born March 15, 1941) was more excited about R&B and doo-wop, and he and Brian would harmonize on Everly Brothers songs. Mike got a hard dose of adult life when, in early 1961, he had to marry his pregnant girlfriend, Frances St. Martin.[7] He supported his young family by pumping gas and working at his dad's factory. When his father's business quickly and unexpectedly failed, Mike's situation became dire, and if some kind of career

could be built on the musical synergy he had with Brian, he couldn't wait to get started.

Unlike the others, Alan (born September 3, 1942) was not born in California, but rather in Lima, Ohio. His father, Donald, had been plant photographer for Lima Locomotive before the family moved West and ended up in Hawthorne, where Alan, blond and 5'4", played football with Brian at Hawthorne High. He shared the musical ambitions of Brian and Mike, but his tastes leaned towards folk music, his favorite act being the striped-shirted Kingston Trio. He sang in his own folk combo called The Islanders, and Brian invited him to sing with him, Carl and Mike.

Alan was eager to get in a studio, so Murry set him up with Hite and Dorinda Morgan, who ran mom-and-pop publishing company Guild Music and had a facility for recording demos. Alan and a couple of friends auditioned some folk standards and were promptly sent back to the drawing board. In late August 1961 he again auditioned for the Morgans, this time with the three Wilson brothers and Mike. (Dennis may not have previously displayed much musicality, but he didn't want to be left out.) The Morgans told them the same stumbling block remained: they needed original material. Good thing Dennis was there, because he boldly interjected that Brian and Mike had been cooking up a song about surfing — one that he had suggested. The Morgans knew nothing about surfing, but figured if there were a lot more kids like Dennis who loved it, then there was a market for surf music. They told the boys to come back when the song was finished.

Brian and Mike got going on their composition, simply titled "Surfin'." They were inspired by L.A. duo Jan & Dean, who proved local kids could achieve national success, as they had with their 1959 top 10 single "Baby Talk." Jan Berry had scored an earlier hit with Arnie Ginsburg — recording as Jan & Arnie — called "Jennie Lee," the name coming from an exotic dancer from San Pedro known as "Miss 44 & Plenty More."[8] The doo-wop vocals on that record are believed to have influenced "Surfin'."

The guys practiced hard. According to legend, when Murry and Audree went on a trip to Mexico City with some British guests, the Wilson boys took the emergency food money their parents had left — topped up with a loan from Alan's mother, Virginia — and rented professional equipment. Dennis, who became the drummer by default, bought a drum kit. Carl played guitar, Alan standup bass. They rehearsed and taped the song in the Wilsons' garage, which had been converted into a music room. Murry may not have been pleased when he and Audree returned to find all the food funds gone, but when the boys played back their song, he could hear the promise in it. "Surfin'" was primitive, but undeniably exuberant.

On September 15, 1961, The Pendletones returned to the Morgans' studio to record their first demos, including "Surfin'," "Luau" — written by the Morgans' son Bruce — and "Lavender," written by Dorinda. The results were encouraging enough that the Morgans signed the group to a publishing contract and booked time at the World Pacific studio to professionally re-record the songs with Hite producing. Although Dennis sang background vocals at that October 3 session, his drumming was deemed not good enough, so the group brought along a fill-in. When that mystery player didn't work out either, Brian ended up putting a shirt down over a drum and playing with his hand. It was all very seat-of-the-pants, but youthful enthusiasm won the day.

Guild Music got the group signed to a local

label run by brothers Robert and Richard Dix, who planned to release "Surfin'"/"Luau" as a single. They didn't care for the Pendletones name, however, and unbeknownst to the group it was changed to "The Beach Boys" from an off-the-cuff suggestion by Russ Regan at Buckeye Record Distributors, which distributed the Dixs' product. The group was not sure about the new moniker when they heard about it, but if that's what it took to get its music out there, so be it. The single was released in various pressings in November and December on the Dixs' X and Candix labels, and the boys had the thrill of their young lives when they heard "Surfin'" on local radio stations KFWB and KRLA.

They promoted that song and another at a show headlined by surf-guitar titan Dick Dale on December 23,[9] but their lack of stage experience was evident. Things went smoother when they played on a bill with Ike & Tina Turner at the Ritchie Valens Memorial Concert in Long Beach that New Year's Eve. The $300 they received made the whole enterprise seem viable, and if they needed further assurance, the popularity of "Surfin'" continued to swell. By March 1962 it had landed at #75 on the *Billboard* national chart.

This initial elation turned to mixed feelings when the group received its royalty check for $900. Murry suspected they were being shortchanged. He added $100 out of his own pocket so that each member got an even $200. Nonetheless, the guys remained excited — except Alan. He felt the payoff hadn't been worth it, and opted for the safer bet of continuing his studies at El Camino College, focusing on dentistry. In February 1962, he announced he was quitting the band. Brian, who had begun stockpiling songs, was livid. Just as things were starting to roll, the band was losing one of its founding members.

Alan's bombshell came just as the group was plugging in. Brian had taken up the electric Fender Precision bass and also wanted a pair of electric guitars in the band. He needed a rhythm player to back up Carl's leads, and David Marks, who had been waiting in the wings, provided an instant solution. In April, when Murry brought the boys into Western Studio to record "Surfin' Safari," the racetrack-themed "409" and the moody ballad "Lonely Sea," their lineup consisted of the Wilson brothers — with Dennis now holding his own on drums — and Mike and David. Unhappy with Hite Morgan's work on

"Surfin'" and looking to protect his sons from the suits — and no doubt to realize his own ambitions — Murry assumed the role of group manager and produced the recordings himself. Candix soon went belly-up and Murry walked away from the deal with the Morgans. He saw something bigger ahead.

He brought the tracks to Capitol Records' young surfing A&R man Nick Venet, who eagerly bought them. Capitol readied a June release for a single featuring "409," backed on the B-side by "Surfin' Safari." The latter actually became the bigger radio hit. It was vastly superior to "Surfin'" and reached #14 on *Billboard* and the top spot in surf-friendly Sweden. On July 16 the boys signed with Capitol, and in August and September they recorded enough material to fill an album. On October 1, the *Surfin' Safari* LP was on record-store shelves. It was raw, ranging from cutesy ("Ten Little Indians," "Cuckoo Clock") to charming ("Chug-a-Lug," "Little Miss America"). It was no artistic triumph, but it was a lot of fun and a fair success, peaking at #32.

The group had gotten off to a promising start. It was about to become a national phenomenon.

David Marks on ...
SURFIN' U.S.A.

Written by: Chuck Berry
Lead vocal: Mike Love
Produced by: Nick Venet
Recorded: January 5, 1963
Released: March 4, 1963
Chart peak: U.S. #3, U.K. #34
Appears on *Surfin' U.S.A.*

"Surfin' U.S.A." not only established The Beach Boys as a top American group on par with The Four Seasons, but the song's clever lyrics also helped take surfing from a Southern Californian craze to something kids all over the country could do — if they only had an ocean. Brian's early influences are all over the classic track, from Chuck Berry to The Four Freshmen, while Carl and David cop some guitar licks from pioneering rock 'n' roll instrumentalist Duane Eddy.

"That's really what made the band unique — the combination of those things," says David. "The way Carl and I married our electric guitars with Brian's jazz voicings and vocal harmonies was the key — something that blended so well and created such a unique sound." In this case, the result was a #3 smash hit in America.

David's role on "Surfin' U.S.A." — and in The Beach Boys' development in general — is sometimes reduced to a footnote, but he helped author Jon Stebbins set the record straight in the 2007 biography *The Lost Beach Boy*. David was part of The Beach Boys' initial wave of success, playing on their first four albums and seven top 40 singles. He believes one of the biggest misconceptions about him "is that

1

Al Jardine and I are somehow adversaries. The fact of the matter is we were in The Beach Boys at the same time. I would say, technically, there were six Beach Boys in the beginning."

Alan has said that "Surfin' U.S.A." was in the works before he left.[1] Brian took the melody from Chuck Berry's 1958 hit "Sweet Little Sixteen" and also used Berry's idea of rhyming off the names of cities where, in the original, all the rockin' was going on. In the commonly accepted version of the story, Brian substituted in the names of surfing hotspots like Del Mar and Doheny, drawn from a list supplied by Jimmy Bowles, brother of his then-girlfriend Judy. However, in a 1994 interview on U.S. TV newsmagazine *A Current Affair*, Mike claimed to have written the words, referring to himself as the group's "surfboard man."

Regardless of who devised the lyrics, Brian then approached Carl and David to work out the guitar sound on their Fender Stratocasters. David gives a tip of the hat to Duane Eddy. "He was one of the people we were studying when we were starting off playing guitars," he explains. "The opening riff to 'Surfin U.S.A.' came from the Duane Eddy song 'Movin' N' Groovin,' which has in its middle part a half-step twang riff that we used in a lot of our other songs."

Although Nick Venet gets producer credit on the *Surfin' Safari* and *Surfin' U.S.A.* albums, there is little doubt Brian was already the band's main creative force and that Murry was also exerting his influence from the control room. "Surfin' U.S.A." demonstrated Brian's growing record-making skills. Despite its borrowed elements, it is far from a mere knock-off. His colorful production makes "Sweet Little Sixteen" sound downright monochromatic by comparison. It was the first song where he double-tracked the lead vocal, which was sung with newfound authority by Mike. Layering two separate performances of the vocal created a fuller sound and would become a signature Brian technique. The song also features Brian's rollicking organ segment followed by Carl's stinging solo, arguably his most memorable ever. David's fills, meanwhile, keep things marching forward. It all adds up to the group's first anthem — a clarion call for kids everywhere to catch a wave.

David likens the way he and Carl gelled instrumentally to the way the group harmonized. "It sounded usually like one guitar when we played together," he says. "We were tight and we learned from the same influences. We listened to the same records and we played together every day after school."

While the pounding drums on "Surfin' U.S.A." sound like Dennis' handiwork, according to David, Dennis was unavailable for the session after breaking his ankle while getting off a drum riser. Veteran player Frank DeVito was enlisted in his place, although some Beach Boys historians insist Dennis plays at least a portion of the final drum track. "He did a really great job," David says of DeVito. "He was trying to play like Dennis, who invented his own drum style, more or less. Dennis had his signature drum riff on 'Surfin' Safari,' so Frankie put that in at the beginning of the choruses of 'Surfin U.S.A.' It was like a high-tech version — a single-stroke buzz roll with that riff."

David rates the early Beach Boys' musicianship as "just as adequate as any other band in the area." Initially they were considered just one of several SoCal surf acts — alongside Dick Dale, The Marketts, The Bel-Airs and The Challengers — but they also had the vocal chops, Brian's writing and Murry's indomitable drive on their side. Because they were a self-contained unit, they were sometimes hired to back up performers appearing on the same bill, including, incredibly, Sam Cooke, Lou Rawls and bluesman Jimmy Reed.[2]

"Surfin' U.S.A." was released with the drag-race number "Shut Down" on the B-side. The latter song also got ample radio play, and the double-sided hit single made the boys stars. "We started getting calls from the Midwest to do tours and shows," David recalls. "When we embarked on our first tour, it really did change our lives. Carl and I had to go to a private school. It wasn't a hardship by any means. We were going with the flow and loving every second of it."

Understandably, Arc Music, Chuck Berry's publishers, pursued the matter of Brian's apparent act of creative borrowing, and in the end Arc got the publishing rights and Berry the songwriting credit. (Berry's name is the only one credited on some releases, and on others it's shared with Brian.) The duck-walking rock 'n' roll legend's alleged anger over the artistic appropriation is dramatized in the 2009 Chess Records biopic *Cadillac Records*.

Just as "Surfin' U.S.A." was enjoying a bitchin' ride on the charts, the group followed up with an LP of the same title. The *Surfin' U.S.A.* album was more than just a quick cash-in on a couple of hit singles. Tracks such as "Farmer's Daughter," "Noble Surfer," "Lana" and "Finders Keepers" exhibit a delightful innocence and show 20-year-old Brian finding his studio legs. The stark "Lonely Sea," written mostly by his friend Gary Usher, was a harbinger of the melancholy to come. Brian's arrangements do laps around his efforts on *Surfin' Safari*, his symbiotic relationship with the rest of the guys quickly evolving. He knew exactly who was best suited for each part, and they each had a knack for memorizing, playing and singing back those parts. And the family harmony blend is magical. Brian soars on the high end while Mike holds down the bottom and his brothers fill the middle. Brian wasn't happy with David's inconsistent vocals — he was going through puberty, after all — and limited his participation in the harmonies. David did handle the leads, however, in concert performances of covers "Louie, Louie" and "Kansas City."

The Beach Boys became famous mostly for their singing, but *Surfin' U.S.A.*'s five instrumentals — the most on any of their albums — are far from throwaways. It is the band's most consistently rocking platter as well as its most surf-themed: they cover two numbers by Dick Dale — "Let's Go Trippin'" and his classic take on "Misirlou" — while Brian comes up with the great original "Stoked" and

Carl and David flip out playing Carl's "Surf Jam." "Carl and I were in our glory with that album," David reflects. "That's what we really loved to do at the time. We were just in love with playing guitars and all the surf music that was going on."

The group — except for Dennis — might not have actively surfed, but with the *Surfin' U.S.A.* LP, which reached #2 in America, they recorded the most popular surf-rock album. *The Book of Rock Lists*, co-written by former *Creem* editor Dave Marsh and Kevin Stein, ranks it the best record of 1963, ahead of such landmark releases as James Brown's *Live at the Apollo* and *The Freewheelin' Bob Dylan*.[3]

It would prove a banner year for the group, but by the fall David would be gone. While many fans assume it was David's departure that October that prompted Alan's return to the fold, the two actually co-existed in the band for awhile. Brian — who in addition to his Beach Boys duties had been producing other artists including The Honeys and Sharon Marie — quit touring in spring 1963. Brian's decision may have been difficult for the rest of the band to accept, but Alan, who no doubt regretted leaving in the first place, was ready to step back in.

"Brian needed the time to write songs and produce records, and the touring didn't allow him enough time to do both things. So that's when Al was reenlisted to come and take Brian's place on the road, playing bass and singing Brian's high parts. For Brian that was an ideal situation," David recollects. But Murry didn't see it that way. He was incensed that Brian wasn't onstage for the fans, and so the Beach Boys leader reluctantly returned to the road later that summer, leaving Alan odd man out again.

And Brian wasn't the only one getting a hard ride from Murry. The Wilson patriarch chastised the whole band for what he deemed unprofessional behavior, which especially in David's case should hardly have been unexpected given his age. (Not smiling onstage was one of his transgressions.) For his part, David found Murry a relentless taskmaster, but is more understanding in retrospect. "His hard-handed discipline came when we were screwing around and not taking care of business," the guitarist says. "To me he was an authority figure — like a school teacher or a parent — and it was natural that he would yell at us for not taking business seriously."

David says his greater grievance was of an artistic nature: even though barely a teenager, he felt stifled, as Murry was dead-set on making Carl the group's unquestioned number-one guitarist. "Murry did tend to turn my guitar down and wouldn't let me play leads. It was frustrating," David says. But the cocky youngster wouldn't be held down, cutting loose with leads at live shows and sneaking in some notes on the studio tracks of "Shut Down" and "Surfin' U.S.A.," where he slips in a Dick Dale–esque downslide. "You can hear little places where Dave the 14-year-old wanted more attention," he admits. "I might have been the first punk guitar player, if you want to put it that way, because I was being aggressive with my rhythm playing." The ambitious youngster had even brought forward his composition "Kustom Kar Show" for potential inclusion on the auto-themed *Little Deuce Coupe* album, but, as Stebbins' book suggests, Brian rejected it under pressure from Murry.[4]

By the summer of 1963, tensions were mounting. While driving to a show in Brooklyn, Murry started tearing into David, to which the exasperated teenager responded that he quit. The rest of the band shrugged it off as an idle threat, but it's what Murry wanted, and to some extent David as well. He stayed on for another couple of months, but the last straw may have come when Murry denied David's parents Elmer and Jo Ann a managerial role with The Beach Boys and a more prominent spot for David. His final show with the band was in San Diego on October 5, 1963.[5]

"My main reason for leaving the band at the time was to pursue my own music. I had this little band on the side," David recollects. He had hooked up with this new group through Mark Groseclose, a drummer who sat in with The Beach Boys at a few gigs after accident-prone Dennis hurt his legs when he crashed his sports car.[6] David took over Groseclose's garage band The Jaguars, which were renamed David Marks & the Marksmen. Not only did the new outfit put his guitar chops front and center, but he would also be chief songwriter and producer as well as sing most leads, which he handled with aplomb. The band signed with fledgling A&M Records, but despite a valiant effort never got off the ground. The group's music would have been lost to time if not for David's self-released 2009 compilation *The Ultimate Collector's Edition — 1963–'65*, a charming document of a young band trying on several styles in search of its sound.

After the Marksmen's demise, David gigged in a few short-lived bands before hooking up with singer-songwriter Matt Moore, with whom he formed The Moon. They landed a deal with Imperial Records and were joined by drummer/producer/engineer Larry Brown and bassist Drew Bennett. The band's two LPs remain cult favorites, especially the lost 1968 flower-power debut *Without Earth*. The group's commercial failure is attributed to Imperial's lack of promotion.

David later joined Colours, a sister band to The Moon led by Jack Dalton and Gary Montgomery. Although similarly revered among aficionados, Colours never found major success and soon folded. Then a promising spot opened up with husband-and-wife country/R&B outfit Delaney & Bonnie, but David was supplanted when Eric Clapton entered the picture. Exhausted by the rock 'n' roll lifestyle, he packed up for Boston to study classical guitar and composition at the Berklee College of Music and then the Boston Conservatory, but quit his studies before long. He still occasionally saw the other Beach Boys, who had long since hired Bruce Johnston as its fifth road member while Brian stayed home. Mike asked David to rejoin the band in 1971,

Mike, Brian, Carl, Dennis and David rehearse for the *Surfin' Safari* album at Capitol Studios in August 1962.
[© Getty/Michael Ochs Archives]

likely to bring the group closer to its roots, and although he appeared onstage at one Beach Boys show, he ultimately declined.[7]

As the '70s unfolded, David played in local bands and jammed with his music-biz cronies while The Beach Boys experienced a major renaissance capped off by their chart-topping 1974 greatest-hits collection *Endless*

Summer. Capitol rereleased "Surfin' U.S.A." as a single from the collection, and it reentered the charts, climbing to #36. This gave an unexpected bump to David's royalty checks, which would allow him to focus on playing and writing for the next two decades. It would also fund 20 years of drug and alcohol use.

Then, in 1997, Mike came calling again and, incredibly, 34 years after he left, David officially took the stage as a reinstated Beach Boy. It was quite a turnaround for someone who had done his best to distance himself from his history with the group. "I gained a new respect for the music, and I learned to appreciate some of the stuff that I didn't play on in the later '60s," he reflects. Although some fans perceived his return as a cynical ploy to replace one Beach Boy with another when Carl was sidelined by lung cancer treatments, David has said he was both surprised and saddened that he would not get to share the stage with his old guitar partner,[8] who passed away on February 6, 1998.

Due to another tumble off the wagon, David's second go-round with The Beach Boys lasted only two years, and their parting seemed a mutual decision. What finally got him to give up the bottle was a diagnosis of hepatitis C, which can lead to cirrhosis and cancer of the liver, especially in heavy drinkers. By 2004 he had beaten his illness, and he has remained a spokesman for public awareness of the disease.

The new millennium saw David raise his public profile, both by embracing his past and pushing ahead. He released a pair of solo albums and the three-CD set *The Lost Years*, a companion piece to Stebbins' book that collects his post–Beach Boys work. He was far removed from the California surf, having settled in Westchester County, New York, with his wife, Carrie. He sat in with The Beach Boys on several occasions and toured with the Legends of Surf Music, an outfit that also featured Alan as well as Jan & Dean's Dean Torrence. Not surprisingly, their Beach Boys–heavy setlist included "Surfin' U.S.A." "It's one of the songs people think of when they hear the name 'Beach Boys,'" he says.

Longtime fans thought it was only right when, in December 2011, it was announced David would join Mike, Brian, Alan and Bruce for the group's 50th anniversary celebration reunion tour and album. David was likewise understandably enthused. "I'm really positive about it," he says. "It will be great."

Dennis Diken on...
SHUT DOWN

Written by: Brian Wilson and Roger Christian
Lead vocal: Mike Love
Produced by: Nick Venet
Recorded: January 5, 31, 1963
Released: March 4, 1963, as B-side to "Surfin' U.S.A."
Chart peak: U.S. #23
Appears on *Surfin' U.S.A.* and *Little Deuce Coupe*

The group realized early on that songs about surfing ultimately would be limiting both creatively and commercially. While "Surfin' U.S.A." ingeniously invited landlocked youth to fantasize about catching a wave, enthusiasm for the subject matter would no doubt soon ebb in the average listener in Topeka. Cars, on the other hand, were the status symbol of American adolescents everywhere, and the band was shrewd enough to include automotive songs on all their early albums. That theme supplanted surfing as the main vehicle for their musical talents.

Capitol had more faith in car songs from the get-go, pushing the hot-rodding "409," co-written by Brian and Gary Usher, as the A-side of its first Beach Boys single. Brian's next batch of car songs was sparked by a new and fruitful creative partnership with Roger Christian, a disc jockey at KFWB. Murry hooked up the pair after hearing Christian on the air explaining why The Beach Boys shouldn't be singing the praises of a Chevrolet 409. Impressed by his automotive expertise, Murry called Christian to suggest he talk with Brian. Meeting at a café after the DJ finished a late shift, Christian shared his journal of car writings, and Brian was instantly taken with his talent for weaving technical terms into compelling narratives. Brian was particularly revved up by a lyric of Christian's entitled "Shut Down," about a fuel-injected Corvette Stingray outracing a Dodge Dart, and composed a song around it. The resulting number transcended its B-side designation to become a hit in its own right. Opening with the group's call to increase the RPMs on the Stingray's tachometer, the song races through 110 glorious seconds of auto vernacular, cool harmonies sung lower than usual, and the band at its most garage-like.

Appearing on the *Surfin' U.S.A.* album in March 1963, the song was also included that October on the *Little Deuce Coupe* LP, which collected the group's three car hits to date alongside nine new songs, all with an automotive theme save for "Be True to Your School." Although the band's very name evokes sand and surf, fans loved this new asphalt-bound direction, sending the record to #4 in the U.S. and making it one of the band's two non-compilation albums to achieve platinum certification in America (*Pet Sounds* being the other).

Back in 1963, "Shut Down" ignited a life-long passion for Beach Boys music in six-year-old Dennis Diken, who would go on to drum for New Jersey rock band The Smithereens, which charted singles "Blood and Roses," "Only a Memory" and "A Girl Like You" in the late '80s. In 2009, Diken released his first solo album, *Late Music*, which contains several songs with more than a trace of Brian Wilson influence. He can still remember how it all began.

"My dad was going to buy me a record that day, and I wanted 'Shut Down,'" Diken recalls. "I remember the store in Lodi, New Jersey. I remember the lady behind the counter. I asked her for 'Shut Down' and she reached and got it and handed it to me. My dad paid for it and we're walking away and I turned it around and I saw 'Surfin' U.S.A.' was on the other side. I had no idea — I thought they were two separate singles, and it blew my mind. I couldn't believe I was getting both of those songs on the one record. It was such a huge moment for me."

"There was something about 'Shut Down,'" he continues. "It's one of the toughest records I've ever heard. By tough, I mean it's got an attitude in the performance, in the vocals and in the lyrics. I knew it was about a hot-rod race, but I still don't know what they're talking about. It's a lot of car jargon."

Nonetheless, when Diken recently started a side-project band, they called themselves The 413s after the Super Stock 413 cubic inch–powered Dart in the song.

Given Diken's area of musical expertise, it's no surprise that he's particularly fond of Dennis' contribution to the recording. "It's one of my favorite rock and roll drum performances," he says. "It's really a great moving, grooving drum track. He really propels the song, and the drumming defines the attitude on that record. Through sheer will Dennis is booting it in a way that only a young player — maybe an unschooled player — can do. It's just his sheer will that's driving that track. What really rings my chimes in anybody who plays an instrument are the spirit, vitality and imagination they bring. And on the tracks where he really shines — and 'Shut Down' is one of them — Dennis was just what the doctor ordered."

It seems too coincidental that Diken is also named Dennis. He knew he wanted to be a drummer ever since he was a child, using Tinkertoy pieces and Lincoln Logs as sticks and beating on the plastic lids on coffee cans. He loved The Beach Boys but didn't know each member's role in the band. Then, one year after picking up "Shut Down," he had another religious moment at the local A&P, where, on an album display rack, he spotted *Shut Down Volume 2*, the latest Beach Boys LP.

"I'm looking at the song titles and I see 'Fun, Fun, Fun' — which I already had on a single — but then I saw the title of the instrumental 'Denny's Drums' and I just froze in my tracks," he says. "Here's my favorite group at that time and the drummer's name is Denny. That forged some kind of spiritual bond between me and Dennis Wilson — at least in my heart and soul."

Diken has managed to get close to his heroes, hanging out with all the original members at some point. He sat in with Brian's band for a 2007 benefit show for New Jersey's Count Basie Theatre that saw local hero Bruce Springsteen hop onstage to play guitar on "Barbara Ann." David Marks was a guest at a Diken solo show where they did "Shut Down," with Marks, who played rhythm guitar on the original track, singing lead. In 2009, Diken joined the touring Beach Boys for a show and hung out backstage with Mike, who talked about the huge influence Chuck Berry had on the group.

"Mike imbibed that Chuck Berry aesthetic

in his singing, where you can take a wordy song like 'Shut Down' and make it work," Diken says. "He used it a lot throughout The Beach Boys' career. Mike is a great lead vocalist and front man. He's a big part of why that band succeeded. The sound of his voice is unlike any other in rock and roll. I love the doo-wop thing on the chorus of 'Shut Down,' when he goes to the low voice. It's fabulous." Mike also plays the song's two-note sax solo. "I told him it's one of my favorite sax solos on a rock and roll record," Diken says with a laugh. "I don't know if he thought I was pulling his leg, but I love it. It's so tough and punky. It's just got that swagger and snotty attitude that is rock and roll."

While critical kudos for The Beach Boys — and The Beatles, for that matter — are usually reserved for their more ambitious mid- to late-'60s albums, Diken believes those groups already peaked with their rawer early records. "They evolved and maybe they got better as players and the music got more complex, but it's not better for me," he says. "I think everything that's great about The Beach Boys is etched in the grooves in 'Shut Down.' Yeah, it's not as sophisticated as the music on *Pet Sounds*, but it still moves me every bit as much. It's about how it affects you. That's what rock and roll or any music is all about. You can appreciate it on different levels, but when you really get down to it, it's about how it makes you feel."

The drummer believes tracks such as "California Girls," "I Get Around" and "Shut Down" will prove eternal. "No matter how many times I hear them on the radio — unlike certain other overplayed evergreens — I just never get sick of them, because there's such quality, there's such vitality, there's such magic in the music," he says. "I think they'll span the ages. There's something in those records that's going to speak to generation after generation."

JOHN SEBASTIAN ON...
SURFER GIRL

Written by: Brian Wilson
Lead vocal: Brian Wilson
Produced by: Brian Wilson
Recorded: June 12, 1963
Single released: July 22, 1963
Chart peak: U.S. #7
Appears on *Surfer Girl*

The smash success of the *Surfin' U.S.A.* album gave Brian enough leverage with Capitol Records to officially assume the role of Beach Boys producer, and his elevated status inspired him to new creative heights. He also convinced Capitol to let him record off-site at Western Studio, where he preferred the bass frequency and thought he could get a "ballsier sound."[1] Western engineer Chuck Britz would become his right-hand studio man for the next four years.

The Beach Boys weren't the only outlet for Brian's expanding songwriting and production talents. He and the band would also record with Jan & Dean, to whom Brian gifted his work-in-progress "Surf City." Co-credited to Jan Berry, it became Brian's first composition to top the charts in the U.S. A more hands-on project was The Honeys, a spunky female trio featuring Ginger Blake, 15-year-old Marilyn Rovell — who would become Brian's love interest after his breakup with Judy Bowles — and Marilyn's older sister Diane. Brian idolized Phil Spector's records with The Crystals and The Paris Sisters and looked to build Spector's Wall of Sound around an all-girl surf group.

For the next Beach Boys single, Brian dug up what he's called his first formal composition, the ballad "Surfer Girl." He had come up with the tune while driving to a hot-dog stand, the melody inspired by "When You Wish Upon a Star" from the Walt Disney film *Pinocchio*. (Brian paid tribute to that song with a cover on his 2011 album *In the Key of Disney*.) His ability to put "Surfer Girl" together in short order came as a surprise even to him. The group took an initial stab at the track (logged as "Little Surfin' Girl") at its February 8, 1962, session at World Pacific with Hite Morgan.

Disarmingly innocent, the song is a tender fantasy about a girl on the beach whom the narrator admires from afar but seemingly hasn't worked up the nerve to approach. It may just be her French bikini that has caused his heart to race, but that's enough for him to pledge his capital-L love to her. The lush background harmonies cushion Brian's touching lead and help sell the would-be lover's earnestness.

The group re-recorded the song in June 1963 and it saw release the following month, just as "Surf City" was cresting on the charts. The change in pace may have cost the group a few male fans who expected more garage-band rock 'n' roll like "Surfin' U.S.A.," but "Surfer Girl" is one of the prettiest songs

Brian ever wrote and gained new female followers, who would scream when it was performed in concert. Capitol bought into Brian's new direction, putting the slow number on the A-side and the shuffling car anthem "Little Deuce Coupe" on the flip. That faith proved well placed, with "Surfer Girl" becoming a #7 hit in the U.S. and "Little Deuce Coupe" making it to #15.

"Surfer Girl" became the title track of the band's third album, which — behind its iconic cover of the guys carrying a surfboard at Paradise Cove — displayed astonishing musical growth. Featuring the two latest hits, the album also boasts the brilliantly arranged "Catch a Wave" and Brian's falsetto-driven "Hawaii," both of which figured in Beach Boys setlists nearly 50 years later. "The Surfer Moon" marked the group's first track with a string arrangement, while best of all was the arrestingly introspective "In My Room."

An early example of Brian twisting traditional doo-wop chord progressions,[2] "Surfer Girl" announced that there was more to The Beach Boys than Chuck Berry rewrites. Twenty-five hundred miles east in New York, a burgeoning folk scene was happening, and its participants had no time for hedonistic

California surf-music. But bespectacled 19-year-old John Sebastian, caught up in the Bob Dylan–influenced singer-songwriter movement and tentatively readying his own career, took note with "Surfer Girl."

"As East Coast kiddies, we didn't get that big a portion of surf music on the radio, so Brian's whole first effort kind of went over — or under — our heads," Sebastian says. "Surfer Girl," he adds, changed that. "That was epic. It still generates a tear to hear it. That was one of the songs that made you want to be a West Coast guy and experience that whole surf culture."

Inspired by the tune and looking for a musical style of their own, Sebastian and producer Erik Jacobsen recorded a couple of surf tunes with a nasal Mike-style vocal, but neither saw release. But both men would score a major success a couple of years later with The Lovin' Spoonful, and Sebastian would establish himself as a great singer-songwriter in his own right.

In the Spoonful's jaunty 1966 track "Jug Band Music," Sebastian situates himself in that exotic West Coast culture. He's an innocent swimmer who accidentally gets smacked by a dude on his board. But the noble surfer dives in the water to rescue the hapless narrator. Sebastian explains that the lyric "was kind of admiration. When you're on the beach, that's what happens — you get wiped out by a beach boy. He's been there. He knows the ropes."

That year, Sebastian and his band got up close and personal with the real Beach Boys, joining them in March and April on U.S. tours. The Spoonful's star was rising at the time with four consecutive top 10 singles, including "Daydream" and "Did You Ever Have to Make Up Your Mind?" and they entertained notions of showing up America's top group at gigs such as the Beach Boys Summer Spectacular at San Francisco's Cow Palace on June 24, 1966. "Brian reminds me that the Spoonful would notoriously show up late so that The Beach Boys would have to go on first. I had totally forgotten that had ever happened and I did apologize," Sebastian says with a laugh. "But it was awfully friendly. We had nothing but admiration for the band."

Sebastian became particularly chummy with Dennis, whom he thought embodied rock 'n' roll stardom. Sebastian and the Spoonful's late lead guitarist Zal Yanovsky marveled at the drummer's live performances and even fantasized about poaching him for their band, especially with word out that Brian had replaced Dennis with Hal Blaine on some of The Beach Boys' records. Using session players was a foreign concept to the Spoonful, who prided themselves on playing their own instruments both onstage and in the studio. They would have been happy to have Dennis.

"In that era, one of the great compliments you could pay a drummer was 'he's an animal,' and Dennis had that quality. I love a guy who hits with both hands on the backbeat," Sebastian says. "We genuinely were hoping to have a little bit more savagery in the drums, and Dennis to us seemed like heaven. And if you don't believe it, stand out backstage after the show. He just couldn't step over the cute California girls, there were so many." The appreciation went both ways, as Dennis in interviews at the time cited the Spoonful, along with The Beatles, as his favorite vocal groups.

Sebastian also became close to Brian, partially for their shared belief that The Ronettes' "Be My Baby" produced by Phil Spector was, as he says, "the best thing less than three minutes ever released." In the early 1970s, when Brian rarely strayed from his Bel Air home, Sebastian would come over to jam. "It wasn't all grimness," he recollects of that period, and he would later share the bill with The Beach Boys for Brian's much-touted onstage return on July 2, 1976, at the Oakland Coliseum.

Sebastian credits Brian with bringing a new vocal sophistication to rock 'n' roll through songs such as "Surfer Girl." "Brian had control of this vocal palette of which we had no idea," he says. "We had never paid any attention to The Four Freshmen or doo-wop combos like The Crew Cuts. Look what gold he mined out of that."

ALICE COOPER ON . . .
IN MY ROOM

Written by: Brian Wilson and Gary Usher
Lead vocals: Brian Wilson and Mike Love with group
Produced by: Brian Wilson
Recorded: July 1963
Released: September 16, 1963, on *Surfer Girl* and
October 28, 1963, as B-side to "Be True to Your School"
Chart peak: U.S. #23

Brian's early collaborator Gary Usher was his main confidant, and that closeness allowed them to explore more emotional terrain in their songs. "Lonely Sea" had injected an anomalous sense of gloom into *Surfin' U.S.A.*, and their follow-up, "In My Room," saw them expand their reach with a timeless anthem of teen alienation.

Usher recalled writing the song with Brian one night after they'd played baseball. Aptly, it was created in Brian's room, which had been the Wilson family music room. Brian sat at the organ, running his fingers along the keys until he stumbled across a promising melody[1] while Usher played bass and called out the words. Within an hour they had the song down. After they played it for Brian's parents, Audree said it was the most beautiful song Brian had written. Even ever-critical Murry had to admit it was good.[2]

Brian had come up with the notion of one's room as a personal kingdom — a haven from prying eyes and a place to laugh, cry, scheme and dream. Since he had been sleeping in the music room, it can be read that he was singing also about music as a refuge. As he recalled more than 30 years later in the documentary *Nashville Sounds: The Making of*

Stars and Stripes, "After I had done the whole song, then I looked back and said, 'Oh, I see what I did. I was writing about myself.'"[3]

"In My Room" was a different kind of Beach Boys song for the radio. The band already had a hit ballad with "Surfer Girl," but that is more of a conventional love song. "In My Room" is a somber ballad that never mentions girls and so doesn't even make it as a slow-dance number. This was the group taking its music to another level. A meditation on the self and the secret emotions young people feel, it added another dimension to the adolescent experience the group was chronicling.

For teenager Vincent Furnier, later to become shock-rocker Alice Cooper, it was the latest record from a group he and his friends loved.

"Before The Beatles, all we listened to was The Beach Boys and The Four Seasons," he says. "Those were the two cool bands. We lived in Phoenix. We had heard that there was an ocean. We weren't sure of it. That whole surf sound came out and it was cool — the tight harmonies and cool records. And we were all drag racing. It was all about how fast your car was. Later I had a Fairlane GT 390 with four on the floor, and we could not keep rubber on the tires. On Friday night you went down to Central Boulevard and drag raced. So to us, they were singing about what we liked doing."

A decade later, Cooper would adopt an anarchic attitude towards education in the classic "School's Out," but for now he was digging The Beach Boys' straight-faced "Be True to Your School," a #6 hit in winter '63. But it was "In My Room" on the flip side that made an even greater impression. "I was 15. I was the perfect age for that," he says. "Your room is your sanctuary. It's your Batcave. It's the only thing you own, so there's a certain holiness to it. 'Mom, Dad — don't come in my room. It's off-limits. It's my own private world here.' All the heartbreak goes on in there and all the elation goes on in there. That's where you get your first taste of responsibility: 'I've got my own room.'"

Brian had to share a room with Dennis and Carl until he was 16,[4] and that memory factored into the song. In those days, he taught them the vocal parts to "Ivory Tower," a '50s love song that had been a hit for Cathy Carr, Gale Storm and Otis Williams and the Charms. Singing it together brought the brothers the harmony lacking outside those four walls, where Murry was part of the

And then there were five. By fall 1963, David had left and Alan (second from left) was back in the group.

equation. On "In My Room," Brian starts off singing the first verse and is soon joined by Dennis and Carl. Brian later recalled that they sound just like they did when they sang "Ivory Tower" all those nights of their youth.

"I love the harmonies," Cooper says. "I guarantee they sat around listening to The Hi-Lo's and all those groups based purely on vocals. Recently I was surfing SiriusXM radio and I came across The Lettermen, and what they were doing was exactly like The Beach Boys." (The Lettermen, known for tight harmonies from their three vocalists, were The Beach Boys' label-mates, having launched on Capitol with the single "That's My Desire"/"The Way You Look Tonight" one year ahead of "Surfin' Safari." Group member Bob Engemann was the brother of Capitol A&R executive Karl Engemann, who had moved over from Warner Bros. Records and brought the group with them. Nick Venet produced The Lettermen's early Capitol hits, and author Steven Gaines suggests it was that association with The Lettermen that brought Murry to Venet's door looking for a record deal for The Beach Boys.[5])

"In My Room" featured a richer vocal blend thanks to the return of Alan, who also plays bass on several other tracks on the *Surfer Girl* LP. He and Mike join the Wilson brothers on the pristine harmonies as the song expands its vocal breadth, and on the bridge Mike shows what a fine balladeer he could be. David was also still around, strumming his guitar behind Carl's moody lead picking. The most noteworthy production touch is a harp in the intro that establishes an otherworldly mood. It is played by Mike's sister Maureen, who did the same on the upbeat "Catch a Wave."

Copying an initiative of The Beatles, the group recorded a German-language version of "In My Room" in March 1964. The title refrain was changed to "Ganz Allein," which means "all alone." But as it turned out,

German record buyers were more than accepting of the band in its original language,[6] so the translated rendition was shelved and wouldn't be heard until its inclusion on 1983's *The Beach Boys Rarities*.

Despite his co-writing triumph, Usher contributed to only a couple more Beach Boys cuts. Murry was suspicious of outsiders in general and of Usher in particular, characterizing him as an opportunist. He did what he could to squeeze Usher out of the Beach Boys scene, although just two days after the "Ganz Allein" session, Brian produced Usher's solo single "Sacramento"/"That's the Way I Feel."[7] Usher produced numerous surf and hot-rod records before collaborating with The Byrds on the classic albums *Younger Than Yesterday*, *The Notorious Byrd Brothers* and *Sweetheart of the Rodeo*. But "In My Room" was his greatest songwriting credit, and he would revisit it, first in a psychedelic 1969 version by his studio group Sagittarius, and then a year later on his *Symphonic Salute to Brian Wilson*.

The song took on greater meaning as it pertained to Brian's life in the early 1970s. Brian would claim to have spent the better part of three and half years "in his room" — although by then that was the one he shared with wife, Marilyn, in their spacious Bel Air home. Much of the time, he was actually hanging out with Three Dog Night's Danny Hutton and Hutton's circle of music friends. One night Hutton brought Brian to a party Cooper was hosting. At the end of the night, Brian invited Cooper and Iggy Pop, the wild lead singer of The Stooges, back to his house.

"He told us he was going to play us the greatest song ever written. I looked at Iggy and I said, 'Let's go!'" Cooper recalls. "So we're sitting there and he sits down at the piano and he goes '*Mama's little baby loves shortenin', shortenin'/Mama's little baby loves shortenin' bread.*' We just start laughing. And he says, 'What are you laughing about? This is the greatest song ever written. *Mama's little baby loves shortenin', shortenin'* . . .' And we went, 'Well, yeah — of course it is.'"

Cooper also remembers Brian out of his room at a mid-'70s music industry party. "I'm sitting with Bernie Taupin and John Lennon. There were probably 10 people at the table, and everybody was a pretty well-known rock star," he recalls. "And I hear, 'Psst!' And I look around and it's Brian. He goes, 'Alice! Introduce me to John Lennon.' I thought, 'What? They haven't met yet?' So I said, 'This

will be great — of course.' I brought him over and I said, 'Hey, John — this is Brian Wilson.' And they went on and on talking to each other. Then Brian said, 'Well, I have to go. Thank you. Bye.' And John sits down. About half an hour later, Brian goes up to Bernie and says, 'Psst! Bernie! Introduce me to John Lennon.' Same thing! Bernie goes over and says, 'John, this is Brian Wilson.' John doesn't lose a beat. 'Oh, good to see you, man.' And as soon as Brian leaves, there's this pregnant pause at the table, and John goes, 'He's not well, y'know.'"

"In My Room" has continued to resonate with other artists. In 1996, country legend Tammy Wynette sang a moving lead on a remake for the *Stars and Stripes Vol. 1* LP, on which country acts perform Beach Boys tunes with the group. (The session is documented on the *Nashville Sounds* DVD.) It was the final recording by Wynette, who died less than two years later at age 55. The cut was held for the album's intended sequel, but when that never materialized, it was remixed as a duet between Wynette and Brian for the 1998 tribute album *Tammy Wynette Remembered*. In 2009, L.A. band Best Coast recorded an up-tempo noise-pop variation, and an instrumental cover serves as the title track of a 2011 album by jazz keyboardist Larry Goldings.

Rolling Stone ranked The Beach Boys' original #212 in its 2010 list of the greatest songs of all time. The following year, *Classic Rock* magazine compiled a list of the 100 greatest songwriters, including both Cooper and Brian. Cooper spoke of Brian as his favorite, referring to the "classic" melody of "In My Room." He says it's a highlight of "the early, innocent Beach Boys music" he loves.

"They were two- or three-minute songs you could sing the first time you heard them. There's an amazing art to that. Getting something as 'simple' as 'In My Room' is harder than writing a 10-minute 'complicated' prog-rock piece," he says. "He really was like a Beethoven. He really was a tortured genius. But he knew how to get it on tape. Young bands send me songs all the time and I listen, and they've got all kinds of image, look and attitude. Then I go, 'Where's the song? This is a riff and you yelling at me. I get it, you're angry. Now write a song about being angry.' I tell them to listen to Paul Simon, Burt Bacharach, Brian Wilson and Paul McCartney. I say, 'This may not be the kind of music you like, but listen to the construction of the songs.' It's just a lost art. The bands that are still here from the '60s are all good songwriters. Those that are just riff bands went the way of the dinosaurs."

HaL BLaIne on...
FUN, FUN, FUN

Written by: Brian Wilson and Mike Love
Lead vocal: Mike Love
Produced by: Brian Wilson
Recorded: January 1, 8, 1964
Released: February 3, 1964
Chart peak: U.S. #5
Appears on *Shut Down Volume 2*

According to legend, a true story told by Dennis inspired Brian and Mike to write "Fun, Fun, Fun" while on tour in Salt Lake City in September 1963. The irresistible slice of white R&B recounts the cautionary tale of a girl who tells her father she's taking his car to the library when she's actually going out joyriding. The chorus is today part of the cultural lexicon, and to many fans the song is the ultimate expression of the carefree good times they associate with the band.

Initially, Brian was stumped by the tempo, trying it fast, slow and in-between before shelving it for a while.[1] Even more doubting was Murry, who thought the song substandard and canceled a session for it. An angered Brian rescheduled[2] and finally got all the elements together, including Carl's guitar intro, which cops Chuck Berry's "Johnny B. Goode" pretty much note for note. (And since the Berry tune was also part of the group's early repertoire, it was impossible for audiences to tell which of the two songs the band was launching into.) There is also a typically great Brian organ solo, but the kicker is his siren-like vocal wail in the tag, which never fails to spur a hoot-a-long.

Also in the Berry mold are Mike's clever

lyrics, which show a keen eye for the teenage scene. It's all so wonderfully innocent: the narrator isn't even vindictive towards the girl whose head gets inflated by her new wheels before being busted by her old man. He still invites her to join him and his friends for less duplicitous fun, fun, fun.

The track is also notable for the drums' driving beat and effortless fills. According to Beach Boys historian Craig Slowinski, the load in this case was shared by Dennis and session player *par excellence* Hal Blaine. "One of my favorite songs," Blaine says of the number. "It just felt so good lyrically. It was just youngsters' lyrics, but it all worked. It was perfect timing for teenagers who were thinking about the beach and having fun. It couldn't miss."

And it didn't, reaching #5 in the U.S., right behind "Dawn (Go Away)" by The Four Seasons, which had been The Beach Boys' chief rival to that point. Occupying the top three spots was a new and more daunting competitor — The Beatles, with "Please Please Me" (#3), "I Want to Hold Your Hand" (#2) and "She Loves You" (#1).

Blaine coined the term the "Wrecking Crew" in reference to himself and his fellow top L.A. session players — trained jazz musicians who, as a loosely defined group, recorded pop and rock 'n' roll records for nearly every producer in town in the 1960s. According to Blaine, the older generation of players turned up their noses. "We were working in movies with some of the old-timers who wore their blue blazers and three-piece suits, and they looked at us kids in Levi's and T-shirts and said we were going to wreck the business," he says. "I started calling us the 'Wrecking Crew' and it stuck."

Brian heard the results of the Crew's work on Jan & Dean and Phil Spector records and made sure to get them for his studio dates with The Honeys and, eventually, The Beach Boys. At first a few players would merely sweeten the track the band had laid down, as Blaine did by adding timbales on "Hawaii." But by mid-1963 Brian saw the occasional need to replace Dennis and tapped Blaine for numbers such as "Our Car Club," where the drums are more prominent than ever. Blaine didn't aim to replicate Dennis' make-it-through-sheer-will drum style from the early albums. "I never even thought about it that way," he says. "I just wanted to hear the song and know what it was about, and that's what gave me the inspiration to do whatever I did."

In assessing Dennis' abilities, Blaine says, "He was a fine drummer. He was a much better piano player. He was the ultimate Beach Boy onstage with the long hair. But he didn't have much training. He was breaking drums all the time. Dennis would do work with the boys and he asked if he could use my drums, and he used to beat the crap out of them. There were huge welts."

But on tracks including "Don't Worry Baby," "When I Grow Up (To Be a Man)" and many others, Dennis, Carl, Al and Brian show themselves to be more than capable of bringing songs to life in the studio. It just often took them longer: in the case of "When I Grow Up," the boys required 37 takes to get the instrumental track down.[3] So while top session players made good money — Blaine was paid $246 (worth about $1,700 in 2012) for the session that yielded "Fun, Fun, Fun" and "The Warmth of the Sun"[4] — they were worth it.

"A lot of it was economics," Blaine says. "Producers called the Wrecking Crew because studio time is expensive. It's a lot of money to make a record. Many of the groups had to rehearse a song two to three weeks before they could even think about recording. We could do 10 to 12 songs in six hours in a double-session."

Brian would rely increasingly on the Crew as his music grew more complex, largely eliminating the other Beach Boys from instrumental sessions in the later *Pet Sounds* and *Smile* eras. The ensemble of outside players was small at the "Fun, Fun, Fun" session, however, with Blaine joined only by bass guitarist Ray Pohlman, Jay Migliori on baritone sax and Steve Douglas on tenor sax.

The Crew was in high demand, booked long in advance. A typical day would be filled with record sessions, overdubs, jingles and movie soundtracks. Blaine remembers lying down beside his drums at Western Studio 3 just to get some rest. He credits his drum tech Ricky Faucher with facilitating the torrid pace. "Ricky was always one session in front of me or one session behind me or both, setting up and tearing down. It's the only way I could do all this work."

Blaine, already in his mid-30s at the time, remembers his initial impression of Brian as just a young musician hanging around a couple of Spector sessions, watching his idol at work. "When we first started working with Brian and the boys, we thought they were just young kids doing their high-school thing," he adds. "And then every time you turned on the radio there they were. All of a sudden The Beach Boys were the biggest thing in the world."

He says in those days Brian was a "very nice, clean-cut kid. We never saw any drugs; we never saw any booze. We all drank coffee and Cokes and had hamburgers and milkshakes and the food so many kids eat. Brian was very good about bringing in food. He was very considerate that way. He was like a big, gentle bear. We never heard him blow up or scream at anybody because he had great respect for the musicians working with him."

The exceptions, however, were Brian's heated exchanges with Murry, who constantly hovered in the booth and added his input. "We could hear the fighting going on," Blaine says. "You could cut that tension with a string. It was just awful. Sometimes Brian would yell, 'Leave me alone!' and then Murry would just suck on his pipe. Murry wanted to be the big boss, and he wasn't. That whole thing was very sad."

When Murry later produced his own Beach Boys knock-off band, The Sunrays, Blaine had the misfortune of being called into service, witnessing more peculiar behavior from the Wilson patriarch. "You could smell the liquor something terrible when he came near you," Blaine

recalls. He adds that before the sessions Murry would pull out a billfold of notes. "Everybody got a two-dollar bill as a tip before we started, and then he'd get down on one knee and say a prayer. It was very weird."

Blaine recalls the mood at Brian's sessions as usually very positive, although sometimes the drummer would have to shush the others so they could get to work. Brian developed a deep trust in Blaine's opinion and made him his studio contractor. That meant putting out the calls to the other musicians, booking studio time, ensuring the necessary equipment was on hand, and then, after a long day of playing, typing up all the contracts back at home. Blaine later passed that responsibility on to Diane Rovell. He and Brian also saw each other socially. "He used to hang out at my house," Blaine recalls. "He loved my piano and he'd sit there and put my little daughter Michelle on his knee and bounce her up and down. She loved it."

As far as Blaine is concerned, Brian could hold his own with the Crew. "He was always a little bit shy, but I don't think he was intimidated. He spoke up for what he wanted or felt we should do. He would walk right up to somebody and say, 'I don't like that thing you're doing at bar so-and-so.'" The sessions would often begin with Brian at the piano singing a new melody, and then the other musicians would join in, with Brian occasionally calling out specific directions. Brian could hear in his head what he wanted from the drums and the other instruments, but possessed a limited musical vocabulary. He favored a simple drum sound, so Blaine stuck to the snare drum and floor-tom afterbeats he used on the Spector records.

"Brian would say, 'Come up with something a little bit different for a bass backbeat, so instead of right on two and four, it would be a little off two and a little before four.' A lot of times the players would do something that flipped him out and he would say, 'I love that. Let's do that,'" Blaine says. Drummer and historian Mike Megaffin sees more of the Spector influence in how Brian relied little on ride or crash cymbals, and at times used hardly any cymbals at all. These were replaced by layers of percussion played by top pros including Frank Capp, Julius Wechter and Jim Gordon.

The Wrecking Crew's glory days would fade as rock bands became increasingly proficient at playing and home studios came into vogue. Brian installed one in his living room. But in the '60s especially, the Crew had it going on. Blaine played on thousands of songs in 40 solid years of hitting the skins. Of these, hundreds were chart hits, and nearly 40 were number ones, including "Surf City," The Crystals' "He's a Rebel" and The Mamas & the Papas' "Monday Monday." And then there's each Grammy Award-winning Record of the Year from 1966 to 1971, including Frank Sinatra's "Strangers in the Night," Simon & Garfunkel's "Mrs. Robinson" and The 5th Dimension's "Aquarius/Let the Sunshine In."

"We loved what we were doing," Blaine says of the Wrecking Crew. "Before, we all were playing six or seven nights a week in smoke-filled nightclubs for $100 a week, and all of a sudden we're making a $1,000 a day. We were driving Cadillacs, Rolls Royces and Lincoln Continentals. You work all your life, you study, you play, you hear the big hit records, and all of a sudden you're on hit records."

Blaine continued making hit records for The Beach Boys for a couple of years after "Fun, Fun, Fun." "Any time I worked with Brian I knew it was going to be great," he says. "It was always a thrill. I couldn't wait to get started."

ROGER MCGUINN ON...
DON'T WORRY BABY

Written by: Brian Wilson and Roger Christian
Lead vocal: Brian Wilson
Produced by: Brian Wilson
Recorded: January 7, 1964
Released: March 23, 1964, on *Shut Down Volume 2* and May 11, 1964, as B-side to "I Get Around"
Chart peak: U.S. #24

The August 1963 appearance of The Ronettes' "Be My Baby" shook Brian to his core. Nothing else he had heard since "Rhapsody in Blue" had made such a profound and lasting impression. He was already a follower of Phil Spector — who produced the track and co-wrote it with Jeff Barry and Ellie Greenwich — but this pop masterpiece would become his all-time favorite record and a never-ending object of dissection and obsession. Opening with its trademark Hal Blaine "bom bom bom — pah" drumbeat, the teen symphony epitomized Spector's Wall of Sound and managed to be tough and streetwise without surrendering its sweet adolescent romanticism.

According to Brian's 1991 memoir *Wouldn't It Be Nice: My Own Story*, he was driving around with Marilyn when he first heard it on the radio. He was so excited he had to pull over, his mind blown by the production detail and how the three chords varied around a steady melody line. His euphoria was short-lived, however, replaced by the fear he would never be able to do anything as good.[1] But as usual with Brian, anxiety gave way to a burning competitiveness. He called up Roger Christian and together they wrote a ballad inspired by Spector's new opus. The title came from a refrain girlfriend Marilyn would use to comfort Brian after grueling days in the studio. "I don't think I can do it. It's not good enough," Brian would say, to which she would respond, "Don't worry baby, it's going to be great."

Brian brought the rest of the band into Western Studio in January 1964 to record "Don't Worry Baby" and other tracks for the *Shut Down Volume 2* album. The song technically remained in the hot-rod genre where Brian and Christian had previously tread, recounting the story of a drag racer whose bragging lands him in the ultimate racing duel. It's the world we know from "Shut Down" and "Little Deuce Coupe," but while those focus on fuel-injected engines and competition clutches making their drivers invincible, the emotional "Don't Worry Baby" is about the driver's dread of screwing up The Big Race. For Brian, that race was with Spector, his father and the rest of the music world. Luckily for the song's narrator, he has a devoted girl by his side, just as Brian had.

In this number, Brian elevates suburban teen melodrama into the realm of art — a musical equivalent to *Rebel Without a Cause*. And the subtext is ripe for the picking — if,

that is, the listener could decipher the words. Coming in after a Dennis drum intro that recalls Blaine's work on "Be My Baby," the group's cascading harmonies buttress Brian's soaring falsetto in a vocal arrangement so lush and complex the lyrics are easily lost. But it doesn't matter, because the singing is pure aural beauty. Brian's lead is one of his defining performances on one of his greatest records. Whether he believed it or not, he had created something that matched — and perhaps even surpassed — his idol.

"Don't Worry Baby" ended up backing the "I Get Around" 45, and while the A-side dominated American airwaves, it reached #24. To some fans, there is nothing secondary about it. To them, it is the ultimate Beach Boys number. *Spin* magazine concurred in a 1989 list in which it ranked the track the 11th-best single of all time.

Another of its admirers — and one whose path crossed with The Beach Boys' many times — is Roger McGuinn, leader of The Byrds. Just as Brian would play "Be My Baby" first thing each day, McGuinn was similarly taken with The Beach Boys. "I remember listening to 'Don't Worry Baby' and 'God Only Knows' just about every morning," recalls the man who made 12-string Rickenbacker guitars and granny glasses ubiquitous in the '60s. "I'd wake up and play those songs. It was really inspirational. It was almost like going to church."

As a young songwriter working for Bobby Darin's publishing company in New York's Brill Building, Jim McGuinn, as he was then known, had penned and sung on the 1963 single "Beach Ball," a Beach Boys/Jan & Dean knockoff for the short-lived group City Surfers. Of course, McGuinn would soon make his mark in L.A. with The Byrds, a rock band arguably as influential for its incorporation of folk, country and jazz as The Beach Boys are for their vocal arrangements and production techniques.

The Jet Set, as The Byrds were initially called, recorded "Please Let Me Love You" and "It Won't Be Wrong" for a fall '64 single on Elektra Records. (The label renamed the group The Beefeaters for the release to make them sound British in the middle of Beatlemania.) Jet Set guitarist David Crosby, who would make his own mark as a great harmony singer, took the demos to Brian seeking his opinion. "We respected The Beach Boys as a professional band and loved their work,"

McGuinn explains. "Brian said, 'Well, you know, you guys are getting there. Keep working on it.'"

When deciding on a new group name, McGuinn and company settled on The Byrds, in part because they hoped for some of that fairy dust that came to "B" bands. "That was our manager Jim Dickson's idea," recalls McGuinn. "He had a philosophy that the B letter was safe and cuddly to little teenage girls — you know, 'Bobby this' and 'Bobby that,' The Beatles, The Beach Boys. The 'B word' would be acceptable — and, in fact, desirable — to young girls, who were the target audience for a rock group at that point. It didn't hurt!"

McGuinn, along with Crosby and their bassist Chris Hillman, would see Brian socially at the West Hollywood apartment of Loren Schwartz, a gregarious employee of the William Morris Agency who knew how to throw a party.[2] His place was, as Brian described, "a black-lighted psychedelic haven" where hip musicians congregated.[3] It is also where — much to Marilyn's disapproval — Brian was introduced to marijuana. Other regulars included key future Brian collaborators Tony Asher and Van Dyke Parks.

The Byrds' breakthrough came after they moved to Columbia Records and hooked up with staff producer Terry Melcher. The son of Doris Day, Melcher had performed with Beach-Boy-to-be Bruce Johnston in Bruce & Terry and together they produced records as Beach Boys sound-alikes The Rip Chords. The Byrds fired Melcher after their second album, and, following the departure of his replacement Allen Stanton, recruited Gary Usher. "By osmosis I think both Melcher and Usher had the sensibility to make pop hits like The Beach Boys," McGuinn says.

In January 1965, Melcher brought The Byrds into the studio to cut an electric version of Bob Dylan's "Mr. Tambourine Man" and had The Beach Boys on his mind, employing the same session musicians Brian had been using. While The Byrds sing on the track, McGuinn is the only member who plays, as only his guitar skills were deemed game-ready. McGuinn recalls Melcher telling drummer Blaine to "get the feel like 'Don't Worry Baby.'" Not only do the two songs share a similar tempo, but the jerky guitar chord that appears in the instrumental break in "Don't Worry Baby" runs throughout "Mr. Tambourine Man."

The Dylan cover topped the U.S. and U.K. charts that summer. Following The Byrds' sudden rise, the group was added to the lineup of the July 3 Beach Boys Summer Spectacular at the Hollywood Bowl, which featured Brian playing with The Beach Boys and performances by The Kinks, The Righteous Brothers and Sonny & Cher. That December, The Byrds returned to #1 in the U.S. with "Turn! Turn! Turn!," Pete Seeger's arrangement of words from the Book of Ecclesiastes, and they performed more dates with The Beach Boys the following June.

But the popular music scene was changing quickly. Three hundred and fifty miles away in San Francisco, bands such as the Grateful Dead and Jefferson Airplane were making their voices heard, and Haight-Ashbury soon supplanted the Sunset Strip as the epicenter of cool. According to McGuinn, the threat from the north didn't exactly unite the L.A. groups. "There was more rivalry among the bands in L.A. than there was in San Francisco, where the bands had more camaraderie," he says.

As with most everyone else, McGuinn saw little of Brian in the ensuing years, but one afternoon in the early '70s Brian showed up unannounced at his Malibu home. After appearing in the security system TV monitors, Brian identified himself and McGuinn buzzed him in. Brian greeted McGuinn and asked, "You got any speed?" McGuinn — who later gave up the drug scene for the Christian life — perused his medicine cabinet and found a bottle of Biphetamine 20s. Brian wanted two.

"So I gave them to him and he took 'em and then we sat down," McGuinn recalls. "He sat down at the piano and I pulled up a chair with a guitar and we started hammering out this beat and a melody. We came up with some words for it. We got one verse and one chorus and that was it. And then I went to bed at midnight or 1 a.m. I got up at seven or eight in the morning, and he was still playing the piano because of the speed."

The song in question, eventually titled "Ding Dang," was something with which Brian would obsessively tinker, and over time it developed the aura of a lost classic. When it finally saw the light of day on the 1977 album *The Beach Boys Love You*, the composition had barely progressed from where Brian and McGuinn had left it. Clocking in under a minute, it proved to be a harmless ditty — another example of Brian's delightful silliness.

McGuinn also hung out with Dennis, whom he characterizes as a "drinking buddy." He remembers the drummer as fun and highly manic. "I got a new Mercedes roadster and let him drive it," he recalls. "He started driving on the wrong side of the Pacific Coast Highway at 60–70 miles an hour. And I'm screaming. It was like in the movies when people are going against traffic and dodging the cars. He was a wild guy."

When the ever-changing Byrds lineup was finally grounded and McGuinn recorded his self-titled 1973 debut solo album, he enlisted Bruce to play piano and sing harmonies, which Bruce would also do on the tour. In 1979 McGuinn joined Wolfman Jack and The Beach Boys for a performance of Chuck Berry's "Rock and Roll Music" on NBC's *The Midnight Special*. The guitarist later lent his signature jangly sound to The Beach Boys' 1986 Melcher-produced cover of "California Dreamin'" and opened for them on that year's tour. His guitar and vocals can also be heard on an alternate version of "Summer in Paradise," title track of The Beach Boys' 1993 U.K. album release.

Part of The Byrds' success can be attributed to how they successfully adapted Beach Boys–style harmonies to a folk sound that suited the times and anticipated much of the pop music of the hippie era. "We were a kindred group," McGuinn says of the relationship between the two great American bands. "I love The Beach Boys and I'm glad they made the wonderful music they did."

Daniel Lanois on . . .
I GET AROUND

Written by: Brian Wilson and Mike Love
Lead vocals: Mike Love and Brian Wilson
Produced by: Brian Wilson
Recorded: April 2, 10, 1964
Released: May 11, 1964
Chart peak: U.S. #1, U.K. #7
Appears on *All Summer Long*

On February 7, 1964, four lads from the port city of Liverpool touched down at John F. Kennedy International Airport, and things would never be the same. The Beach Boys watched helplessly as their homeland succumbed to the considerable charms and talents of John, Paul, George and Ringo in a mania unlike any popular culture had ever known. President Kennedy had been assassinated less than three months earlier, and the nation turned its grieving eyes to The Beatles, who provided an exhilarating distraction.

That month, as The Beach Boys rushed to finish *Shut Down Volume 2*, The Beatles conquered the U.S. charts with "I Want to Hold Your Hand," performed their first American concerts and made three broadcast appearances on *The Ed Sullivan Show*, the first episode alone attracting an estimated 74 million viewers. In addition to stealing the spotlight, the Fab Four represented a further threat in The Beach Boys' backyard since both bands were signed to Capitol in the U.S. and the label started dedicating much of its marketing resources to the Liverpudlians. The company could hardly be blamed: by early April, The Beatles held the top five spots on the *Billboard* Hot 100.

The British phenoms had by then returned to London to film *A Hard Day's Night*, their debut motion picture that would get a well-received summer release. The Beach Boys responded with a less distinguished movie appearance, shooting scenes for forgotten teen comedy *The Girls on the Beach* in mid-April.[1] In the film, the boys provide the titular theme song and perform some fun but awkward lip-synching to "Little Honda" and "Lonely Sea." But even here they are already in The Beatles' shadow, as the plot revolves around three sorority girls promising they can get the Brits for a fundraising concert. The Beach Boys come off as the next-best thing.

There was no escaping it. Seventeen-year-old Carl even hung a Beatles poster on his bedroom wall.[2] Meanwhile, Brian and Mike, as the group's main songwriters, were more than a little concerned. Released amid Beatlemania, *Shut Down Volume 2*, which mixed some of the group's best work with flat-out filler, peaked at only #13 in the U.S. — their first album to miss the top 10 since *Surfin' Safari*. (It would, however, remain on the charts for a healthy 38 weeks.) Since The Beach Boys could not compete with The Beatles' charisma, the two cousins figured the only solution

was to keep making better records.

On April 2, the band began sessions for "I Get Around,"[3] which would be the next single and lead-off track on the *All Summer Long* album. Things got off to an ugly start, however, when tensions between Brian and Murry erupted to the point where Brian fired his father as the group's manager. The friction had been building since the group's January visit to Australia and New Zealand, where they found Murry's puritanical and dictatorial ways suffocating.[4] (Also on this tour, headliner Roy Orbison cautioned Brian that The Beatles, with whom Orbison had toured England in 1963, would supplant The Beach Boys as the world's top band.[5]) After Brian let him go, Murry slinked off to his bed for weeks, displaying depressive behavior eerily foreshadowing that of his oldest son. For now, though, Brian was free of that ever-critical voice that undermined him in the studio. The group hired accounting firm Cummings & Current to look after its finances in the short term and turned its attention to recording.

The new single proved to be one of the band's best fast songs. Sucking in the listener with its memorable vocal intro, the dazzlingly unconventional number then launches right into the chorus, in which Brian, singing miles high with the braggadocio of a modern-day rapper, crows about being cool and making lots of money, while the group repeats the title refrain. The song's various instrumental segues and alternations of the principal theme have been likened to classical composition, and the hand claps are the cherry on the sundae. The song boasts a production and compositional sophistication to which The Beatles could then only aspire, but the casual listener wouldn't necessarily notice all that's going on musically, as it all serves as of one of the group's most fun, upbeat sing-alongs.

The first verse alludes to Brian's need to stretch out creatively, as Mike expresses boredom with cruising the same streets and says he'll find a cooler crowd. Then, in one of the group's last automotive references for a while, he brags that his car is the fastest, and in the most common sense of "getting around," boasts that he and his buddies always score with the chicks. It's all pre-hippie teen attitude, in its way anticipating the free-love movement that evolved as the decade progressed.

Musician Daniel Lanois, 12 years old when the song was released, was instantly captivated by the adolescent world "I Get Around" so potently evokes.

"It's what I call a 'snapshot song.' It's like a Polaroid of a moment or a feeling. I like the way Brian wrote about specifics of a rising culture. He brings the listener in through one philosophical moment — one thought, one emotion — and that is often the most powerful way. You could write a much bigger song, but by writing a small one, you address a big subject. Funnily enough, Brian may not have been personally experiencing all those moments, but he was watching them happen," says Lanois, the Canadian guitarist, singer-songwriter and producer whose moody soundscapes have shaped classic albums for U2, Peter Gabriel, Bob Dylan and The Neville Brothers.

If "I Get Around" provides a snapshot of mid-'60s SoCal teenage life, then *All Summer Long* is the entire scrapbook. The album cover — much imitated to this day — reinforces that theme with a series of photos showing members of the band frolicking on the beach with young ladies. From the groovy motorbike of "Little Honda" to the sun-drenched "Girls on the Beach," the goofy fun at the "Drive-In" and the oldies rock 'n' roll blaring over the radio on "Do You Remember?," the album documents a whole season of teenaged good times. The title track, featuring a unique xylophone intro and piccolo solo, injects a sense of the fleetingness of it all, as befitting the perspective of its songwriters, 23-year-old Mike and 21-year-old Brian. The wistful tune would memorably play over the closing credits of George Lucas' smash film *American Graffiti* nearly 10 years later.

Of course, it wouldn't be The Beach Boys if there weren't a couple of numbers that threaten to kill the buzz. The melodramatic '50s doo-wop-style ballad "We'll Run Away" finds a young couple frustrated by parental objections to their intended nuptials. The end of the innocence, however, is side-two opener "Wendy," which starts bleakly with echoed guitar and bass playing single notes in uni son before picking up the pace. What isn't upbeat is the story about a guy who thought he had the girl, only to find out she slept with another man.

It all builds to the irresistible "Don't Back Down," the group's last early-era song about surfing. With Murry gone as manager, Brian in the song assumes the father-figure role to issue a pep talk to himself and his troops, telling them that no matter what, they can't turn away from that oncoming breaker. The 20-foot wave in question may as well have been the one coming from across the pond. But with *All Summer Long*, Brian not only held his own against The Beatles, he took a Beach Boys album to new heights, loading the record with strong productions from front to back, with the exception of the behind-the-scenes excerpts of "Our Favorite Recording Sessions." The LP reached #4 in the U.S.

Part of what Lanois believes is so culturally significant in this and other Beach Boys records of the era is a guitar that came out of the Orange County city of Fullerton in the 1940s and eventually found its way to Carl, David and Alan. "A lot of The Beach Boys songs were written about the cultural revolution of the time — the beach culture and the rise of rock 'n' roll in California, which is a substantial rise given the Fender Stratocaster was born in the state. It's the very instrument that ended up in the hands of a very non–Beach Boys person like Jimi Hendrix," he notes.

"I Get Around" shook up the music community and the record-buying public, cruising all the way to #1 in the U.S. for two weeks. It marked a key victory for the home boys against the British Invasion, reaching the top on July 4, no less. It also helped The Beach Boys make inroads on the Fab Four's turf, becoming the band's first top 10 hit in the U.K., buoyed by a reported shout-out on British TV from Mick Jagger, who would have heard the song while on The Rolling Stones' first U.S. tour that spring.

If the listener could find it in them to flip over the super-catchy single, they would be treated to "Don't Worry Baby," which completed one of the all-time great two-sided 45s. The two tracks represented the yin and yang of the group's thematic makeup: if "I Get Around" is the ultimate expression of the group's testosterone-fueled competitiveness, then "Don't Worry Baby" reveals the insecurity underneath.

While it may be hard to imagine any link between Beach Boys music and Lanois' atmospheric work, the producer reveals that Brian has called him to discuss the possibility of collaborating. But fans needn't hold their breath: when asked about the likelihood of partnering on a Brian or Beach Boys project, Lanois simply says, "The last thing they need is a Canadian telling them about beaches."

But he and millions of others will always have fond memories of when "I Get Around" hit the airwaves. "I came up through all this music," he says. "I was happy to be there at the inception of it and I'm still rooting for Brian Wilson today."

ALAN BOYD ON . . .

KISS Me, BaBY

Written by: Brian Wilson and Mike Love
Lead vocals: Mike Love and Brian Wilson
Produced by: Brian Wilson
Recorded: December 16, 1964, January 15, 1965
Released: March 8, 1965, on *The Beach Boys Today!*
and April 5, 1965, as B-side to "Help Me, Rhonda"

Following the release of "I Get Around," the group's schedule became increasingly punishing, particularly on Brian. It would all come to a head by the end of 1964, changing the band dynamic forever.

The group had agreed to gift Capitol with an album of holiday songs including their earlier Yuletide hit "Little Saint Nick." Sessions for *The Beach Boys' Christmas Album* — which would also contain four new originals and seven traditional tunes backed by a large orchestra — occupied the second half of June. The band then set out on the five-week Summer Safari tour, which took them to Hawaii and then through the U.S. Southwest, Midwest and West Coast. A show in Sacramento, where the band had a particularly fervent following, was recorded for the *Beach Boys Concert* album that saw release in October. Notable as much for the fans' screaming as anything else, the live LP would become the group's first and only non-compilation album to top the U.S. charts, which it did throughout December.

Meanwhile, there was the matter of following up "I Get Around," which the band did admirably with the mid-tempo "When I Grow Up (To Be a Man)." As young men making teen music for the past couple of years, Brian and Mike co-wrote a song that openly fretted about, among other things, staying hip as time passes. For now they had nothing to worry about, as the single reached #9 in *Billboard*.

The group returned to the road in late August and for most of September, this time making it to the East Coast. On September 27 they followed in The Beatles' footsteps, making their first appearance on *The Ed Sullivan Show*, giving live performances of "I Get Around" — surrounded by three hot rods — and "Wendy." Then it was back home to focus on the next 45, the upbeat "Dance, Dance, Dance," which, driven by Carl's hot 12-string guitar riff, continued the winning streak with a #8 U.S. chart showing.

The boys' rendition of "Dance, Dance, Dance" whipped a Santa Monica crowd into a frenzy at the October 29 filming of the *T.A.M.I. Show*, a classic rock 'n' roll performance movie that saw them headline a stellar bill also featuring The Rolling Stones, James Brown, The Supremes, Chuck Berry, Smokey Robinson & The Miracles, Marvin Gaye and Jan & Dean. Just a couple of days later, Brian and the band embarked on their first tour of the U.K. and Europe, which also included TV appearances. At the airport Brian thought Marilyn was flirting with Mike, which prompted a spat between the couple before the band boarded their plane. For the duration of the flight Brian was wracked with suspicion and dread, and sparked by these feelings he proposed to Marilyn over the phone after touching down. The European tour proved an emotional time for Brian, and he later recalled doing more drinking than he had ever done and channeling his feelings into songwriting.[1]

While the group was staying at Copenhagen's Royal Hotel on a late-November promotional visit,[2] Brian wrote "Kiss Me, Baby,"[3] a ballad that pleaded for the romantic reconciliation he anticipated with Marilyn. The song, to which Mike would add lyrics, may not be among The Beach Boys' best known, but it is a favorite of many fans, including Alan Boyd, director/editor of several documentaries about the band, including 1998's *Endless Harmony: The Beach Boys Story*. "Musically, it goes as deep as many classical pieces and classic standards from the Great American Songbook. This song stands right up there alongside the most moving works by the Gershwins, Irving Berlin or Rodgers and Hart," says Boyd, who became the archive manager for The Beach Boys' Brother Records. "It's always amazed me. The emotions inside the song have got to be real. You can't just manufacture or pretend something like that."

The group returned stateside before the end of the month for more local dates, and on December 7, 1964, Brian married Marilyn, then all of 16. Just over a week later, he went back into Western Studio 3 to record the instrumental track for "Kiss Me, Baby" with his favorite session musicians, including Carol Kaye, who would become his go-to bass guitarist. It was Brian's most ambitious ballad production to date, featuring two basses (Kaye and Ray Pohlman), four guitars (Carl, Barney Kessel, Bill Pitman and Billy Strange), two horns (Peter Christ and David Duke), two saxophones (Steve Douglas and Jay Migliori), two pianos (Brian and 22-year-old Leon Russell) Julius Wechter on bell tree and vibraphone[4] and Hal Blaine alternating on the drums and temple blocks, which produce a percussive sound that would become a Brian trademark. The beautiful arrangement perfectly complements a composition that boasts some of Brian's most arresting changes.

Brian and the band next made a triumphant headlining appearance on the Christmas edition of ABC musical variety show *Shindig!*

Brian played bass at his usual center-stage spot — his recent weight gain evident — and sang the lead on "Papa-Oom-Mow-Mow" and "Johnny B. Goode." Nobody could have guessed it, but this and a subsequent spot on a Bob Hope special would be the last hurrah for the band in this early live incarnation.

Instead of taking a much-needed rest over the holidays, the group, riding its chart-topping live LP, set off on a tour that extended over Christmas and New Year's Eve. This proved to be the breaking point for Brian, who, minutes into the group's flight from Los Angeles to Houston, suddenly began sobbing. He placed a pillow over his face and began to scream, barked at the stewardesses to leave him alone and rolled onto the floor. A shocked Carl and Al, along with the airplane staff, were able to calm him down despite his demand the plane turn around. He made it to Houston and, according to most accounts, was present and somehow able to persevere through that night's show, but spent the next day sequestered and sobbing in his hotel room. The group's road manager took him back to Los Angeles that night, where, at his request, he was met by only Audree.

"Touring was a little tedious," Brian

reflects in *Endless Harmony*. "You had to hop a plane every day, you know, and I was having a little problem — mental problems on tour."[5]

The combination of business and creative pressures, his overbearing father and an unsure start to his new marriage had become a lot to bear. Marilyn particularly objected to Brian's new pastime of smoking pot. Whether his toking was merely something he picked up to alleviate stress or whether it contributed to his anxiety is a matter of speculation. But on some level Brian's airborne episode — which the band described as a nervous breakdown — was premeditated to facilitate his exit from touring, which he had been eyeing since spring 1963.

The rest of the guys, still on the road and now down one man, put out an emergency call to Glen Campbell, whose participation at the group's sessions made him a natural onstage replacement to play bass and sing Brian's parts. Meanwhile, Brian, after a cooling-off period of just two weeks over the holidays, was back at Western in early 1965 commandeering sessions for the group's next album, *The Beach Boys Today!* He showed his studio skills were sharper than ever and was increasingly demanding of both the session players and the group, calling for upwards of 30 takes of a song if he wasn't satisfied. He and the group laid down a vocal track for "Kiss Me, Baby" that sounds like heaven's choir.

"It's very rich and there's a lot happening — a lot of counterpoint and interesting harmonies on top of harmonies," Boyd notes. "There was something about those sad songs of Brian's that really hit me on a very emotional level, and that was one of those tunes I would listen to over and over again. Sometimes even now I'll hear just that part of the song when Mike's voice comes in with 'late last night,' and I'll feel myself getting a little choked up."

Historian Craig Slowinski believes it was after this vocal session that Brian informed his bandmates he was officially retiring from the road to focus on writing and producing.[6] They were shocked — all except Carl, who immediately stepped up in his role as the band's stabilizing force and concert leader. Brian still filled in onstage if Campbell wasn't available and joined the guys for some TV appearances, but a new structure was established whereby Brian mostly stayed home composing songs and recording the instrumental tracks with the session players while the rest of the guys spread the gospel around the world and added their vocal parts when they returned.

A harbinger of the sophisticated music to come, "Kiss Me, Baby" has been a hidden gem. It was buried in the middle of side two of *The Beach Boys Today!* — part of a stunning sequence of introspective ballads that also includes the delicate "Please Let Me Wonder," a cover of doo-wop number "I'm So Young" previously recorded by The Students and Ronnie Spector, "She Knows Me Too Well" and "In the Back of My Mind." Capitol saw the merit of "Kiss Me, Baby," including it on the 1966 *Best of The Beach Boys* compilation, although it didn't make the cut on the following decade's *Endless Summer*. It continued to have its admirers, however, including critic Dave Marsh, who ranked it #289 in his book *The Heart of Rock & Soul: The 1001 Greatest Singles Ever Made.*

For his part, Boyd has helped fans hear the song from a fresh perspective. The *Endless Harmony Soundtrack* LP features Andrew Sandoval's stereo remix of the original mono recording, bringing out both the meticulousness and expansiveness of the track and vocals, while the 2001 *Hawthorne, CA* double-CD collection Boyd assembled with producer/engineer Mark Linett offers an a cappella mix that lays out all the lush ache in the group's

singing. Exposure in Boyd's documentary put the song back on the radar. One of the film's most memorable segments has Brian, more than 30 years after recording it, sitting at a mixing console in his basement studio proudly deconstructing the parts. The vocal layers are so dense that few listeners would have ever made out the words the group sings in the background unless Brian had pointed them out in the film.

"Some people were arguing, 'Do "California Girls" or one of the hits,'" Boyd recalls of his decision to have Brian focus on the number. "I just said, 'No, we've got to pull this one out. It will be new to him since he hasn't really thought about it for a long time.' And he really got into it. I was getting chills in the studio as Brian was listening to it and commenting on it."

And Brian was clearly happy to have rediscovered the tune that so directly reflected his need for love and peace of mind in one of his most turbulent periods. In April 2000, he did a rare performance of it for his solo recording *Live at the Roxy Theatre*. "Let's do a song called 'Kiss Me, Baby,'" he announced to the audience with signature modesty. "It's kind of a sweet little song."

JON STEBBINS ON . . .
DO YOU wanna Dance?

Written by: Bobby Freeman
Lead vocal: Dennis Wilson
Produced by: Brian Wilson
Recorded: January 11, 1965
Released: February 15, 1965
Chart peak: U.S. #12
Appears on *The Beach Boys Today!*

Radio listeners in February 1965 would have been understandably confused by the latest Beach Boys release. The harmonies on the driving rock 'n' roll track were unmistakable, but who was that singing lead? While all the group members had traditionally provided beautiful backgrounds, in terms of the front-and-center vocal, the singles had stuck to a formula.

Yet here was "Do You Wanna Dance?," a fabulous cover of the Bobby Freeman R&B standard, bursting out of the gate with a pleading invitation from Dennis.

"That was a big deal," says Jon Stebbins, California-based author of *The Real Beach Boy — Dennis Wilson*, *The Lost Beach Boy* about David Marks and *The Beach Boys FAQ: All That's Left to Know About America's Band*. "Every Beach Boys hit had featured Mike Love and the anomalies had Brian Wilson singing. So to have this guy singing on your A-side was a totally different sound. It shows how confident Brian was to use him."

Hardcore fans were not unfamiliar with Dennis' raspy tenor. On "Luau," B-side of the 1961 debut "Surfin'" single, he sang a solo line with verve. Then 16, he had a voice like a neighborhood agitator with a tender side, which is exactly what he was. He got his first complete lead on the *Surfin' Safari* charmer "Little Miss America," and his vocals provide the competitive juice to album cuts "Surfers Rule" and "This Car of Mine" and plenty of oomph to Dion's "The Wanderer" on the *Beach Boys Concert* LP. And he can be heard somewhere in the mix on just about everything else.

"Dennis' voice is in a lot of Beach Boys hits," Stebbins notes. "His voice is really prominent in 'I Get Around,' 'Don't Worry Baby' and 'In My Room.' For some reason people always thought his voice was the one least used, but it's not really the case. It's in the harmonies in most of those iconic songs. People hear the bass voice and they always think, 'Oh, that's Mike,' but Dennis sang a lot of bass stuff as well. Dennis had a little more of a sandpapery thing than Mike, but they basically would cover the same parts. Brian gave most of the leads to Mike because Mike had a really commercial sound."

Despite Dennis not being technically the best singer of the bunch, Brian tapped him for a couple of key tracks on *The Beach Boys Today!*: "Do You Wanna Dance?," which opens the LP, and final song "In the Back of My Mind." The latter is a great number, but Dennis doesn't quite find the range to nail it. But he was the right call on "Do You Wanna Dance?," as the single's #12 U.S. chart performance attests. "The song's got a little more edge to it because of his voice," Stebbins says. "Carl and Al are much better singers than Dennis, but Brian knew when to use him. There's a texture there, an emotion — something really essential to the Beach Boys records. Dennis brought something."

What that was, most of all, was sex appeal. It didn't hurt that female fans idolized him as the classic blond surfer dude and referred to him as "the good-looking one" or "the cool one." He plays up that image on the "Do You Wanna Dance?" record sleeve, in which the band is pictured in blue short-sleeved shirts, except for him, center, with his shirt off. He also lent credibility to the group's surf and car anthems since he was the only one who actively participated in those cultures. Naturally the group's fans wanted to hear more from him, and on "Do You Wanna Dance?" he delivers. He comes across masculine and confident. It sounds like he won't break down and cry if his girl refuses him. Of course, we know she won't.

The girls certainly weren't refusing him at a New York taping of *Shindig!*, screaming as he and the band — in all their striped-shirt glory — lip-synched their way through the song. It was quite a sight to see Dennis singing lead while pounding away on his kit. Ironically, it was Hal Blaine who played on the record, not Dennis. But Dennis gets so carried away in the TV performance, which aired April 21, that he adds an impromptu drum flourish audible over Blaine's prerecorded track. He would pull double-duty at concerts as well. A photo from a June 1966 concert at Yankee Stadium shows Dennis drumming and simultaneously singing into a microphone held by Mike. In earlier shows when Brian was around, the eldest Wilson brother would man the drums while Dennis sang the occasional lead at the front of the stage.

"Do You Wanna Dance?" is also notable because it finds the group continuing to leave the old days behind, both thematically and musically. Looking to move on to subject matter that wouldn't be perceived as faddish, they hit the dance floor again as they had on their previous hit "Dance, Dance, Dance." The two tracks would bookend the fast first side of *The Beach Boys Today!*

Freeman's original version, properly titled "Do You Want to Dance?," was a top 10 pop crossover hit in 1958 for the 17-year-old performer, but the song may have been fresh on Brian's mind from Del Shannon's rendition, which got some radio play in fall 1964. The Beach Boys' version actually bears a closer resemblance to an earlier effort by Cliff Richard & the Shadows that similarly adds rock 'n' roll harmonies. The song would continue to be covered through the years, notably by The Ramones and in slow-dance fashion by The Mamas & the Papas and Bette Midler. The Beach Boys' version — the band's equivalent of The Beatles' take on "Twist and Shout" — remains one of the best.

In addition to Carl's lead guitar and Brian's acoustic grand piano,[1] nearly a dozen session musicians play on the track, making their presence thoroughly felt for the first time on a Beach Boys hit. Brian was thinking beyond the basic guitar-bass-drums combo, and helping make this one of the group's more powerful tracks is the three-man saxophone team of Steve Douglas, Plas Johnson and Jay Migliori along with Julius Wechter's timpani,[2] which contributes to the song's symphonic rock 'n' roll sound.

But above all, it is Dennis' performance that makes it memorable. The vocal competition within the band would get stiffer, however — especially with Carl's emergence — and it would be the only hit Dennis would sing. The only other group A-side featuring his lead would be his own composition "Slip on Through," which unfortunately slipped through the cracks in 1970. While that song provided further evidence of what a compelling instrument his voice could be, even more importantly it demonstrated how far he had come as a record-making force in his own right.

ALAN JARDINE ON...

HELP ME, RHONDA

Written by: Brian Wilson and Mike Love
Lead vocal: Alan Jardine
Produced by: Brian Wilson
Recorded: February 24, March 3, 4, 21, 1965
Released: April 5, 1965
Chart peak: U.S. #1, U.K. #27
Appears on *Summer Days (And Summer Nights!!)*

It was supposed to be just an album cut, but there was a hit single somewhere in the grooves of "Help Me, Ronda," and in February 1965 the group went back into the studio to get it right.

According to Brian's memoir, the song came to him while he sat at the piano singing Bobby Darin's "Mack the Knife,"[1] while the documentary *Brian Wilson: Songwriter 1962–1969* claims he found inspiration in the harmonica riffs of Buster Brown's 1960 R&B chart-topper "Fannie Mae."[2] "Help Me, Ronda" (an "h" was added to Ronda for the second, more famous version) may be one of The Beach Boys' most upbeat records, but its lyrics are charged with heartbreak. The opening lines, written by Mike, are a mouthful of despair. Our narrator has been dumped by his fiancée for another guy and turns to Rhonda to help him forget. In a case of art imitating life, Judy Bowles had rejected Brian's proposal a couple of years earlier, sending him running into Marilyn's arms. Author Jon Stebbins pushes the belief that Rhonda was a woman with whom either Mike or Brian had a one-night stand.[3]

"I asked Brian who Rhonda was and he said it was just a fiction," recalls Alan, who got to sing both versions. "I'm sure there was something down there in the psychology of it, but that one was purely a studio creation. We really didn't get into the meaning of the lyrics. They spoke for themselves. Brian had a very fertile mind and it was perfect for our intents and purposes."

In January 1965, Brian recorded the instrumental and vocal tracks for "Help Me, Ronda," which ended up on *The Beach Boys Today!* The session players included Glen Campbell on guitar and Leon Russell on piano.[4] The guitar-driven track is sprightly in the verses but flat in the chorus, and the harmonica solo by rockabilly artist Billy Lee Riley is anticlimactic. The record meanders, and in one of Brian's most peculiar bits of studio trickery, it fades in and out three times before the end. "It's very goofy," Alan notes. "It doesn't have a really good, raw feel. It's more of a laid-back shuffle. It's pleasant but it doesn't really go anywhere. It definitely wasn't a single."

But Brian was convinced it was the foundation for one. In February, he and the boys began recording a new arrangement. "We went back into the studio and tried to pick up the tempo a bit and give it a little extra energy," Alan explains. Brian loaded the record with vocal and instrumental hooks. Mike sings a memorable "bow bow bow bow" bass part while Brian's falsetto leads the swelling "Help me, Rhonda, yeah!" that punctuates the chorus. The harmonica break is replaced with Brian's more vibrant boogie-woogie piano and a stinging Carl guitar solo. Brian also came up with a fat new bass line executed by Carol Kaye.

"She had a knack for getting clarity on her bass that's quite beautiful," Alan notes. "She's an accomplished guitarist, so that probably helped her convert that alacrity on the strings to the bass. I'm sure she used a special pick. Carl said, 'Beach Boys music is music of joy,' and Carol gave the song that joyful feeling."

Arriving at that joyful result, however, involved some hard work and hard times. Alan had sung only one lead before — "Christmas Day" on the 1964 holiday album — and the rhythm and meter in the verses of "Help Me, Rhonda" made it hard to master. More problematic still was an appearance by Murry, who, along with Audree and other family and friends, attended a vocal session at Radio Recorders. A few glasses of wine seemed to make Murry forget he'd been fired as the group's manager and that Brian alone had been producing all the records since *Surfer Girl*. He tried to take charge in the control room, as is documented on a widely distributed tape of his exchange with the group. (Brian had let the recording reel run.)

Although Alan already had laid down a good vocal and only an overdub was required, Murry felt the need to show him how to sing the song, despite not knowing the words. The tension is palpable as he implores Alan to "loosen up, Sweetie" and "syncopate" his vocal. "Be happy," Murry directs, to which Alan forces a laugh and replies, "I am so happy, you can't believe it. I am so happy we're only doing one song tonight." Further highlights from the tape:

> Murry: *Fellas, I have 3,000 words to say. Quit screaming and start singing from your hearts, huh? . . . Dennis, you're flatting. Okay, Mike, you're flatting on your high notes. Let's go. Let's roll. So you're big stars? Let's fight. Let's fight for success . . . OK, fellas — you got any guts? Let's hear it.*
>
> Dennis: *Dad, only 82 words . . .*

Murry: *You guys think you're good? Let's go. Let's go. Fellas, as a team we're unbeatable. Let's go. You're doing wonderful —*

Brian [yelling]: *Oh shit! You're embarrassing me! Now, shut up! God damn it.*

Murry: *I'll leave, Brian, if you're going to give me a bad time. Let's go. Let's go.*

Brian: *I've got one ear left and your big, loud voice is killing it!*

Murry: *Can we hear a chord, just a chord, like we used to when you used to sing clear records? . . . This is going to be a helluva hit. Let's go. Loosen up. Loosen up a little . . . I'm a genius, too . . . Brian, forget who you are, will ya? . . . [To Carl] You've been loafing for two hours. What's the matter — you made too much money, buddy? . . . We need help. We need the honest projection that we used to have.*

Brian: *You want to have, like, the "409" sound, right, on "Help Me, Rhonda"?*

Murry: *When you guys get so big*

*that you can't sing from your hearts,
you're going downhill.*
Brian: *Downhill?*
Murry: *Downhill! . . . Son, I'm sorry.
I've protected you for 22 years, but
I can't go on if you're not going to
listen to an intelligent man . . .*
Brian: *We would like to record in an
atmosphere of calmness, and you're
not presenting that.*
Murry: *Forget it.* [To Audree] *I'm
sorry, dear. We'll never come to
another recording session. Carl,
I'm so sorry . . . The kid* [referring
to Brian] *had a big success and he
thinks he owns the business . . .
Chuck* [Britz] *and I used to make
one hit after another in 30 minutes.
You guys take five hours to do it.*
Brian: *Times are changing.*
Murry: *Don't ever forget: honesty is
the best policy, son. Right, Mike? You
know what I'm talking about, Mike.
We've had our differences,* [but] *you
know what I'm talking about.*

Reflecting now on the incident, Alan says, "I
was having trouble with the part and both
Brian and Murry were trying to help me, but
Brian resented his father's interference and
they began to lock horns. It was a classic
father-son conflict where Brian began to assert
himself as a man. I could only imagine how
difficult that must have been for both of them.
They were struggling over how best to produce the music, but clearly Murry was com-
promised by his closeness to it. He brought his
own values, and it didn't really belong in our
system. One must make way for the new, but
it was difficult for him to lose control."

Despite his father's criticisms, Brian's creative choices were once again validated when
"Help Me, Rhonda" rocketed to the top of
the U.S. charts, where it stayed for two weeks.
The group's second #1 single, it knocked The
Beatles' "Ticket to Ride" out of that spot and
prevented Sam the Sham & the Pharaohs'
"Wooly Bully" from ever getting there.[5] It also
introduced Alan as a singer with a punchy,
commercially appealing voice, and he would
step into the spotlight, flashing a toothy,
Kennedyesque smile as he belted out the hit
on *Shindig!* and *The Andy Williams Show.*

"Help Me, Rhonda" was included on
the *Summer Days (And Summer Nights!!)*
album, even though the earlier version had

New member Bruce (left) suggested the *Summer Days (And Summer Nights!!)* LP include the revamped version of "Help Me, Rhonda," sung by Alan (right). [© AP Photo/HO]

appeared on the previous LP. Certainly there was no way Capitol was going to keep a #1 single down. Brian called on Alan's vocal chops again for the cut "Then I Kissed Her," a rewrite of Phil Spector's "Then He Kissed Me" for The Crystals. But when it came time to shoot the album cover — featuring the guys on a yacht — Alan, run ragged by the group's intense schedule, was nowhere to be found. "I had the flu and Capitol went and shot it anyway. Thanks, Capitol, very much," he says.

Alan did appear on the back of the sleeve, however, as each member penned a message to the fans. The guys' respective personalities shine through here: Brian notes that he's preoccupied with the contents of the album, which is unfinished as he writes, while Mike delights in playing to hundreds of thousands of fans, and Dennis has girls on the brain. Carl apologizes for Brian's non-appearance at shows, while Alan reflects on the physical exhaustion of rock 'n' roll stardom.

"We were all running on empty most of the time, just keeping up with the tremendous demands on ourselves," he says, looking back now. "Everything was organized for us to make more albums and tour. We were the grist for the mill. Of course, it took its toll on Brian."

"Help Me, Rhonda" is such an iconic pre–Summer of Love number that the band later felt the need to update it for the hippie crowd. At shows in 1971 they reinterpreted the song as a laid-back blues with Carl on lead vocal. Alan would sing a pacier rendition of this arrangement on the 1973 *The Beach Boys in Concert* album. That LP is the best showcase for Alan's vocals and documents how much he could sound like Brian, as he takes the lead on "You Still Believe in Me," "Heroes and Villains," "Surfer Girl," "Wouldn't It Be Nice" and "Don't Worry Baby." "I didn't know I could sing that high. I can't now," he says with a laugh.

In Alan's more recent Endless Summer Band, the high end is handed off to his sons Matthew and Adam. While he witnessed firsthand the pitfalls of working with family, sharing the stage with his boys, he says, is smooth sailing: "We're pretty easy with each other. We know the music backwards and forwards. We work quite well together." Matt toured with The Beach Boys as a singer and percussionist starting in 1991, but that ended with the shakeup brought about by Carl's death in 1998. Alan parted ways with Mike, Bruce and David — who was then back in the band

— and formed the splinter group Beach Boys Family & Friends, including his sons, Brian's daughters Carnie and Wendy, and stalwart Beach Boys players Billy Hinsche, Ed Carter, Bobby Figueroa and Richie Cannata.

Mike would end up with the licensing of The Beach Boys' name, so when Alan's band released a 2002 live album — which includes his lead on "Help Me, Rhonda," naturally — it had to rebrand itself Al Jardine, Family & Friends. "God forbid any other Beach Boys go up onstage and actually be a Beach Boy," he quips.

The licensing situation impeded Al's ability to tour extensively in the first half of the decade, but he came on board for Brian's 2006–2007 *Pet Sounds* 40th anniversary U.S. tour. At the first East Coast date in Boston's Orpheum Theater, he was visibly moved by the thunderous applause that greeted him as he walked onstage. "It never gets old. Hearing that kind of response was really encouraging," he says. The audience was especially appreciative of "Help Me, Rhonda," with him and Brian alternating on the vocals.

Two thousand and ten saw the arrival of Alan's first solo album, *A Postcard from California*, recorded in the studio at his Big Sur ranch, where he lives with second wife Mary Ann. The LP looked ahead with new songs while embracing The Beach Boys' past. A harmonica-laden "Help Me, Rhonda" returns it to its bluesy Buster Brown roots, as befitting guest guitarist-vocalist Steve Miller. Alan finally got to sing his signature number again with Mike and Bruce at a February 2011 concert in Simi Valley, California, honoring Ronald Reagan's centennial birthday. That show set the stage for the band's 50th anniversary reunion, a milestone that had Alan reflecting on his decision to ditch studying dentistry and take Brian's place on the road back in 1963.

"I came back into the band to help him out so that he could go about doing his business, and I would be happy doing mine. I enjoyed singing the songs that we started when we founded the band. In fact, I probably should have gotten a share of the writing royalties, because if I hadn't come back, he wouldn't have been able to write all those great songs," he says with a laugh. "We all helped each other out in the long run."

PETER BAGGE ON . . .

I'M BUGGED AT MY OL' MAN

Written by: Brian Wilson
Lead vocal: Brian Wilson
Produced by: Brian Wilson
Recorded: May 24, 1965
Released: July 5, 1965, on *Summer Days (And Summer Nights!!)*

After the scene at the "Help Me, Rhonda" session, Murry's relationship with his sons grew frostier, although his thoughts rarely strayed from them. The bond between him and Audree was similarly coming unglued. A main point of contention between them had always been his harsh treatment of the boys.

Back in summer 1964, Audree told her husband that although she would continue living with him, she was no longer in love with him. To Murry, it was yet another family betrayal. Not one to easily articulate his emotions — and there weren't many sympathetic ears — he immediately channeled his hurt into a last will and testament dated August 7.

The document, now part of the Hard Rock memorabilia collection, spells out Murry's desire that upon his death Audree receive 50% of the assets of the Sea of Tunes Publishing Company, which he had shrewdly set up in partnership with Brian for Beach Boys compositions, and of which, he prematurely stated, he was now the sole proprietor. However, he adds, if Audree is not married to him when he dies, then she is entitled to only 25%, "because she did not love me in the true sense of what a devoted wife or mate represents, and that because of her place in my home as mother of my three sons, did undermine my respect in the home, by devious methods of complacency with the children, defaming me in front of them, swearing and insulting me in their presence, and many other means of hurting my standing as the head of the family."[1]

He proceeds to explain that he had been stripped of this standing ever since 1960 — a period that covers not only his sons' maturation to adults, but also the birth and rise of The Beach Boys. Murry couldn't allow his sons to chart their own course, and that would forever poison the family dynamic. The diary-like tone of the document continues, with Murry lamenting that Audree "told me on this date . . . that she did not enjoy intercourse with me anymore . . . I am a very unhappy, and broken-heated [*sic*] man about my family."[2]

Murry and Audree eventually separated. With money made off Brian's songwriting, Murry bought an ostentatious house in Whittier, a dozen miles southeast of Los Angeles — and a home for Audree one block away. Although no longer man and wife in the traditional sense, they still spent much of their time together, and reportedly made peace with one another in the early '70s.[3] Murry allegedly had one or more affairs,[4] but whether this was in the aftermath of his separation from Audree or was ultimately the cause is not known. In his book *Catch a Wave: The Rise, Fall & Redemption of The Beach Boys' Brian Wilson*, author Peter Ames Carlin suggests Murry's extramarital relationships are what prompted Brian to write "Let Him Run Wild,"[5] which, if true, makes it Oedipal pop predating The Doors' "The End" by more than a year.

On May 8, 1965, Murry directed his bile at Brian, drafting an eight-page diatribe to his son that is also in the hands of Hard Rock. The Wilson patriarch continues to indirectly equate the rise of The Beach Boys in "this vicious music business" with the dissolution of the family — a period he calls "almost a living hell for me" — and he confesses that he "wanted to give up completely on two separate occasions."[6] Seeing his sons climb to the top of the music world — and then prove they could stay there without him — was a bitter pill.

Murry proceeds to justify the "violent punishment" of his children — somehow explaining it was doled out to provide them a sense of security — then complains further about Audree's lack of support. "She was trying to raise you boys almost like girls," he writes. He berates Brian for falling under the sway of "a bunch of phonies" including Gary Usher, and predicts "a short cycle of Beach Boys success." He plays up his own role in the success to date and expresses shock that "such a beautiful young boy . . . could become so obsessed to prove that he was better than his father."[7]

In one area, Murry displays eerie foresight: "I am worried that a continuance of this mockery in handling your lives and careers can only end in personality disasters, one way or the other . . . All three of my sons should immediately be taken out of the music business to salvage the rest of their lives." There are also glimpses of self-awareness: "I am proud of the job I did with my sons as their manager and guiding force, although I know I was wrong in my approach . . . I know I failed my sons many, many times . . . I am not over the fact that I have lost my three sons' love."[8]

The letter curiously ends on a business note, with Murry explaining that he is trying to temporarily keep Capitol from paying Brian approximately $276,000 in songwriting royalties that otherwise would be eaten by the taxman due to Brian's tax bracket. He then suggests he and Brian sever remaining business ties, because "we can no longer work together in a truly honest father and son relationship."[9]

Brian's memoir interprets this as a veiled threat whereby Murry would withhold Brian's money until Brian relinquished his interest in Sea of Tunes to him.[10] Murry believed he was entitled to 100% of it, as the one who had secured the group's record deal, promoted and managed them in their formative years and pushed Capitol to keep supporting them, especially during the British Invasion. A self-made man, he had taken out a mortgage on ABLE Machinery to help the group get off the ground[11] and then gave up the company to pursue the boys' interests full-time.[12] After further badgering from Murry, Brian did give over his interest in the publishing company. In 1969, Murry unwisely sold Sea of Tunes to Almo/Irving Music, a division of A&M Records, for $700,000 — a small fraction of what it was later worth — and kept it all.

Murry's letter to Brian provides a wealth of insight into his conflicted personality, and it made headlines in 2009 after being posted online. Among those who read it with great interest is acclaimed artist Peter Bagge, creator of the popular alternative comic magazine *Hate* and the darkly funny cartoon series

Rock 'n' Roll Dad that features Murry as its protagonist.

"It makes Murry sound *very* complex and even a bit more sophisticated than you would have assumed from some World War II–era suburban blue-collar guy," Bagge says of the letter. "A lot of it sounds like *Dr. Phil*–type pop psychology, but such jargon wasn't commonplace in the mid-'60s. It makes me wonder where he got it from. But it's also classic Murry: alternately using guilt, threats, self-pity and insults to get what he wants."

These facets of Murry's personality have been dramatized in a pair of TV productions that aired on ABC in the U.S. *Summer Dreams: The Story of the Beach Boys* — a 1990 adaptation of Steven Gaines' book *Heroes and Villains: The True Story of the Beach Boys* — boasts a frightfully effective portrayal of Murry by Arlen Dean Snyder. This was followed a decade later by the two-parter *The Beach Boys: An American Family*, which has a far more authorized air to it, executive produced as it is by sometimes group drummer John Stamos.

It was the latter program that inspired Bagge and comedian Dana Gould — a writer/producer on *The Simpsons* — to do *Rock 'n' Roll Dad*. "Dana and I were talking about how much we loved the Murry character, played in grand fashion by Dana's actor friend Kevin Dunn. We agreed that Murry was the best part of the story, and that the show got boring after he stopped appearing in it," Bagge recalls. "Cranky old men are always funny to me — from a safe distance, anyway. Plus all the stories I'd hear and read about him were so over-the-top and entertaining, both because of and in spite of their awfulness."

Rock 'n' Roll Dad first appeared on start-up Icebox.com in 2001 but was cut short at four webisodes after the dot-com crash. The show opener features hothead Murry (voiced by stand-up comic Paul F. Tompkins) bellowing his immortal line "I'm a genius, too" while his glass eye pops out. The storyline begins after Murry has been fired by his sons, and each installment focuses on his attempts to surpass The Beach Boys by recording various bands — including a group of Borneo bush monkeys — and even joining forces with a couple other notorious rock 'n' roll dads: Alfred "Freddie" Lennon (biological father of John Lennon) and Joe Jackson (father of The Jacksons).

Bagge and Gould aren't the only ones who saw the comedic potential in Murry's behavior.

Murry Wilson's more unsavory characteristics provided the inspiration for the *Rock 'n' Roll Dad* cartoon and comics by Peter Bagge and Dana Gould. [© Peter Bagge]

Strangely, so did Brian. It's not clear whether Brian read Murry's letter at the time, but just over two weeks after Murry wrote it, Brian recorded "I'm Bugged at My Ol' Man," one of the most amusing — yet in its way unsettling — tracks the band ever laid down.

The production is spare beside other tracks on *Summer Days (And Summer Nights!!)*, featuring New Orleans–style piano, Greek-chorus group backing vocals, and a warbling Brian lead that is so self-consciously silly it is credited to "Too Embarrassed" on the LP's back cover. He sings as a teenager who enrages his dad by missing curfew, and as a result must endure an increasingly outrageous series of chastisements. Not only must he stay in his room, but his father gets rid of his surfboard, cuts off his hair while he's sleeping, boards his window, disconnects his phone and takes away the boy's radio and listens to it tauntingly outside. A pinnacle of ludicrousness is reached when he suggests his parents are starving him while eating a giant meal themselves. His frustration builds to a scream as he wails that he just wants out.

"That song was obviously supposed to be funny — which it is," Bagge observes. "Brian was using the universal 'my old man's an asshole' sentiment that almost every teenage boy feels to both express but also whitewash his own legitimate anger towards Murry."

If there is one serious shot at Murry in the song, it's at the end when Brian suggests Murry is out of touch, not cool. To Brian, pop music tastemaker of the mid-'60s, this was the ultimate judgment. In the many interviews he has given about his father, depending on how magnanimous he has felt, he has said that Murry either did or didn't know "where it's at." Murry understood the significance of such a statement. In his letter to Brian he takes offense to the fact that Usher called him "a square," and in a 1971 *Rolling Stone* interview, Murry says that when Brian wrote the song, "He meant it as a put-on, but he meant it."[13]

Murry's rivalry with Brian would not recede. His attempt to recreate The Beach Boys with knockoff striped-shirters The Sunrays died a quick death, and then he believed he would outdo his sons by strong-arming Capitol into releasing an album of his own, the instrumental easy listening of 1967's *The Many Moods of Murry Wilson*, which includes a version of Brian's "The Warmth of the Sun." ("Generic schmaltz — tolerable background Muzak" is Bagge's assessment of the LP.)

Outside of the group itself, Murry's shadow looms larger than anyone's in The Beach Boys story. "He was good *and* bad: good in that it's always helpful and maybe even necessary to have a bully representing you, and he obviously had some useful cynical knowledge of the music business," Bagge says. "But bullying your own clients is never wise, and his cynicism and paranoia seemed to have no bounds. He also became the very thing he claimed to despise: a showbiz rip-off artist."

Most telling about Murry's relationship with his sons is the fact that following his 1973 death from a heart attack at age 55, neither Brian nor Dennis attended the funeral. Three years later, while filming the NBC TV special *The Beach Boys*, Brian, just coming out of a long fog of seclusion and drug abuse, sat at the piano with his brothers — by now all bearded men in their 30s — and stumbled through "I'm Bugged at My Ol' Man." In spite of it all, the three of them cracked up. Only they could truly understand how bittersweet that laughter was.

James Mercer on...
GIRL DON'T TELL ME

Written by: Brian Wilson
Lead vocal: Carl Wilson
Produced by: Brian Wilson
Recorded: April 30, 1965
Released: July 5, 1965, on *Summer Days (And Summer Nights!!)* and December 20, 1965, as B-side to "Barbara Ann"

Capitol wanted new Beach Boys product for the summer of 1965 and delivered *Summer Days (And Summer Nights!!)* to record stores just in time. While the album has been perceived as a step back lyrically from the sustained introspection of side two of *The Beach Boys Today!*, it does contain some luscious tracks and formal experiments that would see full flower on the *Pet Sounds* and *Smile* recordings.

Indeed, in a January 28, 2011, tweet, Brian informed followers that the album was his favorite. And why not: few LPs in pop history can boast a suite of songs on par with "Then I Kissed Her"–"Salt Lake City"–"Girl Don't Tell Me"–"Help Me, Rhonda"–"California Girls"–"Let Him Run Wild"–"You're So Good to Me." The public certainly approved, and the record joined *Surfin' U.S.A.* as the only Beach Boys non-compilation studio albums to chart as high as #2 in America. Capitol evidently didn't see its immediate potential in the U.K., however, delaying its release there until June 1966, when it reached #4, riding high alongside *Pet Sounds*.

"Girl Don't Tell Me" recounts a teenage boy's realization that his summer romance is nothing more than that. The song's Beatlesque qualities have been much noted, particularly the stuttered three-note rise in the verses and chorus,[1] which recalls "Ticket to Ride." It's no coincidence. Released on April 9, 1965, "Ticket to Ride" was The Beatles' most recent radio hit when The Beach Boys made their recording. Brian's old Hawthorne buddy Bruce Griffin, speaking to author Peter Ames Carlin, recalled being with Brian when they first heard the John Lennon tune. When Griffin asked Brian what he thought of the bespectacled Beatle, Brian responded, "Well, he knows what he's doing."[2] At a June 18, 2011, concert at Toronto's Massey Hall, Brian introduced "Girl Don't Tell Me" by saying, "Here's a song I wrote for John Lennon."

Both songs are about parting with a girl who doesn't share the narrator's feelings, but the two numbers feel very different. While The Beatles' record breaks ground with the rumbling, dissonant sounds producer George Martin gets out of the band, The Beach Boys' production, which hangs nearly entirely on its strong melody, is simpler and bouncier and in its way just as compelling. While session players handled some *Summer Days* tracks, "Girl Don't Tell Me" is played by the Wilson brothers, roadie Ron Swallow on tambourine and Bruce Johnston in what was probably his first Beach Boys session. The group had hired Bruce after country-star-to-be Glen Campbell announced his departure. Bruce was a keyboardist by nature but had to quickly ramp up his bass chops for the live shows, his first coming April 9, 1965, in New Orleans.[3] On "Girl Don't Tell Me," he plays the celesta — a keyboard that sounds like bells and which helps bring out the lyrics' bittersweet innocence. Carl strums on guitar and adds a 12-string electric solo in the break capped off by Dennis' floor-tom roll and cymbal crash. Eighteen-year-old Carl's suggestions for the guitar sound earned him an assistant producer credit.[4]

"Girl Don't Tell Me" was included on 1974's *Endless Summer* but has been left off more recent greatest-hits packages. It's a hidden gem that has become a favorite of a younger generation of fans. Such is the case for The Shins' James Mercer, who discovered it after his indie band broke out thanks to exposure in the 2004 Zach Braff film *Garden State*. The singer-songwriter picked up a copy of *Summer Days* at a Goodwill store in his hometown of Portland and loved the song so much he added it to his group's 2009 tour setlist.

"I was hooked right off the bat," Mercer recalls. "The melody is modern — it's strange but beautiful. It sounds kind of sci-fi, but it's arranged in a pretty straightforward way. The Beach Boys were already jumping off the early stuff that sounded very rock and roll. I love when a song has an inventive feel to it. This song definitely has that, but it's still really rocking, and they would go on to do that all the time."

There are no harmonies on the track, which gives the song a particularly direct feel. Carl was likely nervous about singing it, and Bruce recalled that Brian made the rest of the guys leave the studio while Carl stepped up to the microphone. Carl had previously taken or shared the lead on "Summertime Blues," "Pom, Pom Play Girl," "Louie, Louie" and "All Dressed Up for School" (which remained unreleased until 1990), but this was his first great vocal performance, displaying the spine-tingling range Brian later used on some of the group's best songs. On "Girl Don't Tell Me," Carl totally sells it as the guy who fell hard for the girl the previous summer and was heartbroken when she didn't stay in touch over the school year. Now it's summer again and they've reunited, but he's determined to not play the fool this time.

"Carl's terrific. The Wilson brothers had a natural gift — that feel for their voices," notes Mercer, who, along with wunderkind producer Danger Mouse, formed Broken Bells and released a dreamy 2010 album that draws Beach Boys comparisons. Referring to The Beach Boys and The Beatles, he adds, "So much comes across in those guys' voices. It's not really so much about the interesting chords they put together or the beats, because those things had been done. Some people's voices just carry a lot."

As with many great Beach Boys' songs, the narrator in "Girl Don't Tell Me" wears his heart on his sleeve. Mercer loves the honesty. "He's not trying to pretend he's some kick-ass rock and roll guy," Mercer says. "He's talking about staying with his grandma during the summer, which is when he and the girl met. It's just so 'California suburbs in the '60s,' which is a comfortable feeling for somebody like me who grew up in the suburbs. I can see this kid making plastic car models in his room, watching *Bewitched* and all that. It's really sincere. It's something everyone can connect with at some point in their adolescence — falling for somebody and it becoming this overwhelming theme of the whole summer."

Mercer is just one of many artists past

and present who have tackled the song. Two months before it even appeared on a Beach Boys single, 12-year-old Keith Green gave a surprisingly credible reading on a 45 release. The U.K.'s Tony Rivers and the Castaways couldn't resist adding Beach Boys–style harmonies to their 1966 version, while The Smithereens include a cover on their 1995 *Rarities: Attack of the Smithereens* collection. The melody has proven universal, holding up well with translated French lyrics on "Ne Dis Pas" by Souvenir on the 2000 tribute album *Caroline Now! The Songs of Brian Wilson and The Beach Boys*. More recently, two Brooklyn bands have put out more rocking renditions: noise-pop trio Vivian Girls in 2008 and country rockers My Cousin, The Emperor in 2011.

So why are so many performers drawn to it? Brian's music, Mercer explains, can connect with anyone who has ever felt shy or been the underdog. "One of the great things about rock and roll is that the whole thing is this hat trick where you take what can be a miserable situation — adolescence or just feeling like a loser — and you make it cool somehow," he says. "And Brian really does that. He makes being in a downturn dramatic, romantic and beautiful."

CAROL KAYE ON...
CALIFORNIA GIRLS

Written by: Brian Wilson and Mike Love
Lead vocal: Mike Love and Brian Wilson
Produced by: Brian Wilson
Recorded: April 6, June 4, 1965
Released: July 12, 1965
Chart peak: U.S. #3, U.K. #26
Appears on *Summer Days (And Summer Nights!!)*

In a 2010 interview with this author, Brian cited "California Girls" as The Beach Boys' main song. "You could call it our anthem. I think it stands out as the best record we've made," he said. Lyrically, it may be a fluffy paean to the charms of American females, but Brian's musical intentions were grand. His inspiration was "Jesu, Joy of Man's Desiring" by Johann Sebastian Bach, whom he credits with inventing the shuffle beat nearly 300 years earlier.

When Brian composed the song, he started with the bass part, and within half an hour he had the chords and melody as well, he recalls in David Leaf's documentary *Beautiful Dreamer: Brian Wilson and the Story of Smile*.[1] And when it came time to record the track at Western Studio, that foundational bass part would be played by Carol Kaye, whom Brian has called "the greatest bass player I've ever met."[2]

Kaye was not a California girl by birth, but rather an Everett, Washington, native who made her mark on the Hollywood session scene. She played guitar in L.A. bebop clubs in the 1950s and explains that a chance record date for Sam Cooke led to her eventual status as the town's fourth-ranked studio guitarist. Then, at a fateful 1963 session, she was asked to fill in on the Fender Precision Bass. "The first thing I thought was 'Yay, this is fun,' and the second thing was I only had to carry in one instrument," she recalls. "If you were a guitarist, you had to carry an acoustic guitar, an electric guitar, an acoustic 12-string, electric 12-string, classical guitar, ukulele, mandolin and Dano bass guitar." She transitioned to predominantly bass work and moved up to number-one call after Ray Pohlman gave up studio gigging to be musical director on *Shindig!*

While female musicians were common in big bands, Kaye was the only woman among the top 1960s L.A. session players, and her achievements would be commemorated in Laura Veirs' 2010 song "Carol Kaye." Kaye says she's played on more than 10,000 sessions, which include classic records for Phil Spector, Ray Charles, The Monkees, Simon & Garfunkel and The Doors. While playing rock 'n' roll required simplification from jazz, she appreciated the way Brian incorporated her instrument. "He took bass up another step," she says. "He saw it as integral in a symphonic orchestra. He used bass as the framework of a hit record. Very few people can write for bass, but his writing was beautiful. There are a lot of jazz musicians who admire him for it." For her part, Kaye got a remarkably clear, funky

bass sound — aided by using a pick — and Brian put it high in the mix.

In "California Girls," she explains, the bass line is a simple part one would find in old country and western songs such as "Tumbling Tumbleweeds." "It worked so well on 'California Girls' and the spirit of the song was great. The way Brian wrote it plus the way we played — it came together so nicely," says Kaye, who was 30 at the time of the song's recording. Brian would often record Kaye's electric bass as well as an acoustic upright bass played by Lyle Ritz. "There's only one bass on most of my records, but Brian wrote for two basses on most of The Beach Boys records, like Phil Spector did. Sometimes we would play together and sometimes Brian would split us apart," she explains.

The song boasts one of pop music's great intros. The sublime opening bars — which constitute Brian's favorite self-penned piece — stand apart from the rest of the song while leading into it beautifully. Carl and session player Jerry Cole open with magnificent electric 12-string guitar chords played in chamber echo, Kaye does her tumblin' bass part, Hal Blaine lightly taps the cymbals, and the subtle, majestic horn of Roy Caton and saxophones of Steve Douglas, Jay Migliori and Jack Nimitz put it over the top. "I love what Brian wrote there. He got a very deep feeling and we all felt it when we first played it," Kaye recalls. The 22-second passage was Brian's proclamation to the rest of the music biz that he was a composer to take seriously. Unfortunately the message was often buried by DJs who talked over the intro until Al de Lory's sexy roller-rink organ comes in ahead of the vocal.

Although Brian was collaborating with great, seasoned players, Kaye insists he alone composed virtually all the music. "On 'California Girls' there was a fill I stuck in at the end of the bridge that he liked. Aside from that, every note I played was his," she says. Brian likely paid particular attention to the bass since it had been his instrument in the band, although Kaye says she wasn't aware of that at the time. "When I finally saw film of him playing bass, I thought he lacked really good technique but he had that feel for it and a definite ear," she says.

Kaye also knew nothing of Brian's drug use. He acknowledges writing the groovy chords to "California Girls" on an early LSD trip. He was eager to see how the drug would stimulate his creativity, and his friend Loren Schwartz, who recounts the story in *Beautiful Dreamer*, happily obliged him with a 125-microgram hit of liquid purple Owsley. It made Brian see notes floating in the air. But whatever Brian did in the writing process, Kaye always found him professional and in control at the studio. She adds that regarding herself and most of her fellow players, "Our drug was the coffee we drank to stay awake."

Plenty of caffeine was consumed the night they recorded "California Girls." Although Brian has called it his favorite session and a very "up" experience, the studio tapes tell a different story. The affair dragged on past midnight and required 44 takes, largely due to difficulty with the tempo and the guitar part in the intro. Fatigue set in and patience ran thin among Brian, engineer Chuck Britz and the dozen-plus musicians. Brian was taking his perfectionism to new heights.

"He'd spend three or four hours on one song, whereas usually in a three-hour record date we'd cut four or five tunes. We played every tune and every take like a hit record. It got a little boring because Brian would change things back and forth all the time. But we stuck it out because we knew what he was doing and we admired him. And that admiration and respect got across to him and helped him to grow and feel safe with us," Kaye says.

Brian did not have a title for the song or seemingly much idea of its lyrical content when he laid down the track. On the session tape, he can be heard calling the song on various takes "You're Grass and I'm a Power Mower" and "Oh Yeah."[3] The vocal track wasn't recorded for another two months, which gave Mike plenty of time to come up with the words. With Murry handling the group's publishing, however, Brian alone was credited on the record. That was rectified in 1994 after a court ruled that Mike had been denied dozens of proper credits.

The lyrics show Mike keeping concert-goers top of mind. Celebrating the qualities of girls on the East Coast, West Coast, in the North, South and in-between allowed the group to give a shout-out to every American female in the audience. According to one member of the touring band, it's the "Midwest farmers' daughters" who cheer loudest when name-checked. The song also features one of Mike's best lead vocals, his appreciation of the opposite sex never in doubt. Brian recorded the vocals at Columbia on the studio's then cutting-edge 8-track recorder, allowing him to triple-track Mike's lead and also record the group's backgrounds over three tracks,[4] resulting in an expansive vocal soundscape.

The record stays true to the group's doo-wop influences, with successive singers stepping to the fore: Mike, followed by Brian on the chorus, then group newcomer Bruce on the repeat. Although Bruce was not yet an official member, the group invited him to sing on "California Girls," making for a memorable vocal debut.

Kaye remembers the other Beach Boys occasionally dropping by instrumental sessions. "They were nice, cute young guys," she recalls. "They would exchange a joke with Hal Blaine. They seemed thrilled that we were playing it for them. My respect really grew for them when I heard takes of the vocal overdubs, because Brian really had to help them shape up to get the best vocal performances. They did a good job."

Their intoxicating vocals on "California Girls" helped make it the group's crowd-pleasing opening number. It was denied the top spot on the U.S. charts, however, making it to #3. The records it trailed over its two-week chart peak were no lightweights, however: Sonny & Cher's "I Got You Babe,"

Bob Dylan's "Like a Rolling Stone" and The Beatles' "Help!"[5]

By the time the politically correct 1980s rolled around, the song's objectification of women really made it seem from another time, yet the tune proved so irresistible that David Lee Roth's 1985 cover — featuring background vocals by Carl and Christopher Cross — replicated the original's #3 showing. In 2010, *Rolling Stone* ranked the original the 72nd greatest song of all time, and it has served as the reference point for identically titled numbers by country star Gretchen Wilson, indie darlings The Magnetic Fields and pop phenomenon Katy Perry, whose 2010 chart-topper had the titular tweak to "California *Gurls*" and who has played The Beach Boys' record as she's walked onstage at concerts. In 2010, the Recording Academy chimed in with its approval, inducting the song into the Grammy Hall of Fame, which honors records "of lasting qualitative or historical significance."

Kaye notes that creating such an iconic song required top players. "Brian's music needed that weight. It needed that experience. It mostly took the jazz players to get that fine technique and feeling," she says. "But we never thought the music would last more than 10 years."

DAVID M. BEARD ON ...

THE LITTLE GIRL I ONCE KNEW

Written by: Brian Wilson
Lead vocals: Brian Wilson, Carl Wilson and Mike Love
Produced by: Brian Wilson
Recorded: October 13, 24, 1965 | Released: November 22, 1965 | Chart peak: U.S. #20 | Appears on *Best of The Beach Boys Vol. 3*

Brian entered Western Studio on October 13, 1965, ready to embark on the most creative period of his career. He had two tracks on the go: the upbeat "The Little Girl I Once Knew" and the ballad "Don't Talk (Put Your Head on My Shoulder)." The *Pet Sounds* recording era was unofficially underway.

Brian was only at the rehearsal stage with "Don't Talk" and wouldn't revisit it until the following February. It required strings, and he felt the need to hone his chops in that area. So, on October 15, under the guidance of arranger Dick Reynolds, his Christmas LP collaborator, he worked with a full orchestra on covers of "Stella by Starlight" and "How Deep Is the Ocean?" and a piece he titled "Three Blind Mice." The tracks were experiments, not intended for release. With "The Little Girl I Once Knew," however, Brian was already in his element. Riding the chart-topping success of "Help Me, Rhonda" and the stunning "California Girls," momentum was on his side.

He came up with an innovative track. The intro launches with a drop-in from Carol Kaye's bass, and Brian underlined her importance by initially labeling the song "Carol K" on the session tape box.[1] A melodic 12-string guitar provides a response before Don Randi's organ comes in with the record's most distinct sound. The verses strut along driven by Kaye and Frank Capp's percussion before coming to an unusual four-beat stop, sustaining the last note. The chorus then bursts in. The same effect follows the second verse. Brian had put a couple of seconds of silence in the middle of the *All Summer Long* cut "Drive-In," but this jarring structure was extreme. The second chorus is followed by a break featuring Randi's swirling organ triplets bolstered by the trumpet and saxophones section.

"Every part of that song is as he envisioned it. Every little part is distinct," notes historian David M. Beard, editor of foremost Beach Boys fanzine *Endless Summer Quarterly* and Beach Boys columnist at Examiner.com. "It's very purposefully recorded. You can hear that Brian is creatively locked into something different — the next thing. That was always his biggest challenge: what is the next thing? At that time he was leading the pack and didn't really have anything to feed off other than what he had just finished doing. But he was very sure of himself and knew what he wanted."

While the track may have pointed to a new direction, the lyrics were in familiar territory, telling the story of a guy who runs into a girl from his past who has now grown up and catches his eye. The group had previously celebrated the blossoming of a teenage girl in the 1964 outtake "All Dressed Up for School," which includes some similar phrases. Some believe "The Little Girl I Once Knew" is about Marilyn.

The lead vocal is handed from Brian to Carl to Mike, who has the most memorable lines, each ahead of the stops, letting the girl know he's coming after her and letting her current boyfriend know as well. If that cocky attitude seems pure Mike, it's because he had a hand in the lyrics. At least, that's what he has told Beard. The song, Mike said, slipped through the cracks in the 1990s legal action to have his writing contribution officially recognized on a number of tracks.

"'Little Girl' is nothing deep, but the words are a perfect marriage with that track," says Beard. "It's powerful when you hear Mike go, 'Look out, babe!' and it just holds, then the whole group comes in. Brian wanted that lyric to register. He wanted you to be dialed in and paying attention."

The vocals are beautifully proportioned in the complex harmony arrangement, with a prominent spotlight for Bruce at the end of the chorus. After the instrumental break, Brian sings a joyous "la doo day" countered by Mike's "pow pow pow" bass vocal, and then the group repeats the chorus. All the ecstatic singing builds to a state of sonic euphoria — a goose bumps–eliciting expression of elation.

The single was released in late November in the U.S. and the following month in the U.K.[2] It found an early fan in John Lennon, whose reaction was quoted in *Melody Maker*: "This is the greatest! Turn it up, turn it right up. It's *got* to be a hit. It's the greatest record I've heard for weeks. It's fantastic. I hope it will be a hit. It's all Brian Wilson. He just uses the voices as instruments. He never tours or anything. He just sits at home thinking up fantastic arrangements out of his head. Doesn't even read music. You keep waiting for the fabulous breaks. Great arrangement. It goes on and on with all different things. I hope it's a hit so I can hear it all the time."[3]

While Paul McCartney is usually portrayed as the Fab Four's biggest Brian fan, Lennon evidently shared that admiration. In fact, in *The Beatles Book* fanzine's 1966 Christmas edition, Lennon cites Brian as the musical person he most admires.[4] One can't help but wonder what ideas Brian and "The Little Girl I Once Knew" may have put in his head. About nine months after making his remarks about the song, Lennon and his bandmates retired from touring so they could stay home and dream up their own fantastic arrangements. On a musical note, Beard adds, "I wonder how much he gleaned from the kaleidoscope effect in the song that ended up in 'Being for the Benefit of Mr. Kite!'"

Dashing Lennon's hope it would be a hit, "Little Girl" didn't even chart in the U.K. One musician's "fantastic" can be an average listener's "weird." *Melody Maker* and *NME* reviewers found the record disappointing compared to its predecessors.[5] It fared better in the U.S., but still made it no higher than #20 on *Billboard*, making it the group's lowest-charting 7" A-side since 1962's "Ten Little Indians." Given the upbeat tone and overall quality of "Little Girl," it remains one of the group's ultimate should-have-beens. It marked the first time Brian had gotten ahead of his audience — and it wouldn't be the last.

"The lyrics are very mainstream, but the track is a bit avant-garde. Fans had grown accustomed to straight-ahead rockers. 'California Girls' had that Bach movement at the beginning, but it was still a rock power-ballad. And the fine-tuned version of 'Help Me, Rhonda' was different but still straightforward," Beard says. A former DJ himself, he suggests the problem lay with a lack of significant airplay. "The thing you could never let happen on radio was dead air. You had to keep the music going, and 'The Little Girl I Once Knew' ran into a problem with its two stoppages. It's been alleged that some DJs liked the song so much that they put the song on a reel and edited out the dead air before playing it."

Capitol apparently didn't have much faith in the song's commercial prospects, releasing the "Barbara Ann" single before "The Little Girl I Once Knew" had even peaked in the U.S. — and likely sealing its doom. "Little Girl" is certainly fun, but Capitol believed listeners wanted a simpler kind of fun, and perhaps they were right. But despite the 45's sales disappointment, Brian continues to refer to "Little Girl" as one of his best productions. Its tepid reception wasn't going to derail his artistic ambitions, and he proceeded to work on *Pet Sounds*. Had "Little Girl" been a bigger hit, it likely would have been on the LP.

"'Little Girl' would fit on *Pet Sounds*. The style and creative dynamic of the recording make it part of that family of songs," Beard says. In terms of subject matter, the LP cut to which it is most closely related is "Caroline, No." But while "Little Girl" is jubilant about a girl's maturation, "Caroline, No" mourns the loss of innocence. Beard suggests "Little Girl" would fit the song cycle's story arc of disillusionment if sequenced at or near the beginning of the record.

The song may have the lyrical and musical feel of *Pet Sounds*, but its structure looks even further down the road. It particularly foreshadows the *Smile* track "Cabin Essence" with its low-key verse making a hard shift into a blaring chorus. "It's the first stake he put in the ground leading to his most important work," Beard says.

The song has been largely unknown except to Beach Boys fans. It did appear on 1968's *Best of The Beach Boys Vol. 3*, but that album sold dismally in the U.S. A new audience would find it on the 1975 gold-selling *Spirit of America* collection, and in 1990 it was included as a bonus track on the twofer CD *The Beach Boys Today!/Summer Days (And Summer Nights!!)*. As interest in the group's more obscure work grew, Brian felt emboldened to open his 1999 concerts with the number. He left the high end of the harmonies to other members of his band, shifting to the middle of the vocal pack, as can be heard on *Live at the Roxy Theatre*.

By giving the song such prime concert placement, Brian reclaimed it as a significant part of his legacy. "It's as fun as any of his best songs," Beard says. "It's also as creative and important as any of the most dynamic songs he's ever written."

Dean Torrence on...
BARBARA Ann

Written by: Fred Fassert
Lead vocal: Dean Torrence and Brian Wilson
with Mike Love
Produced by: Brian Wilson
Recorded: September 23, 1965
Released: November 8, 1965, on *Beach Boys' Party!*
and as a single December 20, 1965
Chart peak: U.S. #2, U.K. #3

By fall 1965, Brian was ready to take his music higher. He had already laid down the magnificent instrumental track for "Sloop John B," but Capitol was mostly concerned with the upcoming holiday season. One year earlier, the group had delivered the concert and Christmas albums — both huge successes. How, they asked, did Brian intend to follow up? For Brian, one thing was certain: he needed time to make his next proper album, which would be *Pet Sounds*. A novel solution was devised: rather than do another live album, he recorded a hootenanny with the band and family and friends sitting around having fun and spontaneously singing some of their favorite tunes. Best of all, the album, to be titled *Beach Boys' Party!*, took only six days to record.[1]

Dean Torrence — the blond, falsetto-singing half of Jan & Dean — would drop in to sing on "Barbara Ann." His impromptu participation was really no surprise given the two acts' long history together. Back in their L.A. high school, Dean and his partner Jan Berry performed in a band called The Barons with Bruce on keyboards. The Beach Boys and Jan & Dean first shared the bill on August 25, 1962, at the Reseda Jubilee in the

San Fernando Valley,[2] but by the time they got together again for a high school Valentine's Day dance in 1963, The Beach Boys, who opened, had a national hit behind them with "Surfin' Safari." As a cost-saving measure, they did double-duty as Jan & Dean's backing band — all except for the injured Dennis, who was replaced by Mark Groseclose.[3] To fill out its set, Jan & Dean sang "Surfin'" and "Surfin' Safari," even though The Beach Boys had played those tunes earlier that night.

"Our first impression was they seemed to be kids who were really interested in learning our stuff," Torrence recalls. "There were times when we had worked with a backup band that didn't learn our material all that well, weren't all that prepared and probably couldn't care less about our set. The Beach Boys seemed to really care and that impressed us, so we were as interested in their careers and making them sound as good as we could. We weren't going to treat them like a bunch of lowly backup musicians. We considered them equals, and in this situation we were teammates."

The positive response to their performance of The Beach Boys songs convinced Jan & Dean, who were occasional surfers, of the viability of surf music, setting them on a course that would bring them their greatest success. And they realized something else. "It reminded us that we didn't want to sound like a duo," Torrence explains. "We were always more interested in being in a vocal group, and now the technology was catching up so that if we couldn't find any other vocalists, we could sing some of those parts ourselves and make our records sound more like vocal-group records."

Jan & Dean were building an album around their Top 30 single "Linda" and decided to incorporate their new favorite pastime in the title *Jan & Dean Take Linda Surfin'*. The LP included the two Beach Boys numbers they had done onstage, with The Beach Boys now backing them up in the studio. "Those were songs that had already run their course for them, so it wasn't as though it was going to hurt any of their sales. It would end up giving them that much more exposure," Dean notes.

Once they knocked off the two tracks, Brian asked if the duo wanted to preview The Beach Boys' next single, "Surfin' U.S.A." After hearing the killer tune, Jan tried to persuade Brian to let him and Dean record it. Brian declined but said they could have a similar tune he'd been working on. "It was about half done," Dean recalls. "We still liked 'Surfin' U.S.A.' better, but the new song turned out to be pretty good." Originally called "Goody Connie Won't You Come Back Home," it now had the working title "Two Girls for Every Boy."[4] Jan would complete the song — renamed "Surf City" — and Dean would chip in some uncredited words in the verses. Jan produced an irrepressible track, and Brian came in to sing some parts.

Both Dean and Brian had strong falsettos, which they combined on "Surf City" and later on "Barbara Ann." "My falsetto has all top-end — a lot of treble," Dean explains. "Brian's had more air and a lot more midrange and bottom, and our phrasing was a little bit different. We realized the two falsettos together were very unique. You get this odd thing going on because of the two falsettos being so different and not having the same phrasing. It's almost like a Doppler effect."

"Surf City" eclipsed "Surfin' U.S.A." on the charts, marching all the way to #1 in the U.S., where it remained for two weeks at the end of July 1963. Unfortunately for Brian, Jan & Dean's contract stipulated that the publishing for all their songs would be retained by Screen Gems, which meant a lot of lost revenue — and hell to catch from Murry. Capitol was similarly unhappy about a Beach Boys sound-alike bringing rival Liberty Records a #1 smash — co-written by its head Beach Boy, no less.

Nonetheless, Brian continued to co-write songs for Jan & Dean, including the hits "Drag City" (U.S. #10), "Dead Man's Curve" (#8) and "Ride the Wild Surf" (#16), and The Beach Boys added the duo's #3 smash "The Little Old Lady from Pasadena" to its live repertoire and recorded it on their chart-topping concert album. While the rewards Jan & Dean reaped from working with Brian are obvious, the impact they had on him was also substantial. Jan's technical proficiency in the studio rubbed off on Brian, and Jan & Dean exposed him to the session players the duo shared with Phil Spector, including Hal Blaine and Glen Campbell. Dean recalls that although Jan and Spector did not get along, Jan introduced Brian to Spector when the antisocial producer was in the studio next door. "That did not actually go all that well" is all Dean says of the encounter.

The Beach Boys and Jan & Dean continued slyly dropping in on each other's sessions despite warnings from their respective record companies. But the participation of the so-called Clown Princes of Rock 'n' Roll on a project like *Beach Boys' Party!* seemed natural, so Jan & Dean asked Liberty for permission, believing their label would be more than happy about the high-profile exposure. "They said, 'Well, then we want in writing that The Beach Boys will reciprocate by doing a project with you where we can use their likenesses and The Beach Boys brand name,'" Dean recalls. "We said we didn't have a project yet, and they said, 'Unless you come up with something we can get in writing, you're not to be on the *Party!* record.' Jan had just bought a new house, and he wasn't that interested in having them hold up any royalties, so he capitulated and said, 'Okay, we promise. We won't.'"

As it turned out, Jan & Dean were working at Western Studio one night when The Beach Boys were in the building recording the album. When Jan got wrapped up in some technical issue, the lure of the nearby revelry proved too great for Dean. "So I said, 'I'm going down to The Beach Boys' studio for a couple of minutes,' and Jan said, 'Don't sing on anything!' I said, 'Don't worry, I won't sing. I don't want to get us in any trouble.'

Within three minutes I was singing. I didn't give a crap. I hadn't bought a new house, so it didn't matter to me," Dean recollects.

Dean found the band and its guests sitting around eating snacks and drinking beers. The concept behind the record was to roll tape while the group performed live and loose covers of songs ranging from doo-wop from their high school days (including The Olympics' "Hully Gully" and The Hollywood Argyles' "Alley Oop") to no fewer than three Beatles cuts. The instrumentation was all acoustic with the exception of an electric bass.[5] It was like an early version of *MTV Unplugged*. Upon Dean's appearance, the group asked if he wanted to sing. Sure, he said, suggesting "Barbara Ann," which he knew well.

The song was written by Fred Fassert for his Bronx doo-wop group The Regents and was a #13 hit in 1961 (as "Barbara Anne"), its "ba-ba-ba-ba-Barbara Anne" refrain proving one of the most infectious — and to some, annoying — sing-alongs in rock 'n' roll history. It was right up Jan & Dean's alley, and they recorded it as filler years earlier in the same studio, sticking closely to the original arrangement. The Beach Boys' version involved even less care. Of the *Party!* session, Dean recalls,

Ever since the first time they crossed paths, Jan &
Dean would be inextricably linked to The Beach Boys.
[Courtesy Dean Torrence]

begins the song, joined by Brian and Dean on the high-end lead — Dean's voice the more prominent. "We were standing right next to one another," Dean says. "If we had done it again I probably would have been moved further back off the microphone, but since this was pretty much one take and I was gone, they were kind of stuck with it. Brian was happy with it the way it was. It was spontaneous; it was fun. He didn't care if my vocal happened to stick out more than it should have — they couldn't give me any credit anyway."

He did get an unexpected mention, however. The Beach Boys and entourage regrouped days later to overdub further background party sounds, and at the end of the song somebody blurted out "Thanks, Dean," and the remark stayed on the finished album. "I almost died when I heard that, because I was denying I was on it," Dean says. Fortunately, he didn't suffer any repercussions for crossing the Liberty brass. "Do you really think they would actually take some time to listen to anything?" he quips.

The tape sweetening also involved adding percussion, including hand claps and Hal Blaine using whatever tools might be readily available at a party. The point is underlined

"We started and stopped it and changed the key because we hadn't really planned to do the song. We were winging it. I had to be back at my studio, so we knocked it out in about 10 to 15 minutes, tops."

On the LP, after everybody sings a few jokey lines of "Baa, Baa Black Sheep," Mike when someone, likely Brian, is heard shouting "It's Hal and his famous ashtray!" A big part of the album's success lies in the group's ability to make the sterile studio environment sound like Sunday afternoon at somebody's beach house, which is where the cover photos suggest it was recorded. The songs and singing are great, but just as important are all the goofs and crackups, which give the listener the sense of actually hanging out with the guys.

"It wasn't manufactured," Dean says. "It wasn't somebody laying on one vocal part and then leaving and then another guy coming in. This really was a bunch of people in the moment enjoying each other's company, and I think that came through. It did sound like people having one hell of a good time."

While *Beach Boys' Party!* is often regarded as a stopgap solution on the way to *Pet Sounds* — which in large part it is — Dean argues that Brian was really into it. Brian had previously captured spontaneous chatter on the track "Bull Session with the 'Big Daddy'" and would go for a similar feeling in substance-abetted fashion on *Smiley Smile*. "Creative people probably have a list 50 miles long of projects to do someday, and it was on his list to do a party record," Dean says.

"Whether or not he would have chosen to do it at that particular time we'll never know, but it certainly worked out for the best."

Released in the U.S. on November 8, the album rose to #6 on the charts, and in the U.K., where it appeared the following February, it reached #3, the band's best performance there to date. Everybody was happy: Capitol got its Christmas present, and Brian was able to return to his more ambitious music. While initially no A-side single was released from the album (the cover of Spector's "There's No Other (Like My Baby)" was on the B-side of "The Little Girl I Once Knew"), DJs took it upon themselves to play "Barbara Ann" right off the LP. Capitol took notice and edited "Barbara Ann" into a 45 and rushed it to market. It rocketed to #2 in the U.S., kept out of *Billboard*'s top spot in consecutive weeks by The Beatles' "We Can Work It Out" and Petula Clark's "My Love," but reaching #1 in the *Cashbox* magazine survey and in faraway Norway.

All artists love a hit record, but Brian — however fond he may have been of *Party!* — found the unexpected success of "Barbara Ann" somewhat bewildering. Just as he was taking Beach Boys music into more serious territory, both Capitol and the public showed what they really wanted from the group was good times. It was a stereotype he and the band would have to fight in years to come. But the group understood about giving the people what they want. They had tested out "Barbara Ann" on *The Jack Benny Hour* on November 3, playing it as straight-ahead electric rock 'n' roll, and following the single's success would perform it live in this arrangement from then on.

Meanwhile, the fortunes of Jan & Dean took a quick and tragic turn. In April 1966, Jan, always in a hurry, was driving to a business appointment in Beverly Hills when he slammed his Stingray into a parked truck on a side street. Eerily reminiscent of the tale he had sung in "Dead Man's Curve," the horrific crash left him in a coma from which he emerged with partial brain damage. Against the odds, he learned to walk and talk again and even got back into the studio, but the vibrant 25-year-old with a 175 IQ was never the same. Dean would soldier on, putting out the album *Save for a Rainy Day*, which despite being credited to Jan & Dean, was really a solo record.

Dean also had his education to fall back on, having studied advertising design at USC. In 1967, he opened the Kittyhawk Graphics

Design Studio. He would produce album covers for numerous artists, winning a Grammy Award in 1972 (along with photographer Gene Brownell) for the sleeve of the self-titled album by the band Pollution. He also designed the covers for The Beach Boys' *15 Big Ones* (his title), *The Beach Boys Love You* and Dennis' *Pacific Ocean Blue* and created the group's retro neon-style logo.

With The Beach Boys riding high again in the '70s, resurging interest in Jan & Dean was inevitable. The duo's biggest boost came from the 1978 CBS TV movie *Deadman's Curve*, which dramatized their story and featured Mike and Bruce in cameos. "Mike called me up and said, 'Holy crap, *Deadman's Curve* must have gotten a lot of exposure,' because right after it aired, nearly every interview he was doing was 75% about Jan & Dean," Dean recalls. "He said, 'There's a whole new awareness of Jan & Dean and the connection with The Beach Boys, and we should exploit that. Why don't you think about joining us on one of our next runs?'"

So, in late summer 1978, Jan & Dean were reunited onstage with The Beach Boys, playing a few of their hits on the Surfin' Déjà Vu tour, so named and with a logo design by

Dean. Jan remained partially paralyzed in his right arm and leg, but was able to make it through.[6] Stoked by the experience, Jan & Dean continued performing live with a couple of different backup bands, but by 1982, their momentum was derailed by Jan's newfound drug problem. At the same time, Mike was taking a hiatus from The Beach Boys in part because of Dennis' substance abuse issues, so he and Dean got together for a series of shows billed as Mike & Dean that were, ironically, sponsored by Budweiser. "Mike was trying to create a little distance between himself and Dennis, whom he wasn't getting along with," Dean explains. "He wanted to make the point to the other guys that Dennis needed to go into some sort of rehab and try to straighten himself out or he was not interested."

Jan got his act together by 1983, and he and Dean resumed touring, which they would do until Jan died of a heart attack in 2004. Dean continued to perform in California and the southern U.S., sometimes under the moniker of The Jan & Dean Show featuring Dean Torrence, other times playing with David Marks, sometimes with Alan Jardine, and sometimes as a guest of Mike's Beach Boys. He and Mike — both of whom have embraced corporate gigs, which some other Beach Boys resisted — also played many private functions.

Dean has spent a good part of his career belting out Beach Boys numbers, and in trying to explain the longevity of the music, he recalls the 1978 stadium tour. After the encore, in which he and Jan joined The Beach Boys on "Barbara Ann" and "Fun, Fun, Fun," they were hustled offstage as the backing band played the vamp and rushed to a waiting limo and private jet to fly to another show later that day. "We'd get to the jet so quickly I was still wiping sweat from my head, and I was still humming one of the songs. And I'm thinking, 'I've sung that song a thousand times, I just got through singing it 20 minutes ago, and it just won't leave,'" he reflects. "That's saying something."

SCOTT TOTTEN ON . . .
SLOOP JOHN B

Traditional, arranged by Brian Wilson
Lead vocals: Brian Wilson and Mike Love
Produced by: Brian Wilson
Recorded: July 12, December 22, 29, 1965
Released: March 21, 1966
Chart peak: U.S. #3, U.K. #2
Appears on *Pet Sounds*

Alan's fondness for folk music led the group to one of its biggest hits. Despite conflicting details about how and when the guys came to "Sloop John B," what is consistent is that Alan suggested Brian record the Nassau sea shanty, the origins of which are even murkier.

The song was originally titled "The John B. Sails" after a sponger boat that, according to legend, went down with its oft-inebriated crew. It tells the story of a seafaring adventure gone awry, marked by a drunken fight between the narrator and his grandfather, and a cook who gets the "fits." The oldest known mention of the song came in a 1916 *Harper's* article by Richard Le Gallienne entitled "Coral Islands and Mangrove-Trees," and Le Gallienne referenced it again two years later in his novel *Pieces of Eight*, which tracks the 1903 discovery of Bahamian treasure. Poet Carl Sandburg included the lyrics and music — featuring an arrangement by Alfred G. Wathall — in his 1927 collection *The American Songbag*. Eight years later, folklorists Alan Lomax and Mary Elizabeth Barnicle were in the Bahamas recording a version by the Cleveland Simmons Group titled "Histe Up the John B. Sail."

The Weavers popularized the song with their early '50s version "Wreck of the John B," and the song was subsequently covered, under various titles, by Bahamian artists Blind Blake Higgs and Joseph Spence as well as Americans Johnny Cash, Jimmie Rodgers, The Tokens, The Brothers Four, Barry McGuire and even Dick Dale.

But it was The Kingston Trio's 1958 version that enthralled Alan. According to Brian's biographer Peter Ames Carlin, Brian knew the song by high school, and a tape exists of him singing it at that time with friends.[1] Brian's memoir claims that the group, at Alan's suggestion, played the song for Hite and Dorinda Morgan at their first audition in 1961.[2] In Alan's telling, during the *Summer Days (And Summer Nights!!)* sessions, he sat at the piano and played Brian a revised chord pattern for "Sloop John B" that he thought would be appropriate for the group. Brian surprised him the next day when he called him down to the studio to play back an instrumental track for the song that he had produced overnight with session players. [3] The notion of Brian arranging and recording the song in less than 24 hours is an attractive one — and Brian has told a similar story — but available studio information indicates *Summer Days* sessions ended June 4, while "Sloop John B" wasn't recorded until more than a month later.[4] Regardless of timeframe, Brian turned Alan's inspiration into an incredible piece of music.

"Sloop John B" is one of those songs people expect to hear every time The Beach Boys take the stage, and as such in 2011 it was the responsibility of Scott Totten, musical director and singer-guitarist for the touring Beach Boys.

"It's such a simple three-chord folk song, and what Brian was able to do with that shows the genius of his arranging abilities," says Totten, who started with the band in 2000 and took over as musical director from Chris Farmer in 2007. "That track really keeps your attention from beginning to end. There are so many signature ideas going on. The record has three guitarists [Billy Strange, Al Casey and Jerry Cole], glockenspiel [Frank Capp] and a baritone saxophone [Jack Nimitz[5]]. There's a ton of great instruments, but it builds. It's really quiet at the beginning, Hal Blaine's drums come in, then there's full-time and all the instruments playing. There's another section where there's stop-time and then there's the end, where Carol Kaye's electric bass and the drums are playing eighth notes to really drive it home. It really has a lot of motion."

The intro, featuring flutes by Steve Douglas

and Jim Horn,[6] is by now so indelible that its sound has traditionally been difficult to replicate onstage. "It's a good example of the studio as an instrument," Totten says. "You can get a great player onstage playing the exact same part in time, but it's not going to sound the same for the audience because you're not in a recording studio with a reverb tank and echo chamber." So the 2011 band simply sampled that part from the record. "The record version's in A-flat and we did it in A, because The Beach Boys have always done it live in A. So we changed the pitch of that part."

Brian let the track gestate throughout the summer and fall of 1965, finally in late December recording the vocals, which are every bit as spectacular. In terms of tempo and harmony, his vocal arrangement bears the closest resemblance to the 1935 version by the Cleveland Simmons Group.

"It seems like the track was done before Brian really had a good idea of what he was going to do with the vocals," Totten notes, pointing to outtakes made available on the 1997 Pet Sounds Sessions boxed set. "You hear all the different versions: where Brian takes the entire lead, where Carl takes the lead, and the early overdubs. You can hear how it's not quite

there yet. There's a version where there's two-part harmony and three parts when the chorus comes in, but then the final version has six or more, including Brian's high falsetto. All of a sudden the chorus really catches your ear."

The song's most transcendent moment comes when the instrumentation completely drops out to spotlight the guys' spine-tingling harmonies. It's a startling effect Brian was itching to get on the radio — one which he had tried on an outtake cut of "The Little Girl I Once Knew" that October.

"Sloop John B" was on the radio all over the world upon its release, reaching #3 in the U.S. (behind The Mamas & the Papas' "Monday, Monday" and The Young Rascals' "Good Lovin'"[7]) and #2 in the U.K. (behind Manfred Mann's "Pretty Flamingo"[8]), making it the group's biggest British hit to date. It topped the charts in The Netherlands, Germany and Norway.[9] The song's success all but guaranteed its placement on the forthcoming Pet Sounds LP, even if it interrupted that song cycle's sustained introspection. Some fans — as well as Alan, Bruce and Totten — lament its inclusion. "I didn't like it on Pet Sounds. I just didn't see how it fit," Totten says.

As a production, however, the cut lives up

to that album's high standard. It takes us on the voyage promised in the title of the preceding instrumental "Let's Go Away for Awhile," and — keeping in mind the LP's vinyl-era origins — makes a satisfying side-one closer. One must also consider why Brian ultimately took on this chestnut and dedicated all his artistic might to reimagining it. He sings with plenty of emotion in the opening verse — much more so than Carl does on an earlier version. It wouldn't be much of a stretch to imagine Murry as the story's grandfather figure who gets drunk and combative. Nor is it hard to find a connection between Brian crying that he wants to go home and his real-life screams when he broke down on that airplane seven months before recording the track.

The original line "dis is de worst trip *since I been born*" was slightly altered to suggest being "on" a trip. The update not only sounds more natural, but also Brian was no stranger to being "on a bad trip," his dalliances with LSD having begun in 1965. While some fans read the line as a drug reference, Totten is not among them: "'65 is when acid was just peaking, if you'll pardon the pun. The majority of America wouldn't have thought of that, whereas in '67 maybe they would have."

However topical the reference may have been, the record has proven eternal. *Rolling Stone* ranked it the 276th greatest song of all time on its 2010 list. It's a perfect record — nearly. In the early takes, the group sometimes sings the line "I feel so *break-up*" — in the original's Caribbean vernacular — but at other times sings, "I feel so *broke up*." While recording the final vocals, signals got crossed and somebody sings "break-up" while the rest sing "broke up." When the 2011 touring Beach Boys performed the song, while Bruce sang "broke," Totten deliberately sang "break" — just to stay true to the original record. This is the degree of reverence the group got from its musical director who was also a lifelong fan — one who, as it happens, was born the very day of The Beach Boys' first album release. "Bruce teased me about it all the time," Totten says. "His view was 'Why would you want to show the audience the mistake? Brian would be embarrassed.' I tried to explain to him that as a fan who's listened to that record since I was a little kid, I love that little part. And if I was sitting in the audience and heard both guys say 'broke up' and not 'broke up'/'break-up,' I would be bummed."

Totten would prepare his bandmates by

sending them an MP3 of the isolated parts they each had to sing. The harmony blend generally saw bassist Randell Kirsch handling the high end, followed down the scale by Totten, then Bruce, guitarist Christian Love (Mike's son) and Mike. The band was rounded out by drummer and sometimes vocalist John Cowsill (of '60s pop band The Cowsills) and Canadian keyboardist Tim Bonhomme. TV star and uber Beach Boys fan John Stamos often sat in as a drummer and vocalist, as he had done off and on since 1985. Many fans believed this lineup had the touring Beach Boys sounding better than they had in years, thanks in no small part to Totten's efforts.

"My thought process 99% of the time was to go back to the arrangements on the records, because that's what people remember. They are not looking to hear our reinvention of the music. They want to hear the music they know and love," he says. "I don't think the band ever really did the record version of the 'Sloop John B' vocal arrangement before. We were really close."

It came as no surprise when Mike told *Rolling Stone* that Totten, along with Cowsill, would be in the 50th anniversary backing band, joining players from Brian's group.[10] (Totten was to share music director duties with Paul Von Mertens from Brian's band.) Totten knows the catalog front to back and has had to ensure The Beach Boys' touring band does justice to "Sloop John B" and the rest of the hits night in and night out, just as Carl did as band leader years before him. "Hopefully Carl was watching over and appreciating what we were doing," Totten says. "It's been an honor to play his parts and it's been an honor to sing with these guys and present this music to an audience."

I JUST WASN'T MADE FOR THESE TIMES

Written by: Brian Wilson and Tony Asher
Lead vocal: Brian Wilson
Produced by: Brian Wilson
Recorded: February 14, March 10, April 13, 1966
Released: May 16, 1966, on *Pet Sounds*

The credits on the most acclaimed albums of the rock 'n' roll era cite lyricists with names such as Dylan, Lennon, McCartney, Jagger . . . and Asher.

Tony Asher was a copywriter at the Carson/Roberts ad agency when he teamed up with Brian, and while the aforementioned performers were out on the road or in the studio making revolutionary records, Asher was donning a jacket and tie to meet with corporate clients. But his chance collaboration with Brian yielded music that can stand beside the best of them.

Asher was in his mid-20s when he first met Brian at Western Recorders. He was overseeing a jingle session and ran into Brian while grabbing a coffee. While more of a jazz aficionado, Asher loved The Beach Boys' early radio hits. "In the summertime I went to the beach every day I could get off work and I would drive along listening to 'Fun, Fun, Fun' or 'Surfer Girl.' I had a lot of affection for and connection to those songs," he says.

They struck up a conversation and Brian asked Asher if he wanted to hear some tracks he'd been working on. Afterwards, they took turns playing song ideas at the piano. Their enjoyable exchange was cut short, however, when somebody called Asher back to his session. As Asher left, Brian told him they should write together sometime.

When Asher returned to his office, he cursed himself for not having taken Brian's number. Luckily, they had a mutual friend in Loren Schwartz. In late 1965, Brian told Schwartz he needed a new writing partner. Mike wouldn't be available since he and the rest of The Beach Boys were heading out in January for a tour of Japan. And besides, Brian wanted the fresh perspective a new collaborator would bring. Schwartz reminded him about Asher and gave Brian his phone number. Brian called Asher at the office, and after convincing the ad man it was really him, explained that Capitol wanted the next Beach Boys album and he didn't have any new songs. Would Asher consider writing with him? "It was such an absurd thing," Asher reflects. "I had never demonstrated any lyric writing to him. The only thing I had demonstrated was some rhythmic feels." Needless to say, he jumped at the opportunity.

After arranging a couple of weeks off work, Asher showed up at Brian's Laurel Way home one January morning at 10 a.m. — as Brian had requested — ready to write. But Brian was still in bed. "I said everything I could think to say to Marilyn. I read *Billboard*. It was 1:15 p.m. before he came out of his bedroom," Asher recalls. Although Brian insisted they shoot for 10 a.m. again the next day, Asher didn't bother showing up until noon, figuring this would be Brian's routine. "I was somebody who would show up on time for an appointment and he was somebody who absolutely never showed up on time," Asher says.

Before getting down to writing, Brian and Asher would spend an hour having coffee. "We would generally reminisce about our girlfriends in high school: the ones who broke our hearts and the ones who turned out to be very different from what we had imagined," Asher says. Although at first slightly impatient with this apparent procrastination, Asher came to see their talks as highly useful. "We'd set a mood and then go write a song influenced by that conversation," he says.

Another influence was The Beatles' *Rubber Soul*, which had stunned the pop world upon its December release. Here was an LP not hung merely on a couple of hit singles; in fact, it contained no singles at all. The U.S. version of the album — which is the one Brian heard[1] — was an especially unified collection of folk-inflected pop songs, and Brian wanted to do something as good. He and Asher found further inspiration in marijuana and, on one occasion, hash brownies. "Thank God it was only once," Asher says with a laugh.

Asher began to understand how Brian had written so many hit songs — he constantly sought other people's opinion, just like at their first meeting. "If a courier came to the door, Brian would say, 'Hey, come here — tell me what you think,'" Asher recalls. "It would crack me up focusing on the courier's reaction at being asked to do that. And then Brian would play him something — and the guy might've had a tin ear for all we knew. But Brian probably learned a lot from that."

Asher and Brian usually wrote together, but on a couple of songs Asher worked on the lyrics back home at night. The first set of words he wrote was for a track originally titled "In My Childhood" that Brian had begun recording the previous fall. Brian was dissatisfied with the lyrics he already had, and Asher transformed it into a musing about the ups and downs of adult romance under the new title "You Still Believe in Me." Asher felt comfortable with their partnership from the get-go. "I wasn't petrified when I handed

that lyric to him," he recalls. "I was hopeful he would like it, but I wasn't shaking in my boots. Usually when you create something like that, it's pretty fragile." Brian indeed liked it and was eager to move forward.

Over the next two to three weeks, they came up with eight compositions for the next Beach Boys album, which would be *Pet Sounds*. The songs' themes of yearning, self-doubt and sadness are evident in their titles: "Wouldn't It Be Nice," "Caroline, No," "Don't Talk (Put Your Head on My Shoulder)," "I Just Wasn't Made for These Times," "That's Not Me," "God Only Knows" and "Here Today." The eventual sequencing creates a rough story arc that launches with romantic innocence before sailing into stormier waters and finally arriving at disillusionment. For many, it is a concept album, but if it is, Asher insists that wasn't by design. "It wasn't like we sat down and said, 'We need a song that does this and a song that does that,'" he notes. "But there could have been some unconscious notion that we should link these songs together in some way."

Asher holds two numbers closest to his heart. "The success of 'God Only Knows' and the regard it's been held in make it a real favorite of mine," he says. He is also particularly

The group poses during the filming of a promotional video for "I Just Wasn't Made for These Times."
[© AP Photo]

fond of "I Just Wasn't Made for These Times." "I've been continually surprised that nobody covered it and it didn't have more of a life of its own. It's a poignant song," he says. It's another number that came out of his coffee chats with Brian. "Neither one of us was a particularly popular kid," he notes. "I think Brian was always very shy. Certainly I was not a guy the girls all wanted to go out with. So we talked about feeling that we were not part of the in-crowd when we were in high school. That's how that song got started."

As much as the song is rooted in teenage emotion, it is also prescient of the creative struggle Brian would face with the album and his more adventurous music to come. Although the rest of The Beach Boys were halfway across the world when the song was written, Brian may have been apprehensive about their reaction — as well as Capitol's — to his introspective new songs. Such concerns — if indeed Brian had them — were perhaps justified.

The album sessions began in earnest in the latter half of January 1966. Asher, who had to return to his day job, was able to attend only a couple of them. Recording was divided among Western, Gold Star, Columbia and Sunset Sound, and often took place in the morning, whereas many other rock 'n' rollers recorded at night. "Brian never planned ahead," Asher explains. "He'd just call up the studio and say, 'Could we come in tonight?' And they'd say, 'No, nights are booked for the next three months. We have time at nine o'clock tomorrow morning.' So they'd go in at nine and work until one in the afternoon."

Calling on his favorite session players, Brian laid down nearly all the instrumental tracks in the absence of the rest of The Beach Boys, who later added their vocal parts. Building on the artistic gains made on *The Beach Boys Today!* and *Summer Days (And Summer Nights!!)*,

Brian's new songs featured his most intricate and exacting instrumental arrangements, sometimes calling for upwards of 20 takes. Asher exerted influence here as well.

"I had a lot of conversations with Brian about arranging and instrumentation," he says. "I'd had a good deal of experience going in the studio and recording with orchestras, and I always paid attention to what instrumentation people used. There were lots of instruments Brian had never heard of. The only jazz connection he had was a vocal connection — The Four Freshmen, The Hi-Lo's and those kinds of vocal groups. He hadn't given much thought to the structure or instrumentation in orchestral jazz compositions."

Asher pushed Brian towards violas, cellos and bass flutes and played him the music of Stan Kenton and The Modern Jazz Quartet, and occasionally he blew Brian's mind with some jazz standard. "I said, 'Brian, there are 200 songs like that — maybe 2,000 — written by Cole Porter, Irving Berlin, Johnny Mercer and all the great songwriters of the Tin Pan Alley days.' He was just not aware of any of those songs."

Brian *was* aware of the theremin, a pioneering electronic instrument invented by

Léon Theremin in Russia in 1920. The instrument was not touched by the player. Its eerie, wailing sound was created by altering the distance of one's hands from the instrument's two antennae — one controlling pitch and the other, volume. Jazz musician Paul Tanner and hobbyist Bob Whitsell developed the electro-theremin in the late 1950s. Also later known as the Tannerin, the instrument approximates the sound of a Theremin with a sine wave generator and a sliding knob manipulated by the performer. Brian invited Tanner to play it in a solo on "I Just Wasn't Made for These Times," which helps articulate the narrator's troubled emotions.

The rest of the track, including Mike Melvoin's harpsichord, Ray Pohlman's electric bass, flutes (uncredited), guitars (Glen Campbell and Barney Kessel), Don Randi's piano, four saxes (Steve Douglas, Plas Johnson, Bobby Klein and Jay Migliori) and Hal Blaine's drums — augmented by bongos, timpani and Frank Capp's Latin percussion[2] — is so spacey it sounds like it floated out of Brian's head. As dense as the instrumentation is, Brian moved it all over to one track and used the other seven for vocals, most of which were filled by his voice alone.[3] Three separate

melodic vocal parts overlap at the bridge; in one, Brian sings about his sadness, in another he suggests he's creatively lost, and in the third, he expresses being misunderstood.[4] It is one of Brian's most personal songs on his most personal album, and would become something of a life statement. It would also provide the title for Don Was' 1995 documentary about Brian.

Much has been made of Mike's allegedly negative reception to the *Pet Sounds* songs. He acknowledges objecting to perceived LSD connotations in "Hang on to Your Ego," which Brian co-wrote with group road manager Terry Sachen. Mike added new lyrics to it and the title was changed to the less druggy "I Know There's an Answer." Mike found Brian overly demanding at the vocal sessions and told him only a dog would be able to discern all the details. He is also said to have found the music too avant-garde for the fans and instructed Brian to not "fuck with the formula."

"To some extent, he was preprogrammed not to like it — as much because he wasn't involved as anything else," Asher says. "I wasn't present when he made the famous remark, if he indeed said it. But if so, he was probably right. You can keep doing the same thing over and over — doing pretty damn good songs over and over is not so bad — but the artists and writers held in the highest esteem in the business are people who really never do the same thing twice."

In a 2010 interview with this author, Mike wanted to set the record straight. "There's been stuff said that I didn't like the *Pet Sounds* album and it's entirely a bunch of crap," he said. "Brian and I both went to Capitol Records to play *Pet Sounds* for Karl Engemann, the A&R guy for The Beach Boys. After we played the album, he said, 'This is great, guys, but couldn't you do something more like 'California Girls' or 'I Get Around'? They were so used to having those hit singles from 'Surfin' Safari' on. When they heard *Pet Sounds* . . . that was a little new, and they really didn't know how to treat that."

One way they treated it was by releasing the compilation *Best of The Beach Boys* — half-filled with old surf and car songs — just as *Pet Sounds* was peaking at #10 on the U.S. charts in July. The band now had two albums in competition, no doubt softening the commercial prospects for each. The greatest-hits package would climb to #8 in America and outlast *Pet Sounds* on the charts by a whole year. "I was very brought down by it," Brian would say of his masterpiece's sales performance, speaking on the BBC Radio 6 music series *Classic Albums*. "I couldn't understand why not that many people were buying it. I think possibly the market wasn't ready yet." Stateside sales for *Pet Sounds* may have been unspectacular, but they were solid, and the album's reputation would continue to move units over the years. It finally received platinum certification in the new millennium. British fans, meanwhile, loved it right off the bat, sending it to #2 in 1966, and the U.K. rock cognoscenti showered it with praise — most notably Paul McCartney, who has called it an inspiration for The Beatles' *Sgt. Pepper's Lonely Hearts Club Band*.

To many, *Pet Sounds* is a landmark of popular music. There are at least three books devoted entirely to the LP. In 2003, *Rolling Stone* named it the second-greatest album of all time — behind *Sgt. Pepper's* — while British publications *Mojo* and *The Times* and Germany's *Spex* ranked it #1. And "I Just Wasn't Made for These Times" remains a fan favorite. One of its most notable admirers is guitarist Ronnie Wood, who selected the track for inclusion on the 2003 *Rolling Stones: Artists Choice* compilation.

And this came out of Brian's collaboration with a lyricist who had never even bought a rock 'n' roll LP.

"For me, there was a certain capriciousness about rock 'n' roll," Asher explains. "We all believed the hot record of the month was great when we were hearing it every day on the radio, but then a few months after you bought it, you'd think, 'They're not playing it anymore and I'm never going to go back and listen to it.' We couldn't have known we would actually listen to them in our sixties."

The best of them, anyway.

JIM FUSILLI ON . . .
CAROLINE, NO

Written by: Brian Wilson and Tony Asher
Lead vocal: Brian Wilson
Produced by: Brian Wilson
Recorded: January 31, 1966
Released: March 7, 1966, as a Brian solo single
Chart peak: U.S. #32
Appears on *Pet Sounds*

In a conversation between Brian and Tony Asher, one of them — Asher can't recall who — brought up the memory of a sweet girl who had been a high-school crush. After graduation they had gone their separate ways, and when they ran into each other years later, she had changed. Her once-long hair was cut short and the qualities he had loved about her seemed to have similarly disappeared. She had hardened. The story led directly to the writing of "Caroline, No," one of Brian's saddest songs.

Fans have long speculated about the girl's identity. The leading candidate has been Carol Mountain, a high-school classmate for whom Brian had unrequited feelings. Perhaps she was his surfer girl. He never forgot her — even when he was a famous, married pop star. Author Peter Ames Carlin tracked down Mountain for his book *Catch a Wave: The Rise, Fall & Redemption of The Beach Boys' Brian Wilson*, in which she recounts how, years after they had last seen each other, Brian would call her in the middle of the night just to chat, waking her and her husband.[1]

Asher says Brian never mentioned Mountain to him. But Asher's first love was a woman named Carol Amen, whom he dated in high school and for a couple of years

97

afterwards. The girl in the song was originally also named Carol, revealed in the line "Oh Carol I know," in which the narrator tells his former love interest he understands how time and experience change people. The line evolved into "Oh Caroline, no" — phonetically the same but, the co-writers agreed, more interesting. It's another example of how their collaboration clicked.

"Brian was always very smart about hiring the right people to say what he needed to say," notes Jim Fusilli, *Wall Street Journal* rock critic, novelist and author of *Pet Sounds*, his take on his favorite rock-era album for Continuum's 33 1/3 book series. "I have a huge regard for Tony Asher. As someone in the advertising copywriting world, he knew how to interpret what the client wanted to say — which isn't to say Brian was his client. But I think he understood the tumult Brian was experiencing."

To Brian, a girl cutting her hair is a powerful symbol of lost innocence, and one he would revisit in "Baby Let Your Hair Grow Long" on his self-titled 1988 solo album. In Don Was' documentary *I Just Wasn't Made for These Times*, Marilyn explains how she always felt "Caroline, No" was, on some level, about her. She had cut her hair to look more sophisticated at the same time her relationship with Brian was changing. Young love had given way to constant bickering about Brian's behavior — no doubt his drug use in particular.

"I'm not sure Brian was really ready to be with strong, independent, opinionated women," Fusilli says. "I think he liked the ethos of the late '50s and early '60s in which the woman was subordinate to the aspirations of the man. Now here we are, it's 1966 and things are changing. I don't think Brian ever thought of the geopolitical context. He was just observing what was going on around him and to him."

In David Leaf's *The Beach Boys and the California Myth*, Bruce says he thinks the song is about Brian's own loss of innocence — his foresight that his ability to do "special things naturally" was soon going to vanish.[2]

"*Pet Sounds* is about a man who looks into the future, doesn't like what he sees and prefers to remain a teenager," Fusilli offers. "This song really expresses that. It's about the innocence and optimism of youth and the loss of youth. It's not so much about a person. It's about an emotion dying, a perspective dying. It's irrelevant who the 'Carol' is. It's more to the point that Brian's facing what we now know would be his abyss."

The song took on great significance as *Pet Sounds*' closing track, giving the album a discernible and pessimistic storyline. "Beginning with 'Wouldn't It Be Nice,' you have a very dreamy, adolescent view of what love and romance is supposed to be, and then you come to the end of the album and none of it is true," Fusilli says. "Through the course of the album — if you take away the instrumentals and 'Sloop John B' — you see him coming to this conclusion, and he arrives at it with 'Caroline, No.' It's a form of resignation and surrender. The last word on the album is 'no.'"

The beautifully mournful track begins with what sounds like a shaker, followed by a hollow, echoed percussion effect revealed by journalist Jules Siegel to be Hal Blaine hitting the bottom of an empty plastic Sparkletts water bottle.[3] It is joined by the bittersweet harpsichord of Al de Lory and guitars of Glen Campbell and Barney Kessel, Frank Capp's '50s-style vibraphone and Carol Kaye's very modern bass. Asher says the bass flutes were his idea, as was the hiring of Bill Green to play flute on the track along with Jim Horn, Plas Johnson and Jay Migliori.[4]

The overall sound is a throwback, but Fusilli finds it progressive in its reach outside of rock 'n' roll. "In many ways it's a jazz tune," he notes. "Some of those chords are jazz chords. There's a major seventh that is so wistful. It just hangs there and Brian's voice goes with it. And the bass flutes and the saxophone are so great. I always felt that because of Brian's high voice he was particularly sensitive to the bottom, and that's why he used instruments like bass flutes and a bass harmonica."

The vocal Brian recorded conveyed all the soul-baring anguish in Asher's words. As Dennis recollected, when Murry heard Brian's vocal on the song, he went to pieces.[5] Murry loved it but suggested speeding up the tape to raise Brian's pitch to make him sound younger. And in this case Brian took his advice. The released version is notably faster than the original recording (which is included on *The Pet Sounds Sessions*) and unfortunately loses some of the nuances of the instrumentation. "I like the un-sped-up version, because to have a boy sing these lyrics makes no sense. But to have a man on the edge of a psychological collapse sing them is a whole different story," Fusilli says.

"Caroline, No" is one of two *Pet Sounds* cuts that features only one voice all the way through without harmonies, the other being "Don't Talk (Put Your Head on My Shoulder)." The longstanding story is the rest of the group was on the road and an impatient Brian simply finished "Caroline, No" without them. But available tour data suggests the group would have been around and Brian could have used them had he wished. "He could have easily put other voices in the bridge. You can anticipate them coming in. But he wanted this to be a Brian Wilson song," Fusilli says. Thirty years later, Brian and the group did record harmonies for a remake sung by Timothy B. Schmit of The Eagles. Backed by Jimmy Webb's orchestration, the cut is the highlight of the *Stars and Stripes Vol. 1* album.

Back in March 1966, Capitol made the remarkable decision to release the song as a single under Brian's name alone, reportedly at Brian's insistence. Asher says he vaguely recollects other members of the group not liking the song — thinking it was not "Beach Boys" enough — prompting Brian to release it himself. Steve Douglas, who plays sax on the track, told David Leaf he pushed Brian to make it a solo record, and when it came out it caused major problems within the group.[6]

But perhaps the controversy is overstated.

Mike, when asked about the song in a 2010 interview for this book, replied he thought it was "absolutely beautiful." When the single was released, the group willingly recorded radio spots promoting it on Brian's behalf. (A couple of these are on *The Pet Sounds Sessions*.) The B-side of the 45 is the *Summer Days (And Summer Nights!!)* instrumental "Summer Means New Love" — also essentially a Brian solo number, and one that also boasted a leap in his arranging abilities. "The single was his first attempt at really asserting himself in public and having the public understand what the music industry already knew — that he was the undisputed leader and creative force of The Beach Boys," Fusilli says.

"Caroline, No" is an artistic triumph but, as a downbeat ballad, not standard hit-single material. Commercial expectations were likely not high, which explains why Capitol followed up its release with "Sloop John B" just two weeks later, when it was still too early to gauge how "Caroline, No" would perform. It would eventually reach #32 on the U.S. charts.

On the album, the song gained a 34-second tag featuring Brian's dogs Banana and Louie barking at a passing train and its blaring horn — an odd ending to such a tender ballad and meditative album. Mike has said this segment prompted him to suggest the *Pet Sounds* title. Some believe the effect inspired the sounds of a dog and other animals on The Beatles' "Good Morning, Good Morning" on *Sgt. Pepper's Lonely Hearts Club Band*. For his part, Fusilli never liked the sound effects and feels they were tacked on to end *Pet Sounds* on a different note. "The song fades out on a reed solo that's so beautiful. 'Caroline, No' is a really heavy way to end an album. The song should have ended and we should have sat there in darkness and pondered the experience we just had, but that's not the way albums were marketed in the '60s. In classical and jazz you did that, but in rock, the next record was supposed to fall down on the spindle and the needle was supposed to drop on it."

But that complaint hardly dims the accomplishment of "Caroline, No," ranked #214 in *Rolling Stone*'s 2010 list of greatest songs of all time. "It's perfectly structured and so smooth from start to finish," Fusilli says. "It's meant to wheedle its way into your subconscious. It doesn't barge in. It makes its statement in a very subtle manner and it's devastating. I don't think *Pet Sounds* would be the same without it, and we wouldn't understand Brian like we do if we didn't have 'Caroline, No.'"

sean o'hagan on...

LET'S GO AWAY FOR AWHILE

Written by: Brian Wilson
Produced by: Brian Wilson
Recorded: January 18–19, 1966
Released: May 16, 1966, on *Pet Sounds* and October 10, 1966, as B-side to "Good Vibrations"

The first song Brian recorded in the proper *Pet Sounds* sessions was "Let's Go Away for Awhile," one of the album's two instrumentals. It would show how far his arranging skills had come.

Whereas Phil Spector previously had been Brian's chief influence, this track shows him taking cues from the more sophisticated, elegant sounds of Burt Bacharach. Described alternately as ear candy, movie music or classical, the delicate piece marked a more experimental phase in Brian's music-making. Indeed, it was later tapped as the B-side to the monumental "Good Vibrations."

Julius Wechter's chugging vibraphone helps launch the fantasia, which incorporates two basses and four slow-burning saxophones before a dozen-strong string section drops in. It all builds in excitement, then comes to a sudden stop before arriving at the heavenly retreat hoped for in the title. The track gets there fast and then it takes it slow, as the group sang years later on "Kokomo," with which it shares a thematic if not a musical connection. The bridge is awe-inspiring, adorned with the exotica of an oboe and a guitar with a Coke bottle on the strings for what Brian described as "a semi-steel guitar effect."

"He really understood how to work with strings and brass sections," notes singer-songwriter Sean O'Hagan, leader of U.K. avant-pop outfit The High Llamas. "It's tricky to know where to put everything — to have enough room to accommodate all those sounds. When the horns just pad, he features the strings, and then the strings play the pads and he features the horns. It's lovely — absolutely fantastic."

Brian composed the track with words and harmonies in mind, but ultimately chose to let the music speak for itself. He once challenged an inquisitive listener to "Try to hum it."[1] You can't. Bereft of vocals it's an abstract piece. The title suggests taking a trip — apropos of the '60s — but this is really a voyage into the music of Brian's mind. The other Beach Boys neither sing nor play on it, and no doubt fans at the time would have been confused to hear such a fanciful piece on one of the group's albums. It's no cousin — not even a passing acquaintance — of "Barbara Ann," released only five months earlier. In a 1967 interview, Brian called it "the most satisfying piece of music I've ever made." Neil Young included it on the soundtrack to his 1974 film *Journey through the Past*.

O'Hagan is another admirer. Growing up in Cork in the Republic of Ireland, he became a Beach Boys fan in the early '80s, just around the time he and singer Cathal Coughlan launched cult band Microdisney. Coughlan suggested they listen to *Pet Sounds* from start to finish. "We were completely blown away," O'Hagan remembers. "The other music we would have been listening to at the time was very fast, angry Agitpop, British punk-funk — Scritti Politti and Gang of Four, things like that. And in the middle of all that, suddenly you're listening to The Beach Boys, and it's like, 'Okay, just tear everything up and go back to the drawing board.'"

For O'Hagan, the album opened up a creative approach foreign to the young U.K. and Irish bands of the time. "Nobody wrote. Everybody jammed," he says. "It was just one riff on top of another and there wasn't really much attention paid to chord structure and songwriting. People would just start up and everybody would join in, the song would build, and it was a collaborative effort. And then hearing *Pet Sounds*, I realized the first thing you put in place is a great chord structure, and after that you can just do what you want. 'Let's Go Away for Awhile' also taught me about key changes. You don't just drone on. When you're stuck and you don't know where to go, stop, change key and see how it feels. That song changes key several times."

The High Llamas pay homage to the piece on their 1994 track "The Goat," which captures a similar feeling and even takes a stab at the harmonies Brian might have included on the original. "Let's Go Away for Awhile" remains a major source of inspiration for O'Hagan. "When I'm writing or when I'm at a low point artistically, I just put it on and it always just turns me completely," he says.

When he first got hooked on *Pet Sounds*, O'Hagan couldn't have imagined that one day he would be going on a surreal adventure with his new heroes.

Around the time of The Beach Boys' 1996 *Stars and Stripes Vol. 1* album, Bruce had come up with an idea to inject some edge into the group. Impressed by The High Llamas' *Hawaii* album, which was clearly influenced by The Beach Boys' esoteric 1966–1973 period, Bruce figured O'Hagan could serve as a link between Brian and the rest of the group and help them reconnect with that bygone creative era. Bruce took up the idea with V2 Records, the fledgling record label founded by

New sounds call for a new look. Brian donned specs around the time he recorded *Pet Sounds*. [© Hal Blaine]

Virgin Group billionaire and Beach Boys fan Richard Branson.[2] The new company wanted to make a splash and became one in a line of industry players wrapped up in the quixotic notion of making *Pet Sounds Vol. 2*.

Certainly O'Hagan wasn't interested in making *Stars and Stripes Vol. 2* and told the band so. "I really politely said, 'You probably don't know this, but right now, all over America and England, there are many boys in

On *Pet Sounds*, Brian turned to the elegant compositions of Burt Bacharach for inspiration. [© Hal Blaine]

their teens and 20s who have stopped listening to indie records, and guess what they are listening to? They're listening to *Pet Sounds*, *The Beach Boys Today!*, *Holland* and *Sunflower*, and they think you guys are kind of gods. This is taking off and you've got a whole new audience. It's time to make that kind of record again,'" he recalls.

O'Hagan flew to the U.S. for various meetings with Brian and the rest of the band, looking to get agreements from all involved and work out a timetable for the project. "I found myself in a very strange position because they were my musical idols," O'Hagan says. "The High Llamas had been banging away on that British indie circuit and I hadn't really connected with an industry at any level. I was scared because it was the first time I encountered real power: the industry, major lawyers, Los Angeles business and personalities against personalities. Suddenly I was out there on the big stage with these people."

He found himself literally on a big stage at Cincinnati's Riverfront Stadium, joining The Beach Boys for an August 9, 1996, show after a Reds game.[3] He remembers Bruce telling him, "If you're going to work with the guys, you've got to play with the guys." O'Hagan suggested they do "Sail on Sailor," which they hadn't played in years. They gave it a solid run-through that night with O'Hagan playing guitar stage-right beside Carl.

O'Hagan and a V2 executive had a meeting at Brian's house with Brian and his second wife, Melinda. "Brian seemed to be happy and he was smiling and giving the thumbs-up, saying, 'I'll do anything, guys,'" O'Hagan recalls. Brian got so excited about the project that he ran to the piano and burst into "Proud Mary." "Do you know this song — John Fogerty?" he asked.

But despite this display of exuberance, O'Hagan was skeptical. "Brian was in a fragile state, as he always is, and he was doing a solo record. Melinda wanted to be sure that whatever happened was the right thing for him," he says. "There were a lot of things to consider."

O'Hagan later followed Brian and Melinda to St. Charles, Illinois, where they temporarily relocated so Brian could make his third official solo album, *Imagination*, with producer Joe Thomas. O'Hagan wasn't fond of the middle-of-the-road musical direction in which Thomas was pulling Brian, and believed Thomas was nervous about leaving him alone with Brian lest he goad Brian into playing an avant-garde note or two.

O'Hagan recalls a rare moment when he and Brian were alone in the studio and Brian began talking about the Moog synthesizer, but mispronounced it as "Mog." O'Hagan recognized the term as British slang for a cat. The exchange descended into an inadvertent Abbott and Costello routine:

O'Hagan [thinking]: *He's talking to me about a cat. Why is he talking to me about a cat?*

Brian: *You like the Mog?*

O'Hagan: *Brian, has a cat walked in? Why are we suddenly talking about a cat?*

Brian: *You like the Mog? I hear it in your music — the Mog.*

O'Hagan [thinking]: *How am I going to get out of this?*

Brian [exasperated]: *Mog! Synthesizers! Mogs!*

O'Hagan: *Yes, I know what you're talking about now. Sorry, Brian.*
Thomas [from down the hall]: *What are you guys talking about?*

As it turns out, O'Hagan and Brian weren't on the same wavelength in a larger sense, either. Despite the many meetings, O'Hagan's dream of getting the guys together for a bold new Beach Boys record never got off the ground. Bruce and Carl had seemed genuinely eager, Alan was friendly and Mike distant, and as for Brian, O'Hagan feels that while the will might have been there, the complications may have been just too much.

"It might have been amazing," O'Hagan says. "Bruce was very much up for it. I wanted to try to deliver something for him, but I just didn't feel as though the intent was there in the band completely. And there were lawyers who were finding this all very amusing. They weren't there saying, 'OK, this is great, let's make some great records again.' They were just saying, 'Hey, this will never happen.'"

WOULDN'T IT BE NICE

Written by: Brian Wilson, Tony Asher and Mike Love
Lead vocals: Brian Wilson and Mike Love
Produced by: Brian Wilson
Recorded: January 22, March 10, April 11, 1966
Released: May 16, 1966, on *Pet Sounds*
and as a single July 18, 1966
Chart peak: U.S. #8

Although "Wouldn't It Be Nice" may be The Beach Boys' most gloriously innocent song, its origins were anything but. In Brian's memoir — which took its name from the cut — he confesses that the tune was inspired by fantasies about Marilyn's older sister Diane. He writes that he would soon afterwards act on those feelings, and the two embarked on a sexual relationship.[1]

He couldn't stop talking to Tony Asher about his sister-in-law and, according to the memoir, used the phrase "wouldn't it be nice" to express his illicit desire. The phrase became the starting point for a song.[2] Brian played a melody for Asher, who realized the many notes meant a lot of words were needed — or at least a lot of syllables. But Brian shot down everything Asher offered up. Asher figured at this rate it would be a long haul, so he asked Brian to put the music on a tape he could take home. When Asher returned with a set of lyrics, they made some changes, and the basic song was there. Mike later added the lullaby-like taglines.

Sung from the perspective of an adolescent boy daydreaming with his girl, "Wouldn't It Be Nice" yearns for the unknown joys of adult romance. It's unusually suggestive for a

Beach Boys song — but that's okay, because they want to get married. And then, according to the narrator, they'd be happy. It's a grand statement about the unwavering optimism of young love.

"The whole song is a big question. It's a rhetorical question, which lyrically is very interesting and makes you want to listen to it more. You can see the naïveté in the narrator, but that makes it even better. That song is all hope," notes singer-songwriter and actress Zooey Deschanel, one half of retro indie band She & Him, along with M. Ward. The California native and star of TV sitcom *New Girl* cites the number as an all-time favorite.

Brian's musical track is one of his most adventurous and perfectly matches the emotional purity of the lyrics. While most of the music on *Pet Sounds* was recorded at Western Studio 3 with engineer Chuck Britz, this song and "I Just Wasn't Made for These Times" were done at Gold Star with Larry Levine. As with many of the album's tracks, Brian made some unorthodox instrumental choices. How many rock and rollers were using not just one, but *two* accordions on a record? (Presumably Brian never forgot the accordion lessons he took as a boy.) Even

standard instruments sound exotic in his production approach. Many listeners believe the song's cheerful intro is played on a harp. According to Mark Linett, who co-produced and engineered the boxed set *The Pet Sounds Sessions*, it is actually Jerry Cole's detuned 12-string guitar run directly into the console with live reverb added.

But it's the jaunty accordions played by Carl Fortina and Frank Marocco that really drive the upbeat song and give it a unique feel. In the bridge, they sound like tender mandolins. Trumpeter Roy Caton and the saxophone team of Steve Douglas, Plas Johnson and Jay Migliori also play a crucial role, providing a jolting transition to the middle eight sung by Mike. Percussionist Frank Capp (who also plays timpani on the track) strikes his bells just at the emotional moment when Brian sings about getting married. Brian required 21 instrumental takes of "Wouldn't It Be Nice" before he was satisfied.

For Deschanel, the degree of precision was well worth it. "I especially like the guitar at the beginning and [Hal Blaine's] drum hit that comes in," she says. "On the surface it's a really well-crafted pop song, but then it has so many layers: production-wise, songwriting-wise and lyrically. It's a perfect record."

One of the composition's most daring aspects is the ritardando before the bridge, when the song slows to a crawl, like a music-box winding down. If you were dancing to the song, what were you supposed to do during this section? And not every musician can master such a tempo change. When The Beach Boys initially played the song live — with Alan taking over Brian's lead vocal — they just skipped the part and jumped to the closing tag (as on *Live in London*, recorded in 1968), but as they honed their skills, they eventually tackled it (as on 1973's *The Beach Boys in Concert*).

"It's a different way of doing a break-down," Deschanel notes. "They do that in classical music, but in pop music, a break-down is usually where you make the arrange-ment sparer. But instead of doing that, Brian thought to make it have a decrescendo and slow it down. It's a whole new way of expe-riencing a song, and it has a particular effect that you just don't hear in other pop songs."

At the vocal sessions, Brian was as demanding of the group as he had been of the musicians, with more time spent on this track than any other on *Pet Sounds*. In Charles L. Granata's book *Wouldn't It Be Nice: Brian Wilson and the Making of the Beach Boys' Pet Sounds*, Bruce explains the song's shifting rhythms posed the greatest challenge, and the group did extra work on it at Brian's house using his four-track recorder.[3]

Brian's lead vocal — which Deschanel describes as "angelic" — is bursting with youthful exuberance, amplified by the group's buoyant backgrounds. The vocals are so lush it took Linett's stereo remix of the mono origi-nal on *The Pet Sounds Sessions* to fully appre-ciate the arrangement. One peculiarity of the stereo mix is the loss of Mike's solo vocal on the middle eight. It had been mixed onto the instrumental track in 1966 and, since it was not available as an isolated element, could not be remixed.[4] On the stereo version the seg-ment is replaced by a version sung by Brian.

Another revelatory aspect of the boxed set is the separate presentation of the vocal and instrumental tracks. "Talk about blowing my mind. I can listen to the song over and over again, but then give me the 'Stack-O-Vocals' and the backing tracks and I'm a happy lady," Deschanel says. "Listening to just the vocals is really exciting. It still sounds fresh. It always makes me happy."

"Wouldn't It Be Nice" was released as a single two months after *Pet Sounds* hit the shelves, and climbed to #8 in the U.S. It was a great bargain for those who didn't already own the album: with "God Only Knows" on the B-side, you got two all-time classics on one 45. (In the U.K., the single was released with "God Only Knows" on the A-side and "Wouldn't It Be Nice" on the flip.) In 2006, music webzine *Pitchfork* included both tracks in its top 10 songs of the 1960s. Filmmakers have long recognized the emotions "Wouldn't It Be Nice" elicits, and it has popped up on the soundtracks of *Shampoo*, *50 First Dates*, *It's Complicated* and the documentary *Roger & Me*, in which the song's happy message is used as a bitter counterpoint to visuals of economic devastation in director Michael Moore's hometown of Flint, Michigan. In addition to Deschanel, other new millennium songstresses who have professed their love for the song include Rebecca Pidgeon, who does a jazz-folk cover on her 2008 album *Behind the Velvet Curtain*, and Taylor Swift, who said that if she ever were to get married, she would walk down the aisle to the tune.[5]

Deschanel recalls first being exposed to the song as a child, listening to oldies radio in the backseat of her family's car. (Her father is Oscar-nominated director of photography Caleb Deschanel, her mother actress Mary Jo Deschanel and sister Emily Deschanel, star of Fox drama *Bones*.) Brian is one of her idols, and in 2008 she got the chance to interview him for the MySpace *Artist on Artist* video series. (The clip is included on Brian's *That Lucky Old Sun* DVD.) Admittedly nervous, she came armed with a bunch of questions for her own education.

"I wanted to find out a lot of recording techniques," she explains. "I had heard that The Beach Boys quadrupled the backing vocals, but they actually tripled them. Ever since our interview, whenever I do backing vocals, everything gets tripled." Her appreciation of The Beach Boys has grown as she has matured as a songwriter and recording artist. "At a certain point they transcended all the other music I was listening to," she says. "You can understand something on one level and then all of a sudden you can have a whole new understanding. It spans the decades in a way the music of very few other artists can."

Minutes after making these comments,

Deschanel joined M. Ward onstage in front of a sold-out crowd of 1,200 at Washington, D.C.'s 9:30 Club for the latest date on She & Him's summer 2010 tour. She picked up a ukulele and gave her first-ever public performance of "Wouldn't It Be Nice."[6] Her slower, almost melancholy interpretation would become part of the duo's regular setlist.

LYLE LOVETT ON...
GOD ONLY KNOWS

Written by: Brian Wilson and Tony Asher
Lead vocal: Carl Wilson with Brian Wilson
and Bruce Johnston
Produced by: Brian Wilson
Recorded: March 10, April 11, 1966
Released: May 16, 1966, on *Pet Sounds*, July 18, 1966,
as U.S. B-side to "Wouldn't It Be Nice," and July 22,
1966, as U.K. A-side
Chart peak: U.S. #39, U.K. #2

According to Brian's memoir, the melody for "God Only Knows" was inspired by a song by The Lovin' Spoonful.[1] While no specific Spoonful title is mentioned and neither the Spoonful's John Sebastian nor lyricist Tony Asher knows of any such connection, it has been suggested the vocal layering in the Spoonful's "You Didn't Have to Be So Nice" is actually the influence.

Whatever the composition's origins, Brian had initial misgivings about Asher's words. He fretted over using "God" in the title of a love song, but Asher insisted listeners would accept "God only knows" as an expression rather than a reference to Him. Regardless of intent, the presence of the word can't be ignored. On one hand, its inclusion could have been perceived as a square move. Traditional religion was playing a declining role in the U.S., as reported in *Time* magazine's "Is God Dead?" issue that hit newsstands just as The Beach Boys finished up the song's vocals. But at the same time there was an elevated sense of spirituality in the West, encompassing a growing number of agnostics and those flirting with Asian and Middle Eastern faiths.

Brian also worried about Asher's opening line, suggesting the narrator won't be in love with his girl forever. But it was merely a verbal trick, as he adds that as long as the sky has stars, he will. He then contemplates the possibility of her leaving, and says that if that were to happen, the world wouldn't end, but he wouldn't see the point in continuing to live. A few simple words in lockstep with Brian's painfully beautiful composition evoke deep feelings of both sadness and elation.

"It gets to the heart of real emotion," observes singer-songwriter Lyle Lovett, who performed the tune at a 2007 gala after Brian was awarded the Kennedy Center Honors. "Art reflects all of life. It's the two sides of everything. Happiness doesn't exist without sadness. That's good writing and that's what makes it transcend being just a catchy pop song." Some even interpret the lyrics to mean that if his girl were to leave him, the narrator would take his own life. Asher denies this was his and Brian's intent, and Lovett doesn't buy it, either. "There has to be a conspiracy theory to accompany anything worthwhile," he says.

Lovett says learning the song gave him a new appreciation for the pure musicality of the words. "The craft of it was revealed in such a wonderful way," he says. "The lyric makes so much more sense from a singing standpoint.

I could see where they might have chosen a certain word because it's sung a certain way. It was an education in the way the words fit together, how they help your voice, and how wonderful the melody is."

Brian recorded the instrumental track at Western Studio 3, which was a small space for the session's 20 or so musicians, all of whom had to be note-perfect as they were being recorded together live. There are many indelible elements: Alan Robinson's French horn at the beginning and end, the layered accordions of Carl Fortina and Frank Marocco, Bill Green's four-note flute theme that ends the joyous intro with a sense of doubt, Jim Gordon's backwards clip-clop percussion, the Merry Christmas sleigh bells (credited on the contract to "Tony" — likely Tony Asher), Carol Kaye's inverted bass line, the string quartet appearing at the second verse and Hal Blaine's closing drum triplets. The song may not have been conceived as religious, but this was the sound of heaven.

The session required 20 takes as Brian honed his arrangement, which at one point included a saxophone solo. The track demonstrates not only the skill of the players, but also Brian's openness to their input. The instrumental bridge lagged, so keyboardist Don Randi suggested doing the part staccato instead of playing the full quarter notes. (The evolution of the idea can be heard on *The Pet Sounds Sessions*.) It became one of the record's most arresting moments — an avant-garde and unusually jarring transition for such a tender love song.

Brian intended to handle the lead vocal but handed it over to Carl, later explaining that he believed Carl could "impart the message better."[2] Also, he was likely sensitive to the fact *Pet Sounds* was coming off like his solo project and he wanted to give the other guys a more active role. Carl, then 19, had to sing with a sense of gravitas he had never before attempted, and he more than delivered. His voice, frequently described as "angelic," lends the track a very spiritual quality.

"It's stunning. It's really brilliant," Lovett says of Carl's performance. "*I've* never been accused of being angelic. I couldn't sing that high when I was eight. I had to sing it a little lower. It had an impact on it. It felt more personal in a lower key. It felt more like one person singing to another person, as opposed to a pop love anthem."

The harmonies also contribute to the record's immortality. It just took Brian some time to find the sweet spot. At a certain point he overcrowded the tape with voices, even calling in Marilyn, Diane and Terry Melcher to join the group on an a cappella tag.[3] (This version is included in the boxed set.) In the final version's tag, Brian and Bruce — and to a lesser degree Carl — overlap their voices in one of pop music's most breathtaking harmonic segments. Brian, on the high end, mimics the French horn part. If they sound like a church choir — abetted by the overdubbing possibilities of the Columbia studio's 8-track recorder — it also may have something to do with the prayer sessions Brian conducted before the *Pet Sounds* vocal sessions. For the group, God *was* there.

Brian had produced his most beautiful record and Capitol wasn't sure what to do with it. There was no doubting its artistic accomplishment, but would fans buy it? The label ended up releasing it as the B-side to the more cheerful "Wouldn't It Be Nice" and the two songs charted simultaneously, with "God Only Knows" scraping into the top 40. But in the U.K., Capitol saw an audience more ready for Brian's grand statement and put "God Only Knows" on the A-side. It would reach

The group in London in 1966. British record buyers sent "God Only Knows" all the way to #2 on the charts.

[© AP Photo]

#2, kept out of the top spot by The Beatles' "Yellow Submarine"/"Eleanor Rigby" double A-side. Years later, Beatle Paul would name "God Only Knows" his favorite song.[4]

It has since been embraced stateside as well. *Rolling Stone* ranked "God Only Knows" #25 in its 2010 list of the greatest songs of all time, and a couple of years later *Pitchfork* declared it the best song of the 1960s. Time.com included it on its 2011 list of the All-*Time* 100 Songs. It is by now a well-entrenched standard, having been covered by a wide variety of artists including Andy Williams, Neil Diamond, Olivia Newton-John, Glen Campbell, David Bowie, Joss Stone, Mandy Moore and Michael Stipe, Weezer's Rivers Cuomo, Dale Earnhardt Jr. Jr. and Taylor Swift. It has cued tears in the feature films *Boogie Nights* and *Love Actually* and served as the opening music for the first three seasons of the HBO polygamy drama *Big Love*. The series finale featured a cover of the song by the Dixie Chicks' Natalie Maines, Lovett's fellow Texan country-music star.

It is not surprising, then, that the song was performed on December 2, 2007, when Brian received the Kennedy Center Honors for lifetime achievement in the arts, along with Diana Ross, Martin Scorsese, Steve Martin and pianist/conductor Leon Fleisher. What *is* perhaps surprising is that Lovett would sing it. A veteran of the Kennedy Center shows, he had previously sung tributes to country legends Johnny Cash, Loretta Lynn and Willie Nelson. While it's a struggle to find any correlation between the oeuvres of Lovett and The Beach Boys (save for the fact they've both covered Murray Kellum's "Long Tall Texan"), Lovett says he's been a fan since his 1960s childhood.

"Growing up in grade school in Houston, there were two identifying factions. You were either what they called a 'kicker' — more of a cowboy — or a surfer," he explains. "The surf culture was so big because of The Beach Boys and the impact of surf music. We were close to the Texas coast and there were people who would take their surfboards down to Galveston when it was stormy enough. I walked the line, but I was really more of a surfer. I had Beach Boys albums and so did my older cousin and I would go to his house and listen to them."

He remembers hearing "God Only Knows" back in the day and liking it, and thought he must be dreaming to be performing it years later at such an important event.

"I felt so honored," he says. He gives plenty of credit to music director Rob Mathes as well as the band and background singers the show producers assembled. He strode onstage to sing his intimate take on the song to a crowd of 2,300. "I recall thinking, 'Just try not to screw up,'" he says. "What a responsibility to sing that song! And those shows are spectacular. You walk out there and look up at the box and there is the President of the United States and all the honorees. It's a tremendous feeling."

Evidently, Brian didn't think Lovett screwed up. In the event's taped broadcast on CBS, he and wife Melinda appeared genuinely moved by the rendition and Brian later said, "I thought Lyle Lovett's version was the best version I ever heard, including The Beach Boys.

The most loving, beautiful version I've ever heard. Unbelievable."[5] When this is read back to Lovett, he laughs and says, "That shows just how creative Brian *truly* is. People sent me that quote and I just couldn't believe it. I said hello to him and his wife at the dinner afterwards and they couldn't have been more gracious. You feel what a soulful, powerful, brilliant person he is when you stand next to him. It just comes off him, as does his kindness. What a gentle spirit he has. And he's sent me a Christmas card every year since."

And there is no better example of what a soulful, powerful, brilliant composer, arranger and producer Brian is than "God Only Knows." It's what Lovett has in mind when he adds, "You just cannot say enough about Brian Wilson's impact on pop music."

AL KOOPER ON...

HERE TODAY

Written by: Brian Wilson and Tony Asher
Lead vocal: Mike Love
Produced by: Brian Wilson
Recorded: March 11, 25, 1966
Released: May 16, 1966, on *Pet Sounds*
and December 18, 1967, as B-side of "Darlin'"

The last backing track Brian recorded for *Pet Sounds* boasts one of the album's most incredible instrumental arrangements.

Asher had framed "Here Today" as words of wisdom from a jilted boyfriend to his would-be successor, warning him that the girl is not all she seems and a romance that seems fine could very suddenly go up in smoke. Asher found it challenging to write to the song's various little sections, and came up with far more words than were used.[1] For his part, Brian said he didn't particularly understand or relate to the lyrics as much as he did to their other collaborations.[2]

At the suggestion of saxophonist Steve Douglas, Brian recorded the instrumental track at Sunset Sound, taking advantage of the studio's unique echo chamber[3] and the talents of young engineer Bruce Botnick, who would go on to co-produce the classic *Forever Changes* album for the band Love. "Here Today" is the most direct precursor to "Good Vibrations" — especially with Ray Pohlman's melodic bass played an octave higher than usual[4] over a chugging, echoed organ. The song's 37-second proto-psychedelic instrumental break starts with a jarring smack from Larry Knechtel's Hammond organ, Nick Martinis' drums, and a tambourine reportedly played by Terry Melcher. Don Randi's piano carries the song downstream, where it submerges in a bass run reminiscent of the effect Bill Wyman uses at the end of The Rolling Stones' "19th Nervous Breakdown," which was all over the radio at the time Brian was in the studio.

Also notable is Brian's punchy use of saxophones — five in all — and a pair of marching trombones. Each of the track's stacked parts seems to be moving in its own direction, at times purposefully out of step with Mike's lead vocal. It creates a slightly uneasy feeling, not unlike how one would feel in a volatile romance.

The cut has achieved some notoriety for the studio chatter and a cough that ended up on the original release. Mike laid down the lead and the rest of the group recorded their background "oohs" and "aaahs" at Columbia. At one point, unaware the "record" button was on, Bruce — and possibly Dennis — started talking about cameras, and Brian shouted directions to his engineer. The inclusion of this background noise on the LP supports the theory that for all the care Brian put into recording, he was more cavalier about his mixes. (The talking was removed for the 1997 stereo remix.)

But this is a mere quibble to legendary musician Al Kooper. "I love the arrangement in 'Here Today,'" he says, acknowledging that the use of keyboards, woodwind and brass have influenced his work. When *Pet Sounds* first appeared, Kooper was part of seminal jazz-folk ensemble Blues Project, and he had already co-written Gary Lewis and the Playboys' chart-topper "This Diamond Ring" and played organ on Bob Dylan's "Like a Rolling Stone." He would go on to form Blood, Sweat & Tears, play with Stephen Stills and Mike Bloomfield on the million-selling *Super Session* album, discover and produce Lynyrd Skynyrd and enjoy an acclaimed solo career.

He points out that the organ break on Blood, Sweat & Tears' 1969 #2 hit "You've Made Me So Very Happy" — which he arranged before leaving the group — was inspired by "Here Today." Elements of the song's arrangement also show up in Kooper's 1968 ballad "I Can Love a Woman" off *I Stand Alone* and in "Lucille" off the following year's *You Never Know Who Your Friends Are*. Of the latter, he says with a laugh, "The verses are very Beach Boys and the choruses are very Four Seasons, so I had both coasts covered."

Kooper had listened to The Beach Boys' records from the beginning and noted their artistic growth. And then he had the good fortune of being blown away by *Pet Sounds* ahead of most everybody else. His friend David Anderle, whom The Beach Boys hired to get their Brother Records label off the ground, arranged for Kooper to come to Brian's Laurel Way home for a private listening of the album a couple of weeks ahead of its release. "That was an amazing night," he recalls. "Brian played me the record, and I wasn't expecting *that*. It completely floored me. He was really proud of it, and if there was a part he liked, he would take the needle and put it back and play that part again. And then he played the whole album again, God bless him."

As a bonus, Brian also played him "Good Vibrations" as a work-in-progress. "I stole millions of things from that song. It just changed my whole outlook about what you could do," he says.

On his website (alkooper.com), Kooper cites *The Pet Sounds Sessions* as his all-time favorite recording, weighed primarily from a production and engineering point of view. "In the garden where naïveté and genius meet, there are bass harmonicas, Stratocasters,

violas, oboes, barking dogs and trains. Put this on and go away for awhile," he writes.[5]

To him, The Beach Boys never went out of vogue. And he was present in June 1967 when negative feelings towards the band were fomented at the Monterey International Pop Music Festival. Kooper performed and served as assistant stage manager at the event, which brought stardom to Jimi Hendrix, Otis Redding, Janis Joplin and The Who. But for The Beach Boys, it would prove a deal-breaker with the counterculture. The group was slated to headline but mysteriously pulled out. Two official reasons were given: pressure from Capitol to complete their next album, *Smiley Smile*, and the distraction of a court date for Carl in three days' time. (As the Vietnam War was escalating, Carl had been drafted but refused to report on the grounds that killing was against his religious beliefs. The courts would grant him conscientious objector status.) But it is widely believed the main reason the group didn't play was that Brian — a festival board official — worried the band would come across as not cool next to the other acts. The U.S. press and public interpreted the group's no-show as an admission that it was passé, and for the most part that's how they treated The Beach Boys for the next few years.

Kooper saw the withdrawal from Monterey as a bad call on the group's part, although he acknowledges their image problem. They were still associated with the surf and car music and continued to wear the corny striped shirts on their most recent tour. "I think they transcended that," Kooper says. "They would have killed — absolutely. Everybody likes The Beach Boys. Everybody has some song they really like, especially in California. We all did stupid things in that time period. I turned down Woodstock because I thought they were charging too much for tickets [$6/day in advance or $8 at the gate]. The weekend of Woodstock I played in Central Park for $2 a ticket."

While Brian didn't perform live with The Beach Boys in those days, three decades later he surprised everyone with his first solo tour. Kooper wrote a review of Brian's June 1999 show in his Boston hometown, calling it "a watershed moment in time that I shall never forget . . . I sat with tears in my eyes and triumph in my heart."[6] He later saw Brian and his band perform *Pet Sounds* in its entirety.

While the masterful use of the studio on *Pet Sounds* makes re-creating it onstage a daunting prospect, Brian pulled it off with his gifted band and orchestral backing at many of the venues. The CD souvenir *Brian Wilson Presents Pet Sounds Live* followed in 2002, and if it contains one recording that arguably improves on the original, it's "Here Today," in which the band really pushes the instrumental break and adds some mystical seasoning with a fitting flute part.

Kooper's friendship with Brian has continued. In 2008, he joined Brian onstage in New York in support of cancer charity Stand Up for a Cure, singing the bridge on "Caroline, No" and playing organ on "Help Me, Rhonda." In November 2009, Kooper came to Brian's Providence, Rhode Island, concert to sit in on sound check and join Brian for a pre-show dinner. Kooper's love for *Pet Sounds* also remains. He will on occasion dig out the 40th anniversary Dolby Digital 5.1 surround sound mix.

"I can only play it about once a year," he says. "It's a religious experience. Whenever I think I'm good at what I do, I put that on and then I'm humbled again."

Jace lasek on ...
GOOD VIBRATIONS

Written by: Brian Wilson and Mike Love
Lead vocals: Carl Wilson, Mike Love and Brian Wilson
Produced by: Brian Wilson
Recorded: February 17–18, March 3, April 9, May 4, 24, 25, 27, June 2, 12, 16, 18, late August, September 1, 12, 21, 1966
Released: October 10, 1966
Chart peak: U.S. #1, U.K. #1
Appears on *Smiley Smile*

Of the many Beach Boys classics, Brian has called "Good Vibrations" "the biggest production of our life."[1] Pushing into even more adventurous sonic terrain than *Pet Sounds*, the single showed him rewriting the rules of songwriting, arranging and recording, and the world happily came along on the trip. In the words of former *Creem* editor Ben Edmonds, it showed "fun could be art and still be fun too."[2]

The song was hatched during the *Pet Sounds* writing sessions, and had it been included on that LP it surely would have put album sales through the roof. However, Brian realized it was going to take time to realize his grandiose vision for the piece and put it aside until after he'd delivered a finished LP to a waiting Capitol.

Brian has often recounted how, as a boy, he asked his mother why dogs bark at some people and not others. Audree explained that they pick up different vibrations from different people. That idea of emotion traveling through space both enthralled and terrified a young Brian. Now, years later, his substance-expanded mind had a heightened interest in numerology, astrology and ESP, and he decided to revisit in song that childhood fascination, albeit with a more positive spin.

In Asher's telling, Brian wanted to call the song "Good Vibes" — as in when you walk in a recording studio and say, "Wow, I like the vibes in this place." Asher convinced Brian that "vibes" was clichéd and would trivialize the song. But then, Brian asked, how would they replace the part in the chorus that goes "I get vibes, I get good vibes"? Asher suggested the iconic refrain we all know and love. Brian initially mocked the idea of repeating "good" four times by playing the entire melody on the piano while singing only the word "good," but he soon came to realize it just might work. Asher then wrote a full set of lyrics about the unspoken communication in boy-girl attraction.

The early tracking sessions prominently feature Larry Knechtel's spacey echoed Hammond organ, a memorable electric bass part of guitar-like clarity (Ray Pohlman, Bill Pitman, Carl, Carol Kaye and Arthur Wright all played bass guitar at various sessions), a mystical piccolo (played alternately by Plas Johnson, Arthur C. Smith and Jim Horn) as well as Tommy Morgan's harmonica and — oddly — Jew's harp.[3] For Brian to convey those scary-sexual vibrations, he called back Paul Tanner to add his electro-theremin (or "Tannerin") as he had on "I Just Wasn't Made

for These Times," giving the record its signature sound.

Brian's incorporation of the wailing instrument continues to cast a spell. Jace Lasek, leader of Montreal indie rockers The Besnard Lakes, was so inspired that he tried — unsuccessfully — to have a Tannerin custom-built for the recording of the band's 2010 album *The Besnard Lakes Are the Roaring Night*. "The original theremin's cool, but everybody who gets it just turns it into a noise machine, holding their hands in the air making goofy sounds," Lasek says. "I want to play the Tannerin the way Brian used it. I love the idea of being able to sweep into notes instead of just playing them individually. I'm still on the hunt for one."

At one point, Brian recorded a complete instrumental track and laid down a vocal using Asher's lyrics. (Capitol unearthed this version for the 1990 *Smiley Smile*/*Wild Honey* twofer CD.) This take has a strong R&B feel and would have been good enough to release at the time, but Brian's brain kept bubbling over with new ideas and he continued on what would turn into a recording marathon.

He wasn't satisfied with the words, and with Asher back at his day job, asked Van

Dyke Parks, whom he was courting to write lyrics for The Beach Boys' next album, *Smile*, to take a stab at a rewrite. Parks declined, preferring to start their partnership on a fresh canvas. However, depending on the source, either he or Carl suggested using a cello — which was played by Jesse Ehrlich — as a rhythm instrument in the chorus. "In the 1960s, having the cello chug along like that was shocking," Lasek notes. It was an innovative use of a classical instrument, but it still sounded like rock 'n' roll.

Brian seemed able to conceive limitless variations on the song's main theme, recording wildly disparate fragments in styles from woodwind-based Eastern mysticism to Sunday morning church service to comical Roaring Twenties jazz. Only a fraction of these made the final record. (Edits of outtake sections appear on the *Smiley Smile/Wild Honey* CD, *The Pet Sounds Sessions*, a 40th anniversary "Good Vibrations" EP and *The Smile Sessions*.) Perceptive of the sound qualities produced at the various studios in town, Brian recorded different segments at Gold Star, Western, Sunset Sound and Columbia. Like a film director finding his story in the editing room, he rebuilt the song by cutting

together the various sections he'd recorded. The transitions between fragments were sometimes seamless, other times startling in their juxtaposition of tone and tempo. Judging by the public's lukewarm reception to the less radically experimental "The Little Girl I Once Knew" one year earlier, here Brian was courting commercial disaster.

He made various mixes of "Good Vibrations" only to later junk them. Finding it hard to satisfy himself, he even considered handing it over to an R&B act to record instead. (According to author David Leaf, Wilson Pickett was one artist for whom the song was deemed appropriate.[4]) But despite his frustrations, Brian knew he was onto something big and stayed the course.

His creative approach continues to resonate with musicians into the new millennium, Lasek included. "I see it as a series of musical segments that have been weaved together, and that's always been the way I've constructed songs," Lasek says. "We play on the idea of surprise and emotion, and 'Good Vibrations' has the strongest element of surprise with all its stops and starts. You feel like you're on a journey within the song. The verse has a texture and the chorus has a different texture because they've been recorded in different rooms. It's a shocking listen the first time. The way it hits me, it excites me and gives me hope."

After Brian took a break from the song for most of the summer, recording continued throughout September. He held at least 16 sessions in total at a cost reported anywhere from $10,000 to $50,000 (approximately $67,000 to $336,000 in 2012 dollars). Had the record flopped on the heels of *Pet Sounds'* so-so sales, the group's standing with Capitol would have taken a serious hit. Brian was allowed a luxury of time and expense that is rare today given industry economics — even for a band that owns its own studio such as The Besnard Lakes. "He was able to go in and spend as much time as he wanted," Lasek notes. "Since our studio is for hire, we book time, but we could get bumped by another band that actually pays for it, and of course we would have to take the money. It takes us a while to get in to actually record."

When Brian's bandmates finally heard the track they were struck by its weirdness — particularly Mike, who was relieved that at least the song was about the relatable topic of sexual attraction. He came up with a nearly entirely new set of words, dictating them as he drove to a vocal session. His lyrics' hyper-awareness of sights and sounds were perfectly in tune with not only the track, but also the burgeoning psychedelic movement. Mike also provided the hook of the record with the R&B-flavored chorus opener, which he also sings and which fits like a glove over the bass part.

Carl, fresh off his stellar performance on "God Only Knows," ended up singing the verses after Dennis evidently gave it a try at one session or more. But Carl's vocal is perfect — so airy it could be floating on a cloud of marijuana smoke and contrasting nicely with Mike's more carnal contribution: the sacred and the profane. The group's harmonies are as tight and thrilling as ever, with Brian ecstatically following Mike on the chorus.

By October 10, the opus was finally released in the U.S., its protracted birth quickly proving justified. It lived up to U.K. publicist Derek Taylor's description as a "pocket symphony."

"The song is almost like a whole album, even though it's only 3 minutes and 35 seconds long," Lasek says. "There are all these things going on and it's constantly changing. You have to be a total genius and maybe on some drugs to pull all that together. Brian has said this and 'California Girls' represent the pinnacle of his ability, and he's right. Those songs are devastating."

"Good Vibrations" was a work of magic and everybody wondered how Brian had pulled it off. Released on October 28 in the U.K.,[5] it took only three weeks to reach #1 for a two-week stay. By December 10, it was #1 in the U.S. as well, making it the band's only chart-topper in both countries. Its most direct competition in the U.S., oddly, was The New Vaudeville Band's old-timey "Winchester Cathedral," which would surrender its #1 *Billboard* spot to The Beach Boys only to reclaim it one week later. While it was widely acknowledged that Brian had done something revolutionary on "Good Vibrations," the Recording Academy inexplicably awarded "Winchester Cathedral" the Grammy for the year's best rock 'n' roll recording.

Capitol planned to include "Good Vibrations" on *Smile* and make it the focus of its marketing campaign for the album, but because that project fell apart, the song didn't see LP release until *Smiley Smile* appeared in September 1967. When Brian reconstructed his aborted album on 2004's *Brian Wilson Presents Smile*, he rerecorded "Good Vibrations" using Asher's original lyrics and expanded the song with a "hum-de-dum-hum-de-duh-oh-oh" chant and an instrumental outro resurrected from the cutting-room floor.

"I saw the *Brian Wilson Presents Smile* concert at Place des Arts here in Montreal and I was choking back tears," Lasek recalls. "It's a hard thing to get people to react like that. Music doesn't really exist — it's just a bunch of vibrations. Brian always talked about that. For a bunch of sound vibrations to affect you emotionally is pretty amazing."

For Lasek, the peak moment of his lifelong Beach Boys love came when he met Brian at the 2008 Ottawa Bluesfest, where Brian performed "Good Vibrations" in his 75-minute set. Lasek was on the same bus as Brian and got an introduction from Nelson Bragg, percussionist in Brian's band. "Brian said, 'Hi, Jace!' and he just grabbed me and gave me the hugest hug," Lasek recalls. "I don't really get star-struck anymore, but I was shaking. He's a living treasure."

And the brilliance of "Good Vibrations," regarded by many as The Beach Boys' greatest achievement, has not dimmed. Among its many kudos, it was voted greatest single of all time by artists, producers and music-industry personalities in a 1997 *Mojo* list, and sixth-best song by *Rolling Stone* in 2010. Even when played more than 40 years later at a Brian or Beach Boys show, it remains one groundbreaking and freaky piece of music.

HEROES AND VILLAINS

Written by: Brian Wilson and Van Dyke Parks
Lead vocal: Brian Wilson with Alan Jardine
and Mike Love
Produced by: Brian Wilson and The Beach Boys
Recorded: October 1966, December 1966–March 2,
1967, June and possibly early July 1967
Released: July 24, 1967
Chart peak: U.S. #12; U.K. #8
Appears on *Smiley Smile*

Brian was determined to push in unexplored directions as he turned to the next album. But to do that, he needed a lyricist who possessed both an imagination as unbridled as his and the skill to put Brian's wild concepts into words. He found those qualities in Van Dyke Parks, with whom he would share an unlikely, glorious, tragic and ultimately redemptive collaboration.

Parks was a cerebral, bespectacled Mississippian with a penchant for Tin Pan Alley. Then 23, he was an aspiring solo artist and former child actor who had appeared in the 1956 Grace Kelly period romance *The Swan* and studied piano at Pittsburgh's Carnegie Institute. His single "Come to the Sunshine" would be covered by Baroque pop-sters Harpers Bizarre, and he added Bach-like organ to The Byrds' "5D (Fifth Dimension)." Parks had been over to Brian's house with David Crosby to listen to a preview of "Sloop John B,"[1] but it was at a 1966 party at Terry Melcher's house that he and Brian really got to chatting.

Parks delivered his patter in the manner of and with frequent references to a bygone era. This impressed Brian, who was contemplating a song with an American history theme, and he proposed Parks write lyrics for him. Brian recorded some incredible music in this period, encouraged by a new circle of friends and supporters that included musician Danny Hutton, David Anderle (who managed both Parks and Hutton[2]), Michael Vosse (a young writer Brian hired as his assistant) and a revolving door of admiring journalists. Brian also found stimulation in an expanding menu of recreational drugs, reportedly including hash, pot, uppers, downers, LSD and even nitrous oxide fumes from Reddi-wip cans.[3] His creativity even spilled over into his everyday home life. Most infamously, he had a giant sandbox constructed around the Chickering piano in his dining room and filled it with eight tons of white sand. He then needed only to dig his toes beneath his piano bench to reconnect with his original source of inspiration.

Parks entered the sandbox and saddled up at the piano beside Brian to begin their songwriting partnership. The first tune they banged out was the Old West–themed "Heroes and Villains." With the British Invasion dominating the culture, they looked to write something quintessentially American. What they had in mind, Brian told the *New Musical Express*, was a "three-minute musical comedy," and it

would be constructed in the modular fashion of "Good Vibrations."

In May 1966, Brian assembled a full complement of studio musicians for some preliminary recording at Gold Star,[4] but put the song on the back burner until the fall so he could finish "Good Vibrations." The composition begat other musical ideas he and Parks wanted to group together in a Western suite. They wrote throughout the summer of 1966 and Brian and the group started recording in the fall. In November, Brian and Parks taped a "Heroes and Villains" demo that incorporated snippets titled "I'm in Great Shape" — an ode to rural living — and "Barnyard," which turns a day at the farm into slapstick ballet. The recording would come to light on 1998's *Endless Harmony Soundtrack*.

Brian had amassed a dozen and a half potential album tracks in some form of completion by mid-December. He and Parks originally planned to call their opus *Dumb Angel* but changed the name to *Smile* to reflect a humorous thread in some of the songs. Capitol printed more than 400,000 LP covers — featuring designer Frank Holmes' welcoming cartoon "smile shop" — in anticipation of a Christmas release that ended up being pushed to late January. As a Capitol audio promo for retailers stated, "With a happy album cover [and] the really happy sounds inside . . . we're sure to sell a million units" — a sales projection referring to the label's entire seasonal slate.

Not all of Brian's bandmates were convinced, however. They had spent the summer on a North American tour with little knowledge of Brian's new companions and compositions. They had just basked in fans' screams for their earlier hits, and this experimental new music married to Parks' abstract lyrics bore little resemblance. Most vocal about his displeasure was Mike, who struggled to find the literal meaning of some of the more obscure lines in "Heroes and Villains." Nonetheless, he and the others dutifully laid down the complex vocal parts.

If Brian's artistic judgment needed any affirmation, it got just that from the U.K. in December. On the strength of *Pet Sounds* and "Good Vibrations," The Beach Boys topped The Beatles as best world vocal group in the *New Musical Express* annual readers' poll. Given such kudos, expectations for a new Beach Boys album were higher than they would ever be.

As 1966 turned to 1967, "Heroes and Villains" concepts kept popping into Brian's head and he continued recording, surpassing 30 sessions for that track alone. The growing number of musical fragments made finalizing an edit exponentially more challenging. He kept missing Capitol's deadlines for the album and single, but closed in on a complete version of "Heroes and Villains." It was to run around six minutes on the album — at the time an extreme length for both radio and a 7" record. So, by February 10, he finished a three-minute mix of "Heroes and Villains" that was likely intended for The Beach Boys' next single.

The cut — which would be relegated to the vaults until its appearance as a bonus track on the 1990 *Smiley Smile/Wild Honey* CD — had evolved substantially from the November demo. It contains a radically different section after the second verse set in a rowdy saloon, where the narrator's reverie about a dancing girl is interrupted by the sudden appearance of a barking lawman. An echoing flutter-tone links to a closing cowboy instrumental, which rides the song into the sunset atop clop-clop percussion. Brian's intention for the second half of the song will never be known for certain. Engineer Chuck Britz explained that

Brian had resolved to put it on the single's flip side under the title "Heroes and Villains Part Two,"[5] but according to Alan Boyd, who co-produced the 2011 boxed set *The Smile Sessions*, Brian denied ever planning a two-sided single. But the three-minute mini-epic A-side alone would have been ground-breaking on 1967 radio. If teenyboppers had found it challenging to dance to the shifting tempos of "Wouldn't It Be Nice" and "Good Vibrations," they would have had to just sit this one out altogether.

By late February, The Beach Boys erected their own roadblock to *Smile*'s release when they launched a $225,000 lawsuit against Capitol that claimed outstanding royalties and demanded termination of the group's contract.[6] Brian, believing "Heroes and Villains" was sure gold, withheld it from the label as leverage. He worked on the second half of the song into March but evidently did not finish it, although some sections were spliced together for the 1993 boxed set *Good Vibrations: Thirty Years of The Beach Boys* and an attempt at a finished "Heroes and Villains Part Two" was made by Boyd and Mark Linett for a 7" single included in *The Smile Sessions*. The latter is a wild musical ride, starting with a snippet borrowed from The Crows' doo-wop hit "Gee" leading into barbershop quartet. It moves to stranger territory with the group mimicking animal sounds, quickly descending into X-rated Looney Tunes. This is followed by harmony, piano, string, brass and cowboy segments. It's only in hearing all these parts that one can truly grasp Brian's vision for the song and his fearlessness to try anything and make it work.

But despite the amazing sounds already committed to tape, *Smile* began to unravel on several fronts. Parks, feeling growing tension all round and not enjoying being grilled by Mike over his lyrics, absented himself from sessions and by April was gone completely, off to record his own album, *Song Cycle*. Without Parks, Brian was in a weakened position to defend his new music to any doubters. Meanwhile, Brian's behavior, likely influenced by his drug intake, had become increasingly erratic and paranoid, casting doubts on whether he could satisfactorily finish the ambitious project. Journalist Jules Siegel's *Smile* postmortem "Goodbye Surfing, Hello God!" in *Cheetah* magazine reported the stories that would become legend. Brian fearing Phil Spector had secretly made the

In Van Dyke Parks, Brian found a collaborator with an imagination that could match his own.
[Jasper Dailey, © David Leaf Productions]

freaky movie *Seconds* with director John Frankenheimer just to mess with Brian's mind. Brian canceling a $3,000 recording session because he picked up bad vibrations. Brian turning away an acquaintance from another session because he thought the guy's girlfriend was a witch. (Author Peter Ames Carlin later revealed that the anonymous acquaintance was in fact Siegel, the author of the piece.[7])

The pressure to claim the pop crown was becoming too much to bear. The Beatles' highly anticipated *Sgt. Pepper's Lonely Hearts Club Band* was slated to arrive on June 1, and Paul McCartney, eager to meet Brian and see what The Beach Boys were up to, visited an April session for the comical track "Vega-Tables" and munched on some carrots and celery for percussion. But instead of trying to go head-to-head with their British counterparts, The Beach Boys ultimately gave up the fight. In May, Derek Taylor made the shocking announcement that *Smile* was canceled. Capitol/EMI, in a 2011 press release ahead of the release of *The Smile Sessions*, took some of the blame, stating "the reason *Smile* did not see release in 1967 had more to do with back room business . . . than anything else." The dispute between Capitol and the group was resolved by July 1967 with the company agreeing to distribute The Beach Boys' upcoming records on the group's own Brother Records label. And then, as the 2011 press release says, "It was agreed that *Smile* was no longer to be the band's next album."

It was supposed to have been Brian's grand artistic statement. Or as Dennis so eloquently put it, "*Smile* is so good it makes *Pet Sounds* stink." But abandoning it was a matter of his older brother's self-preservation. "We pulled out of that production pace merely because I was about ready to die," Brian told interviewer Jamake Highwater in an interview in January 1968. "I was trying so hard. So all of a sudden I just decided not to try to do such big musical things." Indeed, he would rarely attempt such ambitious material again.

Capitol still had an album to release, so, in the span of six weeks, the group recorded the deliberately under-produced *Smiley Smile* as a replacement. Whereas Brian had previously recorded at the top studios in town, he now recorded mostly in a makeshift recording facility installed in his new Bellagio Road home. Just a couple of weeks earlier he was directing *la crème de la crème* of L.A. session players, but now he would work more democratically with the other Beach Boys, who mostly played their own instruments — like in the early days — and share in the production credit. Bruce, meanwhile, largely took a pass on the *Smiley Smile* sessions following the tense and weird *Smile* experience. But for Brian, scaling back allowed him and the rest of the guys to enjoy making music again. "We had so much fun," he told Highwater. "The *Smiley Smile* era was so great. It was unbelievable: personally, spiritually, everything. I didn't have any paranoiac feelings."

The group still eyed "Heroes and Villains" for the next single, and salvaged it along with other *Smile* cuts "Vega-Tables," "Wind Chimes" and "Wonderful" for *Smiley Smile*, rerecording the orchestrated musical sections in simpler, bastardized form. The group's new attempt at "Heroes and Villains" veered markedly from Brian's original intention. Bearing a driving rhythm akin to that of Spector's "River Deep, Mountain High" for Ike & Tina Turner, it is a challenging record, marred by its muddy, homemade sound. Bereft of the "cantina" section and the instrumental passages, it loses nearly all its Western flavor and cinematic sweep. But it did retain Brian's great jazzy melody and a harmonic arrangement only he could have accomplished. While it still offers some startling musical juxtapositions, it also has a somewhat more traditional structure than the *Smile* version, borrowing a chorus from the *Smile* track "Do You Like Worms."

Finally arriving in the middle of the Summer of Love, "Heroes and Villains" fell short of the hype for much of the record-buying public. But while it marked the beginning of the group's commercial slide, it nonetheless climbed to a solid #12 in the U.S. and #8 in the U.K. Although initially it was difficult for many listeners to respond to the song outside of the filter of expectation, it and *Smile* have become the central focus for many Brian Wilson devotees. In the case of Colorado indie popsters The Apples in Stereo, those records are an inextricable part of the band's history.

"I used to argue that 'Heroes and Villains' was the greatest rock 'n' roll song ever written, but it's so far from being a rock 'n' roll song," says Apples in Stereo leader Robert Schneider. "It is so far beyond 'Good Vibrations.' It aims so much higher. It's one of the high points of the whole genre of pop music. It's so dense and complicated. You have a simple progression with three chords, and then you have all these extra notes in the harmonies and the arrangement. If your ear can tolerate all that, you end up finding a lot of dissonant notes. That's the Brian Wilson thing."

While Jimi Hendrix and Cream were blowing people's minds with heavy guitars, on "Heroes and Villains" Brian was committing amazingly progressive sounds to 8-track tape using his band's voices. The group got added vocal help from Billy Hinsche of teen group Dino, Desi & Billy, whose sister Annie had married Carl in February 1966. (He sings the "do do do do do do do do" part.) "There are all these crazy background vocal parts," Schneider says. "The guys are going, 'ah-oonka, ah-oonka,' and there's all these weird sounds going on. It's like they have 16 tracks — one for the instruments and 15 for vocals. I know they didn't have 16 tracks, but that's what it sounds like. You can put it down on one track and it can sound like that when you have a group of vocalists who are the best singers on earth."

"Heroes and Villains" was the first song The Apples practiced. "We didn't learn the arrangement on the record, because we could barely even play," Schneider reminisces. "We chose it because there are just three chords, and so we punk-rocked it up. We were able to hammer it out like The Ramones." The Apples soon got its act together and "Heroes and Villains" would be the only cover song in the band's regular repertoire. Schneider and his cohorts wail and thrash their way through it on the 2001 EP *Let's Go!* "We always intended to release our version of the song on both sides of a single, like Brian allegedly had intended," he adds. "But now that The Beach Boys' 7″ actually exists in the *Smile* boxed set, we don't feel quite the sense of urgency."

It is Beach Boys love that brought together Schneider and founding Apples bassist Jim McIntyre while the two attended the University of Colorado in the early '90s. They formed The Apples with drummer Hilarie Sidney and guitarist Chris Parfitt. Schneider wanted to start a label to release their material, just as the Beach Boys had done with Brother Records, and when musician friends from Schneider's hometown of Ruston, Louisiana, also moved to Denver, they joined him in founding The Elephant 6 Recording Company. Bands in this collective have also included Neutral Milk Hotel and The Olivia Tremor Control, with the later addition of Beulah, Elf Power and Of Montreal. They shared a mutual passion for '60s pop, and *Smile* was their Holy Grail.

"We read about *Smile* and obsessed over The Beach Boys records around it. We built up in our minds what *Smile* was in this empty space where much of it wasn't available to hear," Schneider recalls. "The potential of what *Smile* would have been was the primary thing that inspired us. When we started hearing *Smile* bootlegs, it was mind-blowing. It was what we had hoped it would be, but a lot of those songs weren't finished, so there was still this mystery of not hearing the melodies and lyrics. We wondered, 'What are these songs and how do they fit together? Is this a verse?'"

In 1994, when The Apples recorded their debut album *Fun Trick Noisemaker*, they headed to L.A., setting up at a friend's house in Glendora using Schneider's portable equipment, which he dubbed Pet Sounds Studio. (Today, the moniker is used for a bona fide Denver recording studio that has served as birthplace to albums by The Apples, Neutral Milk Hotel and other Elephant 6 artists.) "We needed to record our first album in California. It had to be that way in the name of The Beach Boys," Schneider says.

The band got more of a Beach Boys experience than they'd anticipated when they ended up playing a Brian Wilson tribute show at Santa Monica's Morgan-Wixson Theatre. They performed "Heroes and Villains" that night, and a fellow musician let them in on a little secret: Brian himself was backstage and was going to close the show. "It felt really magical knowing my hero was in the same building," Schneider recalls.

The Apples got to hang out backstage with the other participants, including Alex Chilton of Box Tops and Big Star fame, and Elliot Easton, guitarist for The Cars. Schneider met Brian's wife, Melinda, who offered to introduce him to Brian. Schneider excitedly ran to his van to get a vinyl *Smile* bootleg for Brian to sign, although he was somewhat hesitant to show it to Brian given Brian's well-known aversion to even discussing *Smile*. Turns out he had nothing to worry about.

"I showed him the record and he looked at the song titles on the back," Schneider says. "He talked to me in an older-man-to-younger-man kind of way. He was completely cool and centered and as kind to me as he could have been in that situation. I told him how I worshipped *Smile* and this was the best music ever recorded, and he said, 'It didn't all come at once. It came in cycles.' In other words, it's a really big effort that you can't just do continuously. You allow yourself to relax sometimes. That was meaningful to me."

Brian's 2004 recording of "Heroes and Villains" on *Brian Wilson Presents Smile* reincorporates the "cantina" section as well as vocal and instrumental passages from the so-called "Heroes and Villains Part Two" in a new sequence. A similarly structured version using the original Beach Boys recordings was later assembled for *The Smile Sessions*. The song was finally presented with the grandeur of Brian's original vision. For Schneider and many others, its belated appearance in the new millenium along with the other *Smile* tracks was a major musical moment. What Brian, Van Dyke Parks and the rest of The Beach Boys tried to do back in 1966–67 continues to cast a mighty shadow.

"It seemed so tragic that this majestically conceived piece of art was left unfinished," Schneider says. "It was a warning, like the story of Icarus: if you fly too high, you get burned by the sun. And yet the story does not lessen your desire to fly — it gives you the idea to try for yourself. A young person hears this story and thinks, 'I could do it. I could make it. I could find a way even though Icarus didn't.' That's how I saw *Smile* — like a map to fly to the sun. Only no one made it all the way there."

CARNIE WILSON ON...
OUR PRAYER

Written by: Brian Wilson
Lead vocal: group
Produced by: Brian Wilson
Recorded: September 19, October 4, 1966,
November 17, 1968
Released: February 10, 1969, on 20/20

Brian described *Smile* as a "teenage symphony to God," and nowhere is that more evident than with "Our Prayer." And as much as any other track The Beach Boys ever recorded, it demonstrates the kind of magic the group created with its voices alone.

Brian took the group into the studio in fall 1966 to record the sections of the a cappella number then known simply as "Prayer," which runs just slightly over one minute and was to open *Smile* as what historian Peter Reum described as a "spiritual invocation." Brian was taking the band's harmonies into decidedly heavier territory. The session tape suggests some influences at play, with Brian quipping about "hash joints" and asking, "You guys feeling that acid yet?" Whatever was going on in Brian's head, he must have been feeling Baroque church music — the kind he had in mind when he said one day he would make music people would pray to. With Brian leading on the high-end, the group's combined vocals — a wordless series of forceful oohs and ahhs — soar to the cathedral spire before coming back to earth with an affirming "hmmn." Divine.

But after *Smile* was put on the shelf, the public would not get to marvel at the song's haunting beauty for another two years. By then, Brian's creative contributions had become fewer and farther between, so when assembling the 20/20 album, Carl resurrected "Prayer" and "Cabin Essence" from the ashes of *Smile*. Brian reportedly wanted no part of it, which likely explains why Carl, Dennis and Bruce did the required vocal overdubbing at Capitol Studios rather than at Brian's home facility,[1] as was the norm for the group at that time. Their additions gave greater depth to the original vocal track, which finally saw release on the boxed set *Good Vibrations: Thirty Years of The Beach Boys*.

"Our Prayer" ended up buried as the penultimate track on 20/20, and based on reviews of the time, few were aware it originally had been intended for *Smile*. But that was finally confirmed with its appearance as the lead-off track on 2004's *Brian Wilson Presents Smile*, on which Brian's newer band displays its own vocal chops.

And they're not the only ones who have more recently taken on the challenge of replicating The Beach Boys' vocal feat. Wilson Phillips, the band consisting of Brian's daughters Carnie and Wendy along with Chynna Phillips (daughter of The Mamas & the Papas' John and Michelle Phillips), sings "Our Prayer" as the closer on its 2010 *Christmas in Harmony* album. "That's always been one of my favorite songs," older daughter Carnie recalls. "When you hear it, you have to stop what you're doing and you go to another place for a minute and 10 seconds and then come back when it's over — or you might not come back. To me, it's one of the prettiest things that has ever been written. Wendy and I have been listening to it for many years."

Carnie points out that she has been hearing Beach Boys music since the womb. She was nine months old when "Our Prayer" was first released. She recalls hanging out as a young girl at Brother Studio and hearing her dad write songs and play piano. She and Wendy made the famous 1972 trip to Holland with The Beach Boys, and as little kids they would often join the band onstage for "Good Vibrations." But it was when she was a little older that she began to really appreciate the music.

"I remember when I was 12, putting on headphones in bed at night and listening to 'Surf's Up' and saying to myself, 'This is my dad who wrote this!'" she says. "I always knew all the up-tempo fun songs, but when I started listening to *Friends* and 20/20 and all those records, it just blew my mind. Wendy and I couldn't get over all those songs."

Of all her father's music, "Our Prayer" affects Carnie the most. "It always has brought me to tears," she says. "I can listen to it and go on an emotional journey. It could take me to a very happy place that is a celebration of voices, harmony and structure, but it can also bring me to a really melancholy place of longing and sadness over the years of the troubled relationship with him and not having a father that was always around. It's a really intense, bittersweet thing for me, but most of all it brings up feelings of being really proud of him and is a celebration of his gift."

And that vocal gift is clearly in the sisters' genes, and not only from their father's side. Their mother Marilyn, of course, sang in The Honeys in the early '60s and a decade later in Spring, whose one and only album Brian co-produced. In 1986, lifelong friend Chynna called Carnie and Wendy with the idea of starting a group. Four years later, Wilson Phillips released their harmony-laden self-titled debut album to sales of five million in the U.S. and millions more worldwide. The sisters parted with Phillips after their sophomore LP and Carnie embarked on a TV career that has included talk show *Carnie!*, a hosting gig on *The Newlywed Game*, reality show *Carnie Wilson: Unstapled* and a seat as a judge on *Karaoke Battle U.S.A.*

Wilson Phillips reunited for 2004's *California,* which includes covers of "Dance, Dance, Dance" and "In My Room," the latter featuring Brian on piano and vocals. The Christmas album came next, along with Wendy's idea to include "Our Prayer." Tackling the intricate arrangement was daunting, but Rob Bonfiglio, Carnie's musician husband, broke down all the vocal parts and presented them to the group on a CD.

"Just following the parts is so unbelievably hard. We had to lay down each part separately. There was no way for us to do it live. There are too many parts," Carnie explains. "Timing can be easy when you're doing a cappella and you have a click track, but here the tempo slows down and speeds up. So Rob made the click track live. It wasn't a machine." All of which makes what The Beach Boys originally accomplished all the more astounding.

At a Christmas 2010 family get-together, Carnie played the new recording for her dad. "He sat back in his chair and looked at me and said, 'That's better than The Beach Boys!'

He was actually screaming," she recalls. He was then silent for a few minutes, as though reconnecting with a long-lost Muse. "'Carnie, come here. I want to tell you something,'" his daughter recalls him finally saying. "'Do you want to know what inspired me to write "Our Prayer"? Bach.' He listened to the way Bach arranged and structured things. He said, 'If you listen to Bach, one part's going up, another part's going down, and that's what this is about.'" It's difficult to imagine many other composers on the top 40 in 1966 having Bach on the brain.

Comments like that from her dad keep amazing Carnie, who was eyeing the release of *Dedicated*, a new Wilson Phillips album of Beach Boys and Mamas & Papas covers. She says that after all these years it's still a thrill to hear one of her father's songs on the radio. "When it comes on, it's like a ball of fire I feel in my tummy, and I go, 'That's Daddy,'" she says. "I'm his daughter, but I'm also a fan."

MARK LINETT ON ...
SURF'S UP

Written by: Brian Wilson and Van Dyke Parks
Lead vocal: Carl Wilson, Brian Wilson and Alan Jardine
Produced by: Brian Wilson and Carl Wilson
Recorded: November 4 and December 16, 1966, and summer 1971
Released: August 30, 1971, on *Surf's Up* and as a single November 29, 1971

"Surf's Up" was written over the course of one night, with Brian coming up with melody lines and Van Dyke Parks responding with words.[1] The *Smile* composition's decades-long evolution would prove as epic as the song itself.

Parks' kaleidoscopic lyrics are heavy on patrician period imagery, summoning diamond necklaces, opera glasses and horse-drawn carriages. Back in 1966, Brian told journalist Jules Siegel what he and Parks intended. The central character is a man at a concert amidst an aristocratic crowd clinging to systems and beliefs that inevitably must fall. The scene dissolves to a dream of ancient times and grand battles at sea. Yet for all the suffering through the ages, the jaded protagonist cannot even shed a tear. In the end, God points the way: return to the pure love one feels as a child.[2]

Visionary or pretentious, it certainly was far removed from anything any rock 'n' rollers were singing, including The Beach Boys, who were closing shows with the likes of "Little Honda." Even the "Surf's Up" title was a bold choice. Brian craved counterculture acceptance and was looking to disassociate the group from its surf-music roots. That's why Parks loved the cheekiness of a title that alluded to that earlier era — so passé by 1966

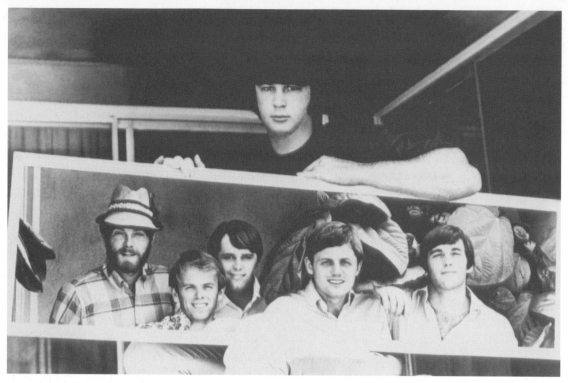

Brian worked on *Smile* while the rest of the group was off touring.
[© AP Photo]

— especially since the song had nothing whatever to do with surfing. In the lingo of the sport, "surf's up" means conditions are good, but this song invokes a tidal wave, portending an occurrence of major proportions. This could be positively interpreted as the rise of a youth movement to better the world. But what the haunted — and haunting — song may actually have been anticipating was the undoing of Brian's music and of Brian himself.

"It's abstract poetry," says producer/engineer Mark Linett. "I don't think one is meant to think too much about exactly what the lyrics mean, but it does have beautiful imagery."

Linett, who became a steady collaborator of Brian's on his first solo album in 1987, partnered with Alan Boyd to put together *The Smile Sessions* for its November 1, 2011, release in double CD, digital and boxed-set configurations. Using the original 1966/67 cuts, they assembled an approximation of what *Smile* could have been, adhering closely to the re-recorded finished version on 2004's *Brian Wilson Presents Smile*, which Linett recorded and mixed. The vocals on some of the '60s tracks were never completed, however. "Brian was a long way from finishing the album when he abandoned it," Linett notes. *The Smile Sessions* boxed set also includes demos, outtakes, vocals-only edits and hours of session highlights from that fascinating period.

Working at Western Studio 3 in November 1966, Brian, engineer Chuck Britz and Brian's session players laid down a sublime instrumental track for the first of the two movements of "Surf's Up." The subtle yet intense arrangement features Al de Lory on upright piano, two basses (Carol Kaye on Fender and Jimmy Bond on upright), percussion (possibly car keys, which Brian wanted Frank Capp to make sound "like jewelry"), Nick Pellico on glockenspiel and Al Casey's plucked electric baritone guitar. Roy Caton's overdubbed trumpet along with four French horns[3] — evoking a Norse call to arms here, quietly anxious there — give credence to the time-spanning lyric. The following month, TV producer David Oppenheim filmed Brian playing the song for the CBS special *Inside Pop: The Rock Revolution*, hosted by conductor/composer Leonard Bernstein and aiming to spotlight the best of contemporary pop music to skeptical middle-agers.

On the program, Brian, alone at his piano, delivers a hypnotic performance. Eyes closed, he taps into his muse as he rarely would ever again. As he trails off, Oppenheim says in voice-over: "Poetic, beautiful even in its obscurity, 'Surf's Up' is one aspect of new things happening in pop music today. As such, it is a symbol of the change many of these young musicians see in our future."[4] The segment didn't air until April 25, 1967, when it further whetted the public's appetite for the long-delayed album. But by then the *Smile* drama was playing itself out, and just one week after the broadcast, the record was officially dead — even though Brian and the band would in fact continue working on it until May 18.

If any Beach Boys had been uneasy about the experimental *Smile* music, at least they came to appreciate the value of its myth. After the group's 1970 *Sunflower* album bombed, they decided to unearth the brilliant song fans heard Brian sing on TV years earlier. No doubt *Smile* remained a painful subject to Brian, and although he agreed to the song's resurrection — or, at least, did not resist it — he absented himself from most of the new "Surf's Up" sessions. Evidently the recording had not been completed in 1967 and presented a puzzle to the rest of the band, who would have to record new sections to piece together with the archived segments. There was no finished lead vocal, but they did have a December 16, 1966, demo of Brian singing the entire song at the piano. They also located the instrumental track — but for the first of the two movements only.

"I've asked Brian if he recorded part two and he doesn't think so,'" Linett says. "Either it was not recorded or the tape was lost, which seems unlikely. So in 1971 The Beach Boys decided to use Brian's piano vocal version for part two and added a little Moog bass and additional vocals."

For part one, the group attempted to marry Brian's vocal to the instrumental track. "They tried to fly Brian's vocal in, but technologically it wasn't feasible," Linett explains. "We have a reel where they transferred the vocal track manually and it didn't work. You need time-compression capabilities. Nowadays it's a fairly simple process."

But back in 1971, the band was forced to record a fresh lead for the opening segment. They asked Brian to sing it, but he declined,[5] so Carl ended up doing it, displaying his peerless ability to reach the high notes. After some careful editing, Carl's section segues smoothly into Brian's vocal in part two. That left part two's closing vamp, which required further adornment. Group members were in Brian's home studio toiling on the track with engineer Stephen Desper when Brian surprisingly appeared, determined to add a final vocal tag. He may have recorded a version at a group vocal session on December 15, 1966, but that tape has never materialized.[6] Perhaps Brian's memory now had been jogged nearly five years later. As it turned out, what he had in mind was a variation on "Child Is Father of the Man," another song earmarked for *Smile*. Alan would sing the lead for this new part, supported by some of the most stunning harmonies of the group's career, delivered by the band — minus Dennis — along with Marilyn and then-manager Jack Rieley.[7]

The new section provided a fitting coda to a crowning achievement. When "Surf's Up" appeared on the group's 1971 album of the same name, *Rolling Stone*'s Arthur Schmidt enthused the song "would have more than given a run to anything on *Sgt. Pepper*."[8]

Digital technology allowed Linett to do what the band couldn't in 1971 — produce a mix featuring Brian's full 1966 vocal for *The Smile Sessions*. But attempting to construct a "pure" 1966 "Surf's Up" raised questions about what to do with the parts added in 1971. Do you leave in the Moog? What about the vocal tag? The respective answers: no and yes.

Linett has mulled over these kinds of issues ever since Capitol hired him in 1987 to coordinate the CD releases of the 1960s Beach Boys LPs. The first catalog release was *Pet Sounds*, which Capitol wanted to follow-up with *Smile*. The label had Linett pull tapes from the aborted album and prepare some mixes, but The Beach Boys chose to withdraw the project. Meanwhile, as Linett recounts, someone made a dub of the tapes and sold it, which led to the tracks being widely bootlegged. Several *Smile* numbers — including the 1966 "Surf's Up" demo — were officially unveiled on *Good Vibrations: Thirty Years of The Beach Boys*, which Linett co-produced with David Leaf and Andy Paley.

The buzz from that release and 1997's Grammy-nominated *The Pet Sounds Sessions* — which Linett engineered and co-produced with Leaf — yet again stoked interest in a full-fledged *Smile* release. But the group once again rejected the idea. Finally, in 2011, all members gave their blessings, surely realizing no other musical offering could make as big a splash in the buildup to the band's 50th anniversary celebrations. But then there was the problem of the *Smile* sections for which no vocals had been recorded. For 2004's *Brian Wilson Presents Smile*, Parks wrote lyrics for songs that had previously existed only as instrumentals, but The Beach Boys in 2011 resisted recording and adding these vocal parts to the 1966/67 tracks.

For Linett, the bonus tracks for *The Smile Sessions* required unprecedented preparation, even compared to *The Pet Sounds Sessions*. "It's miles beyond that," he says. "There were only 14 tracking sessions for *Pet Sounds* [including one for the outtake 'Trombone Dixie'], whereas for *The Smile Sessions* we had to condense more than 70 sessions down to their most interesting and informative bits. Brian was well known for over-cutting. He just cut when inspiration struck him, and there was a lot of inspiration going on."

The rudimentary equipment Brian used to edit his musical fragments into complete songs in 1966/67 makes his accomplishments that much more impressive. On the other hand, it took Linett less than one day to put together the *Smile*-era pieces of "Heroes and Villains," following the structure of Brian's 2004 version. "I had a blueprint, which helps, and digital workstation technology," he says. "Doing that in 1966 — with live mixes and tape and razor blades — would have been a more laborious process. And it wasn't easy to change something — which Brian was doing a lot, since these pieces could be shifted in many ways. He was essentially trying to do digital editing 30 years before it was invented."

While Linett had produced a stereo remix of *Pet Sounds* for *The Pet Sounds Sessions*, the *Smile* album sequence is presented in mono on *The Smile Sessions*, with the studio highlights and some bonus tracks in stereo. That is in part because some of the elements exist only in mono, but there were aesthetic considerations as well. "More so than *Pet Sounds*, *Smile* seems to work better in mono," Linett says. "It seems more integrated that way. It was always Brian's intent that these records be in mono — not because he's deaf in one ear, but because it's the only way to guarantee that the listener is hearing the music exactly as it was created. And remember, in 1966 everybody made their records mono for AM radio. Stereo in rock music was largely a novelty."

That's when Linett was a teenager who'd loved hits like "Dance, Dance, Dance" and "I Get Around." He would become one of Brian's regular collaborators and a key player in The Beach Boys' archival releases. It's part of his job to pore over the session tapes of their classic songs. "Being an engineer, I love listening to the sessions for those records," he says. "I grew up admiring those records, buying those records and wondering how they were made. This is the best way to get a real sense of what it was like in the studio when Brian produced so much great music."

MATTHEW SWEET ON...
WONDERFUL

Written by: Brian Wilson and Van Dyke Parks
Lead vocal: Carl Wilson
Produced by: The Beach Boys
Recorded: July 12, 1967
Released: September 18, 1967, on *Smiley Smile*

"Wonderful" may not be one of The Beach Boys' best-known songs, but it has proven to be among the most durable. One of five *Smiley Smile* songs held over from the *Smile* meltdown, it is the one that was rerecorded in the most radical reinterpretation.

The more simply produced *Smiley Smile* version was recorded in one three-hour session[1] at Brian's home studio with Jim Lockert engineering. The lyrics to "Wonderful" are as intriguing as they are obscure, bearing the unmistakable esotericism of Van Dyke Parks, who was curiously omitted on the original album pressing. The song's story, so it seems, is of a girl whose devotion to God and her parents is thrown askew after a bump-in with a boy unleashes new and confusing emotions. The *Smiley Smile* rendition drops one verse from the *Smile* original but otherwise hews to the original words. Nonetheless, it is a totally different beast, sung by Carl with an eerie sensuality. The spare instrumentation is built on an organ and a piano, with childlike backing vocals. After the third verse, the song takes a left turn into a hash den, where Mike chants nonsense doo-wop while the rest of the guys giggle and talk amongst themselves, with the odd phrase such as "Don't think you're

God" rising above the din. After 35 seconds of this lunacy — which may represent the girl's sexual awakening — the proper song returns, Carl's vocal winding down to a tired, barely audible croak.

The overall effect is one of bizarre menace — *Beach Boys' Party!* on acid. If *Smile* was indeed shelved in part because any band members found the music too weird, it is inconceivable that they would have seen this as any more accessible. *Smiley Smile* alienated the American record-buying public in late 1967, reaching only #41 on the charts, the group's lowest album showing to date. (It made it to #9 in the U.K.) But perhaps it provided some societal good. Reportedly its mellow vocals were used to help soothe patients in a Texas drug clinic and help them recover from bad LSD trips. The album's very strangeness has helped make it a cult favorite.

"Even if it's remnants of *Smile*, I view that time as when Brian really goes abstract — and that's probably why everyone else fought back so hard," says alt-rocker Matthew Sweet. "Van Dyke's lyrics are so cool, and Brian did right by them. He and Brian are trying to capture an impressionistic thing. That time is so experimental, and looking at it now, it's easy to see why it could be overlooked — because people just don't instantly understand really abstract stuff. It takes time to have a conversation about it before we realize what an amazing thing they did."

Growing up in the '70s in Lincoln, Nebraska, Sweet was turned on to The Beach Boys when he heard "All Summer Long" in *American Graffiti* and subsequently bought *Endless Summer*. After relocating to Athens, Georgia, for that city's thriving music scene, he was turned on to *Pet Sounds* by Peter Buck, guitarist for up-and-comers R.E.M. Sweet instantly felt a strong connection to that album but wasn't aware of Brian's role as writer/arranger/producer. In 1985, when Sweet met with Columbia Records' Rick Chertoff and Steve Ralbovsky about signing a record deal, they told him, "We really love your whole Brian Wilson kind of thing," to which Sweet innocently replied, "Who's Brian Wilson?"

"They thought that was hilarious," Sweet recalls. "I did know who Brian Wilson was. It just didn't jump to my mind." They all discussed their shared love of *Pet Sounds*, and then they handed him a copy of *Smiley Smile*. "It's such a cool record to be given, and it also helped me get into the whole idea of where

Brian's head was at regarding art."

The original *Smile* version of "Wonderful" — the only song actually mentioning God by name in Brian's "teenage symphony to God" — was cut at Western, Columbia and Sound Recorders in August, October and December 1966 and January and April 1967.[2] It's proto-psychedelic chamber pop featuring Brian singing lead and playing the harpsichord with the support of a trumpet and the group's parlor-room harmonies. Sunnier and more straight-ahead, the track would be much bootlegged but not see official release until *Good Vibrations: Thirty Years of The Beach Boys*.

"What a lovely version that is," Sweet notes. "It's more baroque, and I really like baroque records from that era. Brian sings it more fully, which works really well with those lyrics. It's got a more serious feel about it, whereas it gets a little trivialized on *Smiley Smile*. That one is so weird in comparison, the way Carl is whispering it. With everyone laughing and making noises there is way more goofiness to it." When Brian was choosing songs for the 2002 compilation *Classics: Selected by Brian Wilson*, he included "Wonderful," opting perhaps surprisingly for the *Smiley Smile* version.

The song clearly holds special meaning to Brian. The title happens to be a pet name he had for Marilyn, as she mentions in A&E Biography's documentary *Brian Wilson: A Beach Boy's Tale*.[3] He recorded the composition twice more: on 1995's *I Just Wasn't Made for These Times*, and then on his 2004 *Smile* reconstruction, staying true to the 1966 cut, although relying on more synthesized textures. That track ingeniously segues into "Song for Children," which Brian and Parks completed for the 2004 release as part of a four-song suite about innocence. Brian chose Rufus Wainwright to cover "Wonderful"/"Song for Children" for the 2009 benefit album *War Child Presents Heroes*.

Sweet has covered several Beach Boys tunes himself, including "The Warmth of the Sun" on *Under the Covers, Vol. 1*, his 2006 album with The Bangles' Susanna Hoffs, and "Sail on Sailor" with Darius Rucker of Hootie & the Blowfish at 2001's *An All-Star Tribute to Brian Wilson* at Radio City Music Hall. While rehearsing for that event, the musicians took a break, leaving Sweet alone with Brian, who was tickling the ivories. "I walked over to him and asked, 'What is that you're playing? It's so beautiful.' He said, 'I know. It's "Blueberry Hill."'" He was just playing the chords, but you never would have known. It was so lovely," Sweet recalls.

In trying to summarize the contribution of Brian and The Beach Boys, people often boil it down to the harmonies, but Sweet sees much more.

"Although I love Brian's harmonies, they just reflect his chord changes," Sweet says. "For me, it's a feeling in the music. It's what the music achieves that is really important. I like stuff that has anxiety in it as well as happiness, and his songs indicate that he felt all kinds of ways. He captured really personal feelings that young people have, and then, as he got older, that growing older makes you have. And he did it all through music. To me, that's a whole achievement beyond just the sound of The Beach Boys."

Danny Hutton on...
DARLIN'

Written by: Brian Wilson and Mike Love
Lead vocal: Carl Wilson
Produced by: The Beach Boys
Recorded: October 27, 1967
Released: December 18, 1967
Chart peak: U.S. #19; U.K. #11
Appears on *Wild Honey*

In fall 1967, with *Smiley Smile* befuddling critics and garnering weak sales, the group had to chart its next move. They had planned to release a live album drawn from a pair of August shows in Honolulu featuring Brian temporarily reclaiming his stage spot from Bruce. But the tapes were deemed not up to snuff and the project, slyly titled *Lei'd in Hawaii*, was shelved. What to do?

Inspiration, remembers Brian's longtime friend Danny Hutton, came from the pantry. "I was in Brian's kitchen and he said, 'Yeah, man, I want you to hear this!' and he pointed to this jar of wild honey and he said, 'We did this song "Wild Honey" and Carl is so soulful on it!'" Hutton recalls.

Fueled by Paul Tanner's two-note bee-like electro-theremin riff (referenced in Bruce Springsteen's 2012 single "We Take Care of Our Own"), the tune continued in the R&B mold of the group's previous flop single "Gettin' Hungry," but minus the *Smiley Smile*-era weirdness. Carl wails like Stevie Wonder, affirming his new role as the group's main lead vocalist. One of the great Beach Boys hits that never were, "Wild Honey" — which returned the band to the Capitol label after releasing the previous album and two singles on its own Brother Records — went no higher than #31 on the U.S. charts (#29 in the U.K.), but provided the name and template for the group's next LP.

The album sessions carried on the Stevie Wonder vibe, most directly on "I Was Made to Love Her," a cover of Wonder's #2 hit from that summer. While R&B had been a big part of the band's early days — when it built songs on borrowed Chuck Berry riffs — much of the new material was inspired by the more vocally emotive soul music on the Motown, Stax Records and Atlantic labels. It was a surprising direction for what had been perceived as a white-bread group and opened them up to further derision if it failed.

Brian and Mike, who shared a fondness for the genre, co-wrote nine of the album's 11 songs. The sound continues *Smiley Smile*'s lo-fi DIY aesthetic, with much of the recording done in Brian's home studio, with strings, horns and other instruments added at Wally Heider Studios. "It was all real simple compared to the other stuff. They were going for that. It was back to the basics — 'Let's do a bunch of jammin'; let's go for a funky sound,'" notes Hutton, who had enjoyed a front-row seat in the control booth during the *Smile* sessions.

The Irish-born Hutton had first run into Brian when cutting demos at Gold Star. He had worked for Hanna-Barbera Records, the animation house's fledgling rock label, where he scored the minor solo hit "Roses and Rainbows." When he later signed to MGM, his manager, David Anderle, brought him over to Brian's house, and soon he and Brian regularly hung out together. That was in 1966. "Brian was it. He was the man. He was on the top of the mountain. I knew it. Everybody in L.A. knew it," Hutton recalls. "As far as being in control of himself, in control of the studio and people, the group — he was right there. He was like a rocket."

He believes Brian's production mastery started to slip, however, once he had the home studio installed. "It was a whole different animal," Hutton says. "It wasn't that professional thing where he's going in to Western and he's got it booked for X amount of hours. All of a sudden, he can sleep until whatever time he wants. He'd get up and wander and go to the kitchen. The man loves to eat. Then The Beach Boys were there a lot more. I don't think on a production level that's necessarily good. It's the old story: if you cut a track and then have the musicians come in and ask the bass player what he thinks, he'll say, 'The bass is too low, turn it up.' Everybody's kind of 'me me me.'"

Simultaneous to the *Wild Honey* sessions, Brian was trying to produce an album for Hutton's new band, which featured fellow lead singers Cory Wells and Chuck Negron. Brian eyed the group, which he named Redwood, for Brother Records. "Anderle said they wanted to bring in all fresh talent and Brian was going to be able to do stuff that he normally couldn't do with The Beach Boys," Hutton explains. Earlier, there had even been talk of Brian giving "Good Vibrations" to Hutton for a solo record. But as for Brian depriving his own group of his biggest production, Hutton says, "I don't think that ever would've really happened."

But Brian did have Redwood record his composition "Time to Get Alone," a beautiful ballad treated to a grander production than anything The Beach Boys were doing on *Wild Honey*, and which featured Hutton's considerable involvement. The sessions at Wally Heider's were marked by Brian's typically quirky behavior. After a vocal recording, Brian exited the booth, asked the musicians what they thought and left the room. Outside, he placed a call to his astrologer J'nevelyn,

who informed him that he was on a down cycle.[1] Convinced the vibes were bad, he went home, leaving everybody in the studio wondering what had happened to him. The next day, Brian, who had a major aversion to L.A. smog, came in with an oxygen tank and mask. He would take hits from the tank then go sprinting in the alley behind the studio. "He's just a very unique man," Hutton says.

Redwood also cut Brian's "Darlin'," which, according to some accounts, was so named after Hutton's frequent use of the term. The song is a rewrite of the 1964 single "Thinkin' 'bout You Baby" that Brian and Mike had penned for Sharon Marie. The original is one of Brian's best Spectorish girl-singer productions, and Marilyn and Diane covered it on the 1972 *Spring* LP. Brian cleverly resurrected the forgotten song's great melody for Redwood, believing it suited the group's gutsy vocals. He loved Spector's records with The Righteous Brothers and wanted to make similar white soul.

"He played 'Darlin'' for us on the piano and we loved it," Hutton recalls. "We did that at his house. He played the piano on the basic track. He rushes a little when he plays the piano on that. He called a bass player from Motown to come down and play on it, and then they brought in horn players. The piano wasn't tuned correctly, so the horns were flat. We put a rough lead vocal on it and that was it."

That really was it, because Brian's work with Redwood stopped soon afterwards. Various explanations have been given for the halting of the project, including the claim that Brian was dissatisfied with the group's vocal performance[2] — doubtful given his initial enthusiasm — and that Redwood was dissatisfied with how much it was being paid for its time in the studio.[3] According to Hutton, it was about other Beach Boys wanting both the Redwood songs and Brian's full attention.

"'He's giving away those hits like he did with Jan & Dean!' — I see their point," Hutton says. "I get Mike Love saying, 'Hey, Danny, man, I know about this album thing you want to do. What about a single or something? *We've* got an album to do, man. I don't know what you guys are doing. We gotta get in this room. We gotta start working.'"

But Hutton's band was determined to make its own LP and so didn't sign with Brother, relegating Redwood to another what-if in the Brian Wilson story. "As incredible as The Beach Boys were, they could really never get into the super-soul area," Hutton says. "Cory, our singer, could go into Righteous Brothers and beyond. He could go into Bobby 'Blue' Bland and Sam & Dave territory. We'd do anything. We could do ballads and we did intricate harmony. It would have been very interesting if it had continued."

Brian and his main band convened at Wally Heider's to build the "Darlin'" instrumental track and add the vocals, including another Carl lead. The result was one of the group's catchiest records — a heartfelt, upbeat love song. Record buyers showed their love in turn, sending the group back to the U.S. top 20. The song should have been an even bigger success but was ahead of its time, anticipating the blue-eyed soul of such '70s acts as Todd Rundgren and Chicago. "I think it was good," Hutton says of The Beach Boys' version. "Carl had a beautiful, angelic voice."

(In 1986, when the group was in Waikiki taping their anniversary TV special *The Beach Boys: 25 Years Together*, they invited Hutton and Wells — Negron was out of the band — to perform "Darlin'," giving them a chance to show what they would have done with the record, alternating on the verses and providing a rougher edge.)

"Darlin'" became a Beach Boys concert staple and was included on all three of the group's subsequent live albums, where it benefitted from punchier presentations, especially on *Live in London*, recorded in 1968. Brian gives his own solid performance on *Live at the Roxy Theatre* and told *Goldmine* that he found it the most difficult number to sing because of the "range of the vocal and [how] the words tie together."[4]

The song was the high point of the *Wild Honey* album, which improved on *Smiley Smile*'s chart performance (#24 U.S., #7 U.K.). Some hardcore fans, still stinging from *Smile*'s nonappearance, were left feeling empty by the album's apparent lack of ambition. But when many of rock's leading lights produced more direct, rootsy records — Bob Dylan's *John Wesley Harding*, The Byrds' *Sweetheart of the Rodeo*, The Beatles and The Rolling Stones' *Beggars Banquet* — it seemed The Beach Boys had been ahead of the curve. Some critics retroactively embraced the LP's strong songwriting and idiosyncratic humor, hailing it a minor masterpiece.

Meanwhile, all that remains of Brian's Redwood fling is "Time to Get Alone," which finally saw release on the 1993 collection *Celebrate: The Three Dog Night Story, 1965–1975*. The song was already familiar as The Beach Boys had put their vocals atop the instrumental track for their own version on 1969's *20/20* album. Hutton believes the stifling of Redwood was a contributing factor in Brian's artistic retrenchment. "Brian must have thought, 'Holy crap — I've got three pretty good lead singers who can sing any kind of harmony and I can get soulful,' and all of a sudden he hears, 'No, come on back and just do the Beach Boys stuff.' I don't think that helped him creatively."

But things more than worked out for Hutton and company. They changed their name to Three Dog Night and became a top act of the late '60s and early '70s, scoring 21 consecutive U.S. top 40 singles, including the number ones "Mama Told Me Not to Come," "Joy to the World" — *Billboard*'s top seller for 1971 — and "Black and White," deftly turning outside composers' material into smash hits. The potential revenue on which Brother lost out is staggering to consider, but Hutton believes signing with The Beach Boys' label would have brought complications. "We probably would have taken four or five Beach Boys hits away from them, so in a way it was the best thing for everybody," he says.

While Three Dog Night was basking in its initial success, Brian was retreating from the spotlight. But he stayed close with Hutton, who was plugged into the L.A. scene and who would introduce him to the next generation of hot musicians, including Elton John. While Brian is often perceived as having spent all of this period in bed, he was actually often at Hutton's Laurel Canyon house with the likes of Ringo Starr, Harry Nilsson and Billy Preston,[5] partying through the coke-filled early '70s.

"He and [Little Feat's] Lowell George would drive over and we'd all just sit and get crazy and listen to music," Hutton recalls. "It was a safe place to go. It was tough for him. It stopped being 'Brian the eccentric genius' to 'the nut case who's lost it.' Then it was the start of our group taking off like a rocket. I was there for him. It wasn't like, 'Thanks for what you did, you're not doing anything now, we don't need you, bye.' I love the guy."

Marilyn, however, was less than thrilled with the amount of time Brian was spending at Hutton's, reportedly sending over friends to bring him home on several occasions.[6] "She hated it. 'Is he at Danny's again?' But I have only very fond memories of her. I got a Christmas card from her recently, so she still loves me," Hutton says.

He adds that he and Brian remain the best of friends. Brian has a standing invitation to the Hutton Sunday dinners. "He's like a brother. I think he trusts me more than about anybody in the business," Hutton says. "There've been a lot of ups and downs and we stuck together."

LITTLE BIRD

Written by: Dennis Wilson and Stephen Kalinich
Lead vocal: Dennis Wilson
Produced by: The Beach Boys
Recorded: February 29, 1968
Released: April 8, 1968, as B-side of "Friends"
Appears on *Friends*

Fans had several reasons to be surprised by the first Beach Boys 45 of 1968. "Friends," the lilting waltz on the A-side, marked a return to the glorious harmonizing of *Pet Sounds* overtop a great, jazzy track. Its title suggested greater band unity, and that sentiment extended from the lyrics through the full group vocals to the more democratic songwriting, credited to all three Wilson brothers and Alan. No doubt the group also hoped to remind listeners of its long-standing friendship with them. But the American public turned out to be fair-weather friends, as the song charted no higher than #47 (#25 in the U.K.), the group's lowest performance to date for an album's lead-off single.

An even greater revelation was B-side "Little Bird," the first solo composition by a group member other than Brian to be included on a 7". While the artistic growth of everybody in the band was inevitable, the fact that Dennis led the way was surprising. Wasn't he the guy who got into the band strictly at his mother's insistence? Wasn't he just eye candy for the girls? As it turned out, he had a hitherto dormant gift for melody akin to Brian's, and had absorbed more from his brother than people realized. Once Brian had taught him chords on the piano,[1] he also displayed a great feel for playing keyboards. As early as January 1967, in the middle of the *Smile* sessions, he recorded the musical track for his composition "I Don't Know" and would soon work obsessively on his music.

One might have expected Dennis' first released song to be a surf-rock retread, but instead he showed his spiritual side, which had been awakened in December 1967 when he met the Maharishi Mahesh Yogi at a televised UNICEF benefit concert in Paris in which The Beach Boys performed. He brought other members of the band to learn Transcendental Meditation from the Maharishi, and although he ultimately did not have the patience to be a regular TM practitioner, as Mike did, the Holy Man from Rishikesh left a lasting impression on the Wild Man from Hawthorne.

To help put this newfound spirituality into words and music, Dennis chose an unlikely songwriting partner. Stephen Kalinich was a young poet from New York state who had formed a band with his friend Mark Buckingham called Zarathustra and Thelibius. It was hardly a commercial-sounding moniker, and clearly Kalinich's ambitions didn't lie in the mainstream. But in 1966 Brother Records staffer Arnie Geller took note of Kalinich

and arranged a meeting with Brian, who had a fondness for arty outside collaborators and signed him to Brother. Carl produced Kalinich's "Leaves of Grass" — a pretty song inspired by the Walt Whitman poetry collection of the same name — but it did not see release in its time because of its perceived marijuana reference.

While it was always assumed Kalinich would write with Brian, he gravitated towards Dennis, sensing the drummer's nascent compositional skills. "His music is pure. It's so heartfelt," Kalinich says. "He heard one of my poems once and came up with the melody spontaneously and sang a section of it back to me. Even Brian's never done that."

The pair's collaborations would nearly always begin with Kalinich writing the words, followed by Dennis supplying the music, and then the lyrics would be adjusted as needed. Kalinich says this approach gave them real chemistry. "This was a volatile, lovely, electric, fantastic relationship — sometimes harmony and sometimes discord, but we worked it through," he says.

Kalinich got inspired to write "Little Bird" as he looked out the window of Dennis' Sunset Boulevard house — a mansion once owned by

Will Rogers — and spotted a feathered creature. He came up with lyrics about a singing bird and a talking trout that impart calming words of wisdom to the narrator. It was a long way from *Wild Honey*. After completing the lyrics, Kalinich left them on Dennis' piano.

The resulting record is a small wonder. Dennis introduced a new style for his vocals: intimate, nasal and upfront in the mix, as though he's whispering in your ear. His intense delivery is tempered by the group singing a silly, joyous "na na na na" refrain. Instrumentally the track is adorned with banjo, a Beatlesque cello, horns and appropriately bird-like trumpet. Most amazing is the song structure, which incorporates half a dozen different sections in less than two minutes. If this mini-symphony bears the earmarks of a Brian production, it's no coincidence.

"I always claimed Brian wrote the bridge and changed my words around, but he also changed the whole melody," Kalinich explains. "I talked to Brian recently and he said, 'Well, I touched it up, arranged it and produced it.' So he calls that an arrangement, but it's really a rewrite. Brian didn't take credit. He was trying to help his little brother."

Around this time, Dennis and Kalinich also wrote "Be Still," one of the most distinctive Beach Boys tracks of the era. Clocking in at just 1:22, it features Dennis, backed only by organ, singing at his croakiest about Zen self-awareness, harmony, liberation and the connectedness of all things. It was inspired by a Christmas card Kalinich received that quoted, "Be still, and know that I am God" from Psalm 46:10. "A lot of people have written about stillness — a lot of saints — but to put it in a Beach Boys rock 'n' roll framework, I thought, was different," Kalinich says.

Both songs would appear on the forthcoming *Friends* album, which was Dennis' coming-out party as a creative force. "I so love those songs," Kalinich reflects. "It's like they were gifts to Dennis and me. I was fortunate enough to have an exciting partnership, because when we created, that was God or divine love in action. The songs are talking about acknowledging the spiritual self and getting our ego and the limited little self out of the way. Dennis' music expressed that, although he didn't always in his life and I haven't either."

Kalinich says he doesn't judge Dennis for his indulgences with women, booze and drugs, but the one thing that did irk him was his friend shutting him out of songwriting credits, as on the rocker "All I Want to Do." Kalinich says he wrote not only words for the song but also part of the melody, but was not credited. Of course, Murry could have played a hand in the omission. Kalinich adds that the "Little Bird" contract prepared by Murry entitled him to only 25% royalties despite his co-writer credit, which stands to this day. "And I wrote the words first," he says. "You don't realize at the time how bad it is. I got little of the publishing then because I wasn't smart enough to know."

Many of the ideas he shared with Dennis were never realized and many that were have not been made available for public consumption. The stunning ballad "A Time to Live in Dreams," recorded in November 1968, finally saw the light on the 2001 collection *Hawthorne, CA.* There was talk of a whole album of 50 or 60 similarly inspirational one-minute pieces. And then, Kalinich says, there is "Mona Kana" (the Brian-like orchestral track of which has surfaced on bootlegs), an unfinished song about Helen Keller, as well as, locked in the vaults, "Writing Poems" and the irresistibly titled "Mabel Sitting at the Kitchen Table" and "I Don't Want Much, Just a Country or Two, and Maybe a Planet When It's All Through."

Kalinich worked with Brian as well, first in late 1969 on a spoken-word record of his poems, with Brian directing the musical accompaniment. One of the cuts features Brian on organ while Kalinich reads a version of "Be Still" that contains many more passages than on the original. The album, titled *A World of Peace Must Come,* would remain unreleased until 2008. They also co-wrote the enjoyably quirky "Child of Winter (Christmas Song)," released in 1974, as well as the Golden State gospel of "California Feelin'", for Brian's American Spring side project. (The group's name was changed from Spring to avoid confusion with a British act of the same name.) Kalinich co-wrote the sentimental "You've Touched Me" and "A Friend Like You," a duet with Paul McCartney for Brian's 2004 album *Gettin' in Over My Head.*

In the mid-1970s, Kalinich and Dennis would embark on a crazy-ambitious project called *Life Symphony* that was to incorporate Kalinich's poetry, Dennis' music and live performance. It explores capital-T themes including war, peace, drugs, innocence and the divine, and was conceived to take the form of a stage show, a movie — which would have starred Dennis, who had already appeared in Monte

Hellman's existential car-race film *Two-Lane Blacktop* — and two or three albums. "We were going to do a video with the concept of two babies, a male and a female, floating throughout the galaxies, and they meet and come down to earth to try to help the planet. It was pretty trippy," Kalinich explains.

Feeling restricted by his exclusive Brother Records deal, Kalinich broke his contract with The Beach Boys in the mid-'70s, but continued working with them. He, Dennis and Carl co-wrote "Rainbows," an exhilarating ode to love and nature that appeared on Dennis' 1977 *Pacific Ocean Blue* album. Kalinich says that at one point Dennis asked him to produce the solo record, but he declined.

In 2011, Kalinich released the album *California Feeling*, which includes a cover of "Little Bird" performed by Carnie and Wendy Wilson — a fitting tribute to his friend. As with all of us, Kalinich says, there were many sides to Dennis. "To really know Dennis you had to see the excitement and the enthusiasm and the energy," he says. "Bios show the negative and the drink and all that, but there was a spiritual side combined with the other that was just magnificent. And I feel fortunate that was my relationship. I saw the dark and the light and I still loved him."

MEANT FOR YOU

Written by: Brian Wilson and Mike Love
Lead vocal: Mike Love
Produced by: The Beach Boys
Recorded: April 1, 1968
Released: June 24, 1968, on *Friends*

Nineteen-sixty-eight was a dark year around the world — and not a particularly bright one for The Beach Boys. In January, the North's launch of the Tet Offensive escalated the Vietnam War, while, come spring, France would be rocked by widespread strikes and protests. In America, Rev. Dr. Martin Luther King was felled by an assassin's bullet on April 4, and presidential hopeful Senator Robert Kennedy was similarly killed just two months later.

Nationwide riots in the wake of King's murder forced The Beach Boys to cancel a planned tour of the southern U.S. The group had begun the year simply looking to make some warm and peaceful music — therapy after their turbulent 1967. In February, Brian had started building tracks for the group's next LP, *Friends* — its first in stereo. He used session players more than he had since *Smile* — albeit in smaller combos — which lends the album a more polished sheen than the pair that preceded it.

A major influence on the new songs — which are often startling in their tranquility — was the band's new hobby, which got its most literal nod in the oddly dissonant closing number simply titled "Transcendental

Meditation," co-written by Brian, Mike and Al. Mike, who had been the most taken with TM founder Maharishi Mahesh Yogi, left with sessions underway to join The Beatles, Donovan and Mia Farrow in Rishikesh for two weeks of study at the Maharishi's academy.

Upon his return, Mike devised the idea of sharing the bill with his guru on a 17-day May U.S. tour that would feature a Beach Boys performance followed by a lecture on TM. The match proved a poor concert draw and the whole enterprise was canceled after just four days.[1] Adding insult to injury, John Lennon and Paul McCartney later denounced the Maharishi at a New York press conference and in an appearance on *The Tonight Show*, with McCartney referring to the Beach Boys/TM tour as a "flop." Now the group was getting the thumbs-down from the two main Beatles, who had been among their biggest boosters.

It seemed every move The Beach Boys were making — its tacky new white stage suits included — was putting them further out of step with the American record-buying public. When the album followed in June, its frigid reception in America — it limped to #126 on the *Billboard* chart — was telling. Meanwhile,

the two reigning bands across the pond — against whom The Beach Boys could hold their own but two years earlier — were defining the times with near-simultaneous releases. While The Rolling Stones were lamenting the plight of a "Street Fighting Man" and The Beatles were talking "Revolution," the friendly, non-confrontational *Friends* album arrived on U.K. shelves. The group's loyal British fans appreciated the musical tonic to all the upheaval, and sent the album to #13.

Brian has in the past called *Friends* his favorite Beach Boys album, as its music and lyrics reflect the kind of inner peace he aspired to but could rarely find in life. Over the years it has developed a cult following among fans and musicians, including Ira Kaplan, cofounder of venerable indie three-piece Yo La Tengo.

Known for its deep repertoire of cover tunes, Yo La Tengo has included a number of Beach Boys songs in its setlists over the years. It has also recorded punky, amped-up versions of the early, vehicular-themed "Little Honda" as well as "Shut Down" and its instrumental sequel "Shut Down, Part 2," the latter pair released by the band under the pseudonym Condo Fucks. Kaplan is quick to point out, however, that "It's not like that period of theirs means an iota as much to me as what came later."

Growing up in the '60s in the New York suburb of Westchester County, Kaplan had little affinity for the cars and surf mythologized in the group's early hits. "I was so England-centric as a youngster that I didn't really enjoy them," recalls Kaplan, who is today based out of Hoboken, New Jersey, with bandmates Georgia Hubley (his wife) and James McNew. "I could enjoy The Byrds, but not The Beach Boys. I don't think it was really until 'Good Vibrations' that I really started to like them at all — and even then in a limited way."

What eventually won him over was the group's performance at the June 27, 1971, closing concert of the Fillmore East, which he heard live on New York radio station WNEW-FM. Playing on a bill that also included The Allman Brothers Band, The J. Geils Band and Country Joe McDonald, The Beach Boys delivered an 11-song set mixing early hits with newer material. Backed by a horn section and additional supporting players, they appeared "in all their 13-man splendor," according to a review in *Rolling Stone*.[2] "I remember loving every song they played," Kaplan recollects. "I remember them doing 'Cotton Fields' and a

lot of the old songs that all sounded great to me at that point. And after that I really started to seek out their records."

He has the greatest affinity for the smaller-scale post-*Smile* albums, and, pressed to choose, names the concise *Friends* — with a total running time of 25:32 — as his favorite Beach Boys record. "I always come back to *Friends*," says Kaplan, who was a music critic before launching his performing career. "It's got such a beautiful sound to it. And it's so short. It's such a *piece*. That record just seems so at peace and comfortable."

The track that especially thrills him is opener "Meant for You," which, running at 38 seconds, is the shortest song the group ever released. With its delicate organ and piano and an uncharacteristically subdued Mike vocal, "Meant for You" is a call for serenity and establishes the album's aural landscape. Kaplan likens it to jazz great Thelonious Monk's 53-second horns-only take on the hymn "Abide with Me," which opens the classic 1957 album *Monk's Music*.

"You just can't even imagine how somebody thinks they are going to start a record with a snippet like that. It sucks you right in," he says. As it makes such a wonderful greeting, Brian rerecorded "Meant for You" to also open his 1995 album *I Just Wasn't Made for These Times*. Whether it's because Brian had become unable to complete some of his musical ideas or because he was experimenting with musical form, he would record a number of similarly brief musical fragments starting in the *Smile* era.

Yo La Tengo also covered the Beach Boys shorty "Ding Dang" (57 seconds) for an annual fundraiser in support of New York radio station WFMU during which callers who made a pledge could request any song for the band to play on the spot. Highlights from the 1996–2003 shows were subsequently collected on the CD *Yo La Tengo Is Murdering the Classics*, which also features a stab at "God Only Knows." "We keep trying to convince people that it's not really that easy to play those songs off the cuff," Kaplan says. "There was some disastrous attempt at 'Good Vibrations' once."

For Kaplan, another *Friends* highlight is "Busy Doin' Nothin'," a look at a day in the life of Brian, backed by a bossa nova beat. "It still seems so completely mysterious all these years later," he says of the cut. Also featured on the album are "Wake the World," a subsequent concert staple that manages in its 89 seconds to musically express the passage of eerie night to joyous day, and the gentle "Passing By," the melody of which is entirely hummed by Brian. The longer instrumental "Diamond Head," likely inspired by the group's trip to Hawaii the previous summer, recalls *Smile* in its many shifting parts, minus the intensity. It all adds up to a unique LP.

So why, then, if Kaplan prefers the more esoteric late-'60s Beach Boys output, does his band lean towards recording songs from the more innocent days? He simply chuckles and replies, "We do those earlier songs because they're easier."

MIKE KOWALSKI ON . . .
DO IT AGAIN

Written by: Brian Wilson and Mike Love
Lead vocals: Mike Love and Carl Wilson
Produced by: Brian Wilson and Carl Wilson
Recorded: May 26, June 6, 12, 1968
Released: July 8, 1968
Chart peak: U.S. #20, U.K. #1
Appears on 20/20

No doubt the canceled tour with the Maharishi and disappointing chart performance of the "Friends" single had the group longing for the simpler, sunnier times of yore. That feeling was reinforced in Mike when, as he recalled in an interview for *The Beach Boys Twentieth Anniversary Special*, he went surfing in San Onofre with old friend Bill Jackson, just like they did in high school. Stoked by the experience, he went over to Brian's the next day intent on writing a song about it. Brian pounded out a melody on the piano and a hit was born. In the *Endless Harmony* film, Brian said he thought it was the best of his collaborations with Mike.

Assembling at Brian's home studio, the band laid down a four-track recording of the song — titled "Rendezvous"[1] — that bore little resemblance to the mellow preciousness of the *Friends* album. Borrowing the guitar rhythm from *Wild Honey*'s "A Thing or Two," they went for the surf-rock feel that made their name. Mike's lyrics look back at the days of hanging ten and hanging out with the girls on the beach, inviting all the old faces to reunite. The group may have initially felt sheepish about the song's unabashed nostalgia, but ultimately embraced it, renaming it "Do It Again."

Brian, working with Carl, wanted to retain the track's rawness yet make the production special. He sings at the top of the full, wordless harmony mix, his voice remarkably recreating the sound of a horn. Elsewhere, saxophonist Ernie Small fattened the rhythm, hand claps increase the catchiness, and a heavy guitar solo made the song feel at home on the airwaves in 1968. Most memorable is the funky, in-your-face beat that hooks the listener from the get-go. Dennis played the original drum track, and, according to author Keith Badman's book *The Beach Boys: The Definitive Diary of America's Greatest Band on Stage and in the Studio*, busy jazz-rock player John Guerin recorded additional drums and overdubbed tambourine and wood blocks.[2]

Mike Kowalski, whom The Beach Boys hired that year as a touring percussionist/drummer, explains that the drum part is played "straight-ahead with conviction. I'd say 80% of the songs were pretty much straight-ahead. It's a two and four beat with the hi-hat, a strong snare beat and heavy bass-drum beat." It may not have been a difficult part, but engineer Stephen Desper processed it into the most distinctive drum sound on any Beach Boys record.

In a 2002 online Q&A with fans, Desper confirms the main part is played by Dennis. He explains that the effect, which sounds like the drums are being filtered through a synthesizer, was achieved by two tape-delay units with four of the playback heads moved close together so that one drum strike was repeated four times about 10 milliseconds apart, and then the repeats were blended with the original.[3] The result is so strikingly modern that French pop duo Air sampled it 30 years later on "Remember," a cut from its acclaimed *Moon Safari* LP.

With a strong single in the can, the group now had to do it again on the road. But first they needed a rhythm section for their orchestra, which already included Ernie Small's horn ensemble. The plan was for the orchestra to warm up the audience with big-band numbers and then back up The Beach Boys' set. Bruce recommended Kowalski and bassist/guitarist Ed Carter — both of whom he had gigged with — and their keyboardist friend Doug Dragon, son of Oscar-winning Hollywood composer Carmen Dragon.

Kowalski and Carter had recently returned from England, where they played with Gary Thain as The New Nadir. Kowalski also had drummed for Pat and Lolly Vegas, who opened for The Beach Boys at Anaheim's Melodyland Theater in 1965.[4] (Pat and Lolly later formed the R&B-flavored rock band Redbone.) Kowalski had never owned a Beach Boys record — being more of a jazz, R&B and Latin music aficionado — but he appreciated the group's harmonies and early Chuck Berry influence, and when he heard "When I Grow Up (To Be a Man)," he knew something extraordinary was going on. He was at his parents' Hollywood home — his father was a film and television assistant director — when Bruce invited him to a tryout at the nearby Moulin Rouge theater. Kowalski, then 23, recalls Alan being there, while Mike and Brian were absent. It was the other Wilson brothers running the show — especially Carl.

Kowalski joined the touring band, playing everything from congas to tambourines, shakers, wood blocks, bells and timbales. He would drum in the warm-up then move to percussion for The Beach Boys' set, taking over the drums when Dennis came up front to sing. The group also hired Carter and Dragon, the latter soon being replaced by his brother Daryl, the future "Captain" of Captain & Tennille. Another Dragon sibling,

Dennis, later played percussion and drums while their sister Kathy added flute to Beach Boys studio recordings.

"Carl wanted it to groove," Kowalski says of the group's concert sound. "You obviously had to stick to the record, but there was room to play how you felt it. Carl wanted it to sound 'live.' So with Ed on bass, Doug and Bruce on keyboards and Carl and Al playing guitars in perfect sync, the groove and the pocket were magical. We all felt it, and it rocked."

The new rhythm trio was thrown into a whirlwind two-month North American tour. "What a great gig," Kowalski recollects. "These guys were big. You take any gig you can get, and if it was that one, I'll take it! And being with my lifelong friend Ed was great. It was work and I was glad to have it."

Meanwhile, "Do It Again" had climbed to #20 in the U.S. by summer's end. It was a definite commercial improvement over "Friends," but still represented a somewhat muted response given the record's quality. But it was enough to land the group TV appearances on *The Dick Cavett Show*, *Happening* and *The Ed Sullivan Show*, where they sang it over a prerecorded track along with "Good Vibrations."

Although its popularity waned at home in the late '60s, the group still met an enthusiastic response in the U.K.
[© AP Photo]

The group spent much of the fall recording tracks for its upcoming *20/20* album, which turned out to be a wonderful hodgepodge with creative contributions from each member. Brian curiously extended "Do It Again," which was the lead-off track, with a special effects tag as he had done on "Caroline, No." This time he added a dozen seconds of construction sounds from the *Smile* sessions' "Workshop" fragment.

Listeners in the U.K. had no reservations about the new single, sending it all the way to #1 by the end of August. (It also topped the charts in Australia.) The band flew to London in late November to capitalize with a European tour. A show in Paris was reportedly canceled due to poor ticket sales, but in England, Wales and Scotland, the group had to schedule two shows per night at most venues to meet demand.[5] The December 8 shows at North London's Astoria Theatre were recorded for *Live in London*,[6] the group's most cohesive concert album. Bolstered by Kowalski, Carter, Daryl Dragon and the horns, the live sound was bigger than ever, and the group clearly feeds off the crowd's enthusiasm. The audience adds to Kowalski's percussion by clapping along heartily to Dennis' beat on "Do It Again."

"They went crazy," Kowalski recalls of the European fans. "It was like Beatles time. The band was received overwhelmingly — better than in the States. I don't know why. But they sure were big. You figure, following up on that #1 hit, you go there and you're

going to get mobbed, and they did."

Kowalski returned to England in 1969, where he recorded with The Incredible String Band and Nick Drake. He soon returned to the U.S. and continued working with The Beach Boys intermittently. His time away from the band allowed him to pursue his love for the blues, playing with such legends as Johnny Otis, Big Joe Turner and Charlie Musselwhite. "Every time Carl would call me, I would be there if I could and then I'd go do something else," he explains.

In 1971, Kowalski was pressed into Beach Boys drum service after Dennis reportedly put his hand through a glass door and suffered nerve and tendon damage that prevented him from playing. Kowalski became the main guy for the upcoming tour, which included a July performance in New York taped for the ABC special *Good Vibrations from Central Park*. Later that month he recorded the drum track for the *Surf's Up* cut "Don't Go Near the Water" by Al and Mike. The band soon took on drummer Ricky Fataar of The Flame, which had been a Beach Boys opening act. With the injured Dennis moving to keyboards or singing on the front line, Kowalski and Fataar alternated on drums, percussion and keyboards. With Dennis Dragon also in the mix, Kowalski bowed out when the group went overseas in 1972 to record its *Holland* LP. But he returned the following year for dates recorded for another exceptional live album, the two-record *The Beach Boys in Concert*. Kowalski drums on album highlight "Marcella."

He left again but returned in 1977 and played drums on *M.I.U. Album*, which Dennis wanted no part of. In the late '70s and early '80s, with Dennis in and out of the band, Bobby Figueroa was handling much of the live drumming duties. Kowalski returned in 1981, and with Figueroa on hiatus, found himself filling in for Dennis on a number of occasions. After Dennis died in 1983, Kowalski and Figueroa alternated on drums and percussion throughout the '80s until Figueroa left for good.

In that time, Kowalski played "Do It Again" again and again. For many years, touring player Mike Meros provided an assist. "He would start off with his polyphonic keyboard and play that part on the keys along with the drums so we could get that sound from the record," Kowalski explains.

The drummer says he got along with Dennis and Carl "like a house on fire" and recalls how difficult it was continuing after Dennis' 1983 drowning and then again after Carl succumbed to cancer in 1998. "It was shocking with Carl — with Dennis, obviously, too. But with Carl, it felt different, real different. It was strange, him not being there. But you had to live with it. What else could you do? Either that or not play," he says.

In 2007, Mike Love looked to shake things up and Kowalski's tenure ended. Then 64, he left The Beach Boys as the band's longest-serving drummer — even longer than Dennis. John Cowsill of '60s pop group The Cowsills, who had been playing keyboards for the touring Beach Boys, moved over to drums.

Kowalski could then enjoy a slower pace after 26 consecutive years on the road with the band. He still did some shows with Dean Torrence and tended to his horses in Ventura County. "I remember when I was young, thinking, 'Jesus, am I gonna be playing rock 'n' roll when I'm 50?' All in all it was good," he says. "I had a long run on the roller coaster."

GREGG JAKOBSON ON ...
FOREVER

Written by: Dennis Wilson and Gregg Jakobson
Lead vocal: Dennis Wilson
Produced by: The Beach Boys
Recorded: January 9, March 12, 14, 17, 1969
Released: August 21, 1970, on *Sunflower*
and March 1, 1971, as B-side to "Cool, Cool Water"

"Forever," one of The Beach Boys' most beautiful love songs, came out of a dark time. Dennis' association with Charles Manson is the most notorious chapter in the band's history, and one in which Dennis' friend Gregg Jakobson would also find himself entangled.

Jakobson got his start in the music business contracting recording sessions for producer-friend Terry Melcher. He first met Dennis in Honolulu in July 1964 while accompanying Bruce & Terry, who were opening for The Beach Boys. "Dennis and I hit it off right away," Jakobson recalls. "He didn't want to sit around and drink Mai Tais, so we were always surfing or riding motorcycles around the island, chasing girls."

Jakobson, who has been diagnosed with attention deficit disorder, believes Dennis had ADHD — the hyperactive form — which may explain why they made such fast friends. As Dennis' songwriting blossomed in the late '60s, Jakobson collaborated with him on "Forever" and the similarly excellent "San Miguel" and "Celebrate the News." Years later, he co-wrote half the tracks on Dennis' solo album *Pacific Ocean Blue*, which he also co-produced.

As similar as the pair may have been in

disposition, somebody had to play the disciplinarian or no work would get done, and Jakobson assumed that role. "That was probably part of my job," he explains. "I was always one to go on the move with him — and he was always on the move. I probably slowed us both down a little bit, like dragging an anchor. I had a tendency to do that, especially when we were recording. I would say, 'C'mon Dennis, let's not do that,' and 'Dennis, instead of doing that, let's do this,' or 'Hey, let's finish this off before we go look for girls.'"

It was girls that lured them into Manson's circle. Vincent Bugliosi, the former L.A. assistant district attorney who prosecuted Manson and members of Manson's hippie "Family," chronicled the tale in the bestseller *Helter Skelter: The True Story of the Manson Murders*, co-written by Curt Gentry. According to Bugliosi, it all started in late spring 1968, when Dennis picked up a couple of young women, Ella Jo Bailey and Patricia Krenwinkel, and took them back to his house on Sunset Boulevard. The girls later brought over the scruffy, diminutive ex-convict spiritual leader they called "Charlie" along with the rest of the Family. Once they were inside Dennis' Hollywood mansion, they had no intention of leaving.[1]

When Dennis informed Jakobson of the houseguest who had brought along a school bus full of young and easy women, Jakobson thought he should check it out for himself. Manson subsequently ingratiated himself with a parade of rock stars and rich kids who came by to get stoned and party with the dispossessed girls who obeyed his every whim. "Manson used to tell me, 'The only reason I have all the girls around is to attract the guys.' He wanted the guys. He wanted the gang, to have 'the movement,'" Jakobson recalls.

In addition to Manson's girls and drug connections, Dennis was intrigued by his new friend's songwriting abilities — which he had developed in prison after being schooled on guitar by gangster Alvin "Creepy" Karpis — as well as his off-kilter philosophies. As a 23-year-old who had achieved fame and fortune largely on the back of his older brother, Dennis strove to make sense of it all, and so figures such as Manson and Maharishi — who professed wildly disparate worldviews with equal conviction — were powerfully seductive. In an interview at the time with the U.K.'s *Rave* magazine, Dennis confided, "Sometimes the Wizard frightens me — Charlie Manson who is [a] friend of mine who says he is God and

Dennis met second wife Barbara Charren around the time he wrote "Forever," and the beautiful ballad is often associated with her. [© Ed Roach]

the devil! He sings, plays and writes poetry and may be another artist for Brother Records."[2]

Dennis and Jakobson tried to convince Melcher to help Manson land a major-label deal, describing the musical style of Manson and the Family as "three guitars, 30 voices, all raised in peaceful hymns."[3] Dennis brought Manson and his female entourage to Brian's home studio to record several cuts — despite Marilyn's disapproval of the unhygienic

bunch[4] — and the resulting tapes remained in The Beach Boys' possession.[5] The extent of the group's participation on Manson's recordings, if any, is not known. For his part, Jakobson mostly found Manson to be an intriguing character. "I wanted to film him," he says. "Charlie was interesting musically only if you were looking at him. A big part of it was his presence — the way he would play the guitar and sing about the flies landing on his head. You needed to be there or at least to have pictures with it."

Despite their initially strong connection, Manson's spell over Dennis faded after displays of his violent temper and as the Family's freeloading ways became too much to bear. Dennis, generous to a fault, later said the Family took him for $100,000 in food, clothing, car repairs and doctors' bills for gonorrhea treatment.[6] This made him feel justified in retitling Manson's composition "Cease to Exist" as "Never Learn Not to Love," changing the words — which particularly irked Manson — recording it with The Beach Boys and taking the sole credit.[7] (The disturbing Beach Boys cut — excellently produced by Dennis and Carl — is featured on the B-side of the group's 1968 single "Bluebirds Over the

Mountain" and on the 20/20 LP. They even performed it on *The Mike Douglas Show* in April 1969. Manson's more bare-bones version can be heard on the collection *Lie*.) Before summer's end, Dennis just wanted to flee Manson's crazy scene. He moved out of the house before his lease expired, leaving the Family to face eviction, and Manson relocated them to Spahn Ranch, an old filming location for Hollywood westerns. According to some historians, Dennis expressed his relief at being free from "the Wizard" in his spacey Jakobson collaboration "Celebrate the News," B-side of The Beach Boys' 1969 "Break Away" single.[8]

"We were at the end of our close association with Manson," Jakobson says. "It was the '60s. We partied with [the Family] for a while and it got old. I moved Dennis to a big old house above the Pacific Coast Highway in Malibu and somehow Manson found us. Dennis was really bummed that Manson even knew where that house was. At that point Dennis was really trying to avoid the whole thing. He was over it, and when Dennis was over something, he was totally over it."

Dennis could always find refuge at Jakobson's Beverly Glen house, where he'd crash in a downstairs room with a bed and piano. It was a convenient motorcycle ride away from Dennis' estranged wife Carole Freedman, their daughter, Jennifer, and Dennis' stepson, Scott. It was at Jakobson's house that "Forever" was hatched late one night. Jakobson recalls coming up with the opening line.

"Dennis loved it," he says. "As usual, it came really fast. I was always amazed how he had a reservoir of melody lines sitting there waiting for a lyric. We would finish off 80–90% of it and then in the next day or two we would fine-tune it — maybe throw out or add a word or put in some chorus parts. Most of the time when we did it, it would just all be there. That's the way it's supposed to be. It's not supposed to be pulling teeth."

The song reflects on a love affair, with the narrator declaring his eternal devotion just as the lovers will temporarily part. In a later interview with Beach Boys historian Peter Reum, Dennis explained that he was looking to express his feelings towards women as a whole.[9] The composition shows a romantic side of Dennis that stands in sharp contrast to the free-love ways he embraced with Manson's girls. Around the time he and Jakobson wrote it, Dennis started a relationship with Barbara

Charren — who became his second wife — and it is often assumed the song was written for her. Dennis worked on the basic track in January 1969 at Brian's home studio before moving to Gold Star in March for instrumental and vocal overdubbing.[10] Keyboardist Daryl Dragon, who became a frequent Dennis collaborator, said he was heavily involved in the instrumental production.[11]

The track is sparse, opening with an acoustic guitar strum backed by subtle steel guitar. If the country-and-western sound was atypical, the melancholia recalled Brian at his most heartfelt. The lushness is in the harmonies, which come in a torrent of emotion in the song's midsection before settling down to a final verse delivered with a moving crack in Dennis' voice. The final, effective tug at the heartstrings comes from a wailing counterpoint by Brian, who is said to have arranged the vocals. A group-vocal take appears on the *Hawthorne, CA* collection, and following the performance, Brian, evidently blown away, is heard uttering, "Wow, man. You know, let me hear some of that."

Meanwhile, things were far from harmonious with Manson, who had taken to stockpiling vehicles and weapons. He felt betrayed when nothing materialized with Melcher, which may in part explain the rage he felt towards the estate at 10050 Cielo Drive, where the producer had lived with his girlfriend, actress Candice Bergen. But they had moved out, and in early 1969 filmmaker Roman Polanski and his actress-wife Sharon Tate had moved in. It was there in the early morning hours of August 9 that members of the Family, operating under Manson's direction, took the lives of Tate and her unborn child, hair stylist Jay Sebring — who had coiffed The Beach Boys — Abigail Folger of the Folgers Coffee family and her boyfriend, actor Voytek Frykowski (Polanski was away). Another victim was Steven Parent, a teenager who happened to arrive on the grounds to visit property caretaker William Garretson.

As Los Angeles reeled in the revelation of the horrific events, the Family struck again the night of August 10, killing Leno and Rosemary LaBianca, a wealthy couple seemingly chosen at random. According to Bugliosi, shortly afterwards Manson tracked down Dennis — who apparently had no idea about Manson's connection to the murders — and asked him for $1,500, but Dennis turned him down. "Don't be surprised if you never see your kid again" was reportedly Manson's reply, in an apparent reference to Dennis' stepson, Scott.[12] But by the end of the year, police had put together enough pieces of the puzzle to put Manson and his accomplices behind bars. Manson apparently phoned Dennis the night of his arrest, but Dennis wasn't home and a friend took the message.[13]

Some members of the Family who remained free made further threats against Dennis, and, frightened, he refused to testify at the 1970 trial. Until his death he had little to say in public about Manson. He no doubt harbored guilty feelings about ever introducing him to the Hollywood scene, and friends noted that he became increasingly nervous and paranoid.[14] Daryl Dragon went so far as to attribute Dennis' subsequent self-destructive behavior to his fear of Manson ever getting out of prison or putting a hit on him.[15] Jakobson, meanwhile, took the stand and was able to relate in great detail Manson's feelings about death, women and his wildly imaginative interpretation of the Book of Revelation and The Beatles' self-titled LP usually referred to as the "White Album." Manson saw The Fab Four as angels whose arrival was anticipated in the Bible, and believed songs off their 1968 double-record prophesied the black man's rise over the white man. After that would come to pass, Manson said, his family would emerge from its desert hideout and take over.[16] The Tate-LaBianca murders, staged as though committed by black revolutionaries, were intended to set these events in motion.

"I used to tell Manson he was full of shit. I wasn't buying his philosophy," Jakobson says. "He kind of enjoyed it. It wasn't adversarial. I represented a challenge to Manson, because he couldn't get me over on his side. I wasn't buying into the whole end-of-the-world and the black-white thing."

Meanwhile, Beach Boys business continued. "Forever" had been tagged for a record tentatively titled *Reverberation* that was to fulfill The Beach Boys' final album obligation to Capitol, but it ended up instead on the 1970 *Sunflower* LP for distributor Reprise Records. To many fans, that album is home to Dennis' best work. Unfortunately, sales were weak, as they were for a single with "Forever" backing "Cool, Cool Water." Nonetheless, Brian clearly had an affinity for his brother's song and whipped up another vocal arrangement for the 1972 *Spring* album, with Carl joining him on backgrounds. Carl sang lead on it at Beach

Boys shows in the 1980s, but otherwise the gorgeous ballad was relegated to obscurity.

That changed in 1991 when it was sung by actor and occasional Beach Boys drummer John Stamos on a wedding episode of his popular sitcom *Full House*. The band looked to capitalize on this exposure by recording a Stamos cover of "Forever" for its 1992 album *Summer in Paradise*. A video was shot crediting the song to Stamos' band Jesse and the Rippers, and Mike, Carl and Bruce appear singing backgrounds. Stamos' respect for the song is evident, but with its screeching metal guitar solo, this version is a time-capsule piece. A decade later at his live shows, Brian would sing a lovely rendition dedicated to Dennis.

Dennis' original, meanwhile, will indeed last forever. The legacy of his relationship with Jakobson is the great songs they wrote, "Forever" being the most celebrated. The two friends went through a lot together and shared adventures that were wild to say the least. "And looking back on it," Jakobson adds, "I say, 'God, I'm lucky to have lived through some of them.'"

SCOTT McCAUGHEY ON...
THIS WHOLE WORLD

Written by: Brian Wilson
Lead vocal: Carl Wilson
Produced by: Brian Wilson and Carl Wilson
Recorded: November 13, 1969
Released: June 29, 1970, as B-side of "Slip on Through"
Appears on *Sunflower*

As The Beach Boys' first decade drew to a close, the band was gasping for a fresh start. The '60s had been nearly as cruel as they had been kind, seeing the group soar to the pinnacle of American popular music only to find itself on a fast and bumpy descent. Record sales had grown soft and U.S. concerts were sparsely attended — the low point coming at a Thanksgiving 1969 show at the Corn Palace in Mitchell, South Dakota, that drew under 200.[1] But the group could still count on packed houses in the U.K. and Europe, and had spent that June on a hectic overseas tour that saw them play in recently occupied Czechoslovakia — the first Western musical act to do so.

The band blamed Capitol for much of its commercial downturn at home. They believed the label hadn't fully supported *Pet Sounds* or any of the new material that followed, preferring instead to repackage old hits. Even these collections had dramatically diminishing returns. Kids grooving to Cream's *Wheels of Fire* and The Doors' *Waiting for the Sun* had little use for The Beach Boys' 1964 recording of "Frosty the Snowman" on *Best of the Beach Boys Vol. 3*, which crawled to a pathetic #153 on the U.S. charts in summer 1968.

Relations with Capitol were severed on April 12, 1969, when the group launched another lawsuit against the company, this time demanding $2 million for unpaid royalties and production fees. (As part of the eventual 1971 settlement, the group retained the rights to its albums from *Pet Sounds* on.) All eyes turned to Brian to conjure a hit record that would reverse their fortunes, and he stepped up with the buoyant "Break Away," which he co-wrote with Murry, who is credited as Reggie Dunbar. While a sizable #6 hit in the U.K., it could muster no better than #63 in the U.S.

Despite the ongoing cold shoulder from the American public, the band was on fire in the studio, amassing 40–50 tracks in the couple of years following 20/20. Eleven of those songs were penciled in for the final album owed Capitol, but the group ultimately decided to hold on to this material for a new record deal. It fulfilled its obligation to Capitol with *Live in London*, initially released only in the U.K. in May 1970.

Record companies were hardly beating down their door, but in November the group found a welcoming home on the Reprise imprint at Warner Bros., where president Mo Ostin respected their accomplishments and believed they could work their way out of the recent slump. The band was stoked: Warner Bros. would pay them a handsome upfront sum (reportedly $200,000–$250,000 per album, or $1.1 million–$1.4 million in 2012 dollars) to distribute new Beach Boys product on the band's Brother Records label, which had been inactive since 1967.

The relationship got off to a rocky start, however, when Warner Bros. rejected the group's 14-song album submission, titled *Sun Flower*.[2] But the company did see fit to release "Add Some Music to Your Day" (written by Brian, Mike and Brian's friend Joe Knott) as a U.S. single on February 23, 1970. But despite wonderful harmonies and a lead vocal passed among the group, the soulful ballad couldn't help the band rise above its image problem and stalled at #64. That spring, Capitol released an Alan rerecording of the 20/20 number "Cotton Fields" on a 45 — the final single owed to the group's former label. The charming reimagining of Huddie Ledbetter's down-home standard hit #1 in Australia, South Africa and Norway and #5 in the U.K. In America, however, it didn't even break the Hot 100.

A second attempt at a Warner Bros. album, titled *Add Some Music* and consisting of a new 12-song lineup, was delivered in May and met with another refusal. Undeterred, the group put the finishing touches on a new 7" that updated its classic sound while maintaining the high standard of its two-sided smashes from the early days. The A-side "Slip on Through" is a funky Motown-flavored marvel written and sung by Dennis, while the flip side, Brian's "This Whole World," is every bit as impressive.

Brian recalled writing "This Whole World" one night while sitting at the piano in his Bellagio mansion, "stoned and confused."[3] The tune looks at boy-girl love on a global scale, rejoicing in the hippie ethos of being free. It's a classic bit of Brian introspection with a bright, upbeat vibe largely absent since *Summer Days (And Summer Nights!!)*. Old fashioned rock 'n' roll with doo-wop trimmings, it dazzles with its unorthodox structure and numerous key and chord changes — all in less than two minutes.

"You could actually say it's an A/B/C/A/B/C construction, yet it seems to never repeat itself once. Every section has something new and different going on," notes Scott McCaughey, an indie music fixture since the 1980s as leader of Young Fresh Fellows and The Minus 5, member of The Baseball Project and multi-instrumentalist for R.E.M. "On this cut Brian may have topped Phil Spector when it comes to 'little symphonies for the kids.' It's got hope and exuberance, yet a bit of sadness in there, too. Perfect."

Brian sings backgrounds with Marilyn and Diane, and he called in session musicians Jerry Cole and David Cohen to play guitars, John Conrad and Ray Pohlman on basses, Dennis Dragon on drums, along with Gene Estes,[4] whose chimes and bells lend the song its retro sweetness.

McCaughey is floored by Carl's lead vocal, which displays typically glorious range. "I've waxed eloquent so many times on Carl's singing that I imagine people must get annoyed with me," he says. "His vocals are invariably terrific — right from 'Girl Don't Tell Me' — and he did an amazing job singing some of Brian's most beautiful and demanding songs in concert throughout the '70s and '80s, when I saw them often."

"This Whole World" boasts one of Brian's fullest vocal arrangements with "oom-bop-dit-it" backgrounds coming and going and building to a spine-tingling intersection of four vocal parts. "That's one of the most brilliant things about it — it builds to that majestic a cappella ending and then fades so quickly. You want it to go on forever," McCaughey says.

According to writer Keith Badman, a far longer version of the song was recorded but has yet to surface.[5] A clue to its contents may have emerged a couple of years later when Brian and co-producers Stephen Desper and David Sandler remade the song for the *Spring* album featuring Marilyn and Diane. That rendition, beginning in languid tempo, shifts startlingly into a danceable adaptation of the nursery rhyme "Star Light, Star Bright" — a classic Brian juxtaposition. It likely pricked up the ears of Swedish Beach Boys fan Benny Andersson, who was then crafting a similar sound with ABBA.

"This Whole World" and "Slip on Through" would appear on the album finally titled *Sunflower*. Third time proved the charm, with Warner Bros. giving the green light after the group replaced six of the tracks with holdovers from the Capitol era (Dennis' rocking "Got to Know the Woman" and his ballad "Forever," Bruce's sweet "Deirdre," and the haunting love song "All I Wanna Do" by Brian

and Mike), Dennis' raucous "It's About Time" and Brian and Mike's "Cool, Cool Water," which had its origins in the *Smile* era. The LP boasts an expansiveness of sound achieved thanks to engineer/mixer Stephen Desper's fine work and the use of a state-of-the-art 16-track recorder, one of several technical specs ballyhooed on the album's back cover.

It's around this time that McCaughey, a California kid who hadn't related to the car and surfing songs, tuned in. "I discovered a different appreciation of The Beach Boys," he recollects. "That run from *Friends* to *Holland* — that's when I really dug deep, and those discs still have a special hold on me. It seemed like they had moved on to a whole new language, albeit one that used some of the same vocabulary. I started going to see them live as often as I could."

He recalls seeing his first Beach Boys show at California Polytechnic State University in San Luis Obispo around March 1973. It was one of a series of benefit concerts for Mike's Love Foundation, which pushed for prison reform based on principles of Transcendental Meditation.[6] For McCaughey, it proved an unforgettable experience. "Somehow my friends and I worked our way backstage and chatted with the band and got autographs," he recalls. "Speaking to Carl, who was with Audree, was the most memorable. He was kind as could be. I told him how I loved the band's early material but that the newer songs were even more special to me. He said, 'That means a lot,' and I believe he was nothing but sincere."

Sunflower's appearance in August 1970 was met with enthusiastic reviews that were self-conscious about their enthusiasm. *Rolling Stone*'s Jim Miller proclaimed the group had "finally produced an album that can stand with *Pet Sounds* . . . a stylistically coherent tour de force. It makes one wonder though whether anyone still listens to their music, or could give a shit."[7] Unfortunately, in America, few did. The group had delivered a timeless album in an era when hipness was the currency. It peaked at a disastrous #151 in the U.S., although fared far better in the U.K., making it to #29. The U.S. singles "Slip on Through," "Tears in the Morning" and "Cool, Cool Water" missed the charts entirely.

The new decade that had held such promise began with crushing disappointment. Brian, who had shown renewed interest, seemed especially hurt. If he gave his all and hardly anyone listened, then what was the point? He retreated further from Beach Boys sessions. The optimism with which the rest of the group had approached *Sunflower* — and which suffused its luminous contents — yielded to despair. But the band would find a way to make something positive out of that.

ADAM MARSLAND ON...

LONG PROMISED ROAD

Written by: Carl Wilson and Jack Rieley
Lead vocal: Carl Wilson
Produced by: Carl Wilson
Recorded: April 3, May 4, 1971
Released: May 24 and October 11, 1971
Chart peak: U.S. #89
Appears on *Surf's Up*

As Brian became an increasingly unwilling participant in the group's recordings, Carl was ready to fill the void. As with Dennis, he had learned at his big brother's side. Sometimes he'd been the only other Beach Boy at Brian's tracking dates, sitting in the control booth playing guitar into the board. He possessed both an innate musicality and the patience for long hours in the studio. Ever since Brian had abdicated creative control, Carl had taken a more hands-on role. He broke through producing the group's gorgeous 1969 cover of The Ronettes' "I Can Hear Music," which became an international hit (U.S. #24, U.K. #10). After Dennis had asserted himself as a songwriter on the last three LPs, *Surf's Up* showed what Carl could do.

"The Wilson brothers all had a unique ability to verbalize emotions through sound," notes California indie rocker Adam Marsland, who, along with his Chaos Band, recorded the 2006 tribute album *Long Promised Road — Songs of Dennis & Carl Wilson*, named after Carl's first released composition. "They were not really lyric guys, but they could make their music express pictorially. There's such extraordinary sensitivity to what Brian did, but at a certain point he couldn't do it anymore. He was too scared of his feelings, of what was going on and what music was doing to him."

Each of the Wilsons did his best work teamed with more skilled wordsmiths. Carl's first and best lyrical partner would be Jack Rieley, an enigmatic character in The Beach Boys story. A DJ at L.A.'s KPFK, Rieley entered the band's circle in summer 1970 when he walked into the Radiant Radish — a health-food store ever-quirky Brian co-owned for a short time in West Hollywood. He found Brian himself minding the store that night and asked if he would sit for an on-air interview. Persuaded by Rieley's gift of the gab, the usually reticent Brian agreed and later came down to the station with Mike and Bruce. *Rolling Stone* would run excerpts from the subsequent interview.

But Rieley had more in mind. He sent the group a six-page follow-up memo outlining why their popularity had declined and what kind of publicity campaign could reverse the situation.[1] They knew little about him but liked what they heard, and Carl championed him as the group's new PR man and general guiding force. The ambitious Rieley later supplanted Nick Grillo as the group's manager. Showing affinity for the songs of the Wilson brothers in particular, he would write lyrics with all of them in his quest to push the group into what he considered more relevant terrain.

His first credit was on "Long Promised Road," the title of which recalled both The Beatles' swansong ballad "The Long and Winding Road," which had topped the charts in June 1970, and the opening line from The Hollies' "He Ain't Heavy, He's My Brother," which cracked the top 10 months earlier. Like those numbers, Carl's song opens softly and slowly, with the narrator lamenting the daily struggles that stand in the way of happiness. But after the first verse, the song takes off, as he assures us he will overcome all obstacles. The song rides a slow-fast dynamic — with the interruption of a dreamy bridge — until ultimately building momentum with a guitar solo and heading full-throttle into the fade, with Carl repeating a tagline that suggests the song is addressed to the narrator's love interest.

Rieley's words are arty, but the directness of Carl's music cuts through any pomposity. The lyrics could very well be addressing the band's woes at the time. Carl had taken the torch from Brian, bringing back the anguished self-expression of *Pet Sounds* — although with the notion of rising above misery, not submitting to it. The song also rivals the complexity of some of the *Pet Sounds* tracks.

"I've worked out many Beach Boys songs and 'Long Promised Road' was the hardest," Marsland says. "Carl had a very peculiar way of playing the piano. He would play notes that are right next to each other. On 'Long Promised Road,' he almost never lands on the root of the chord. The first chord is an E minor seventh over C. In the left hand he's playing the C, and in the right hand he's playing a D, an E, a G and a B. It's very close to taking your elbow and laying it down on the piano. He's using all these voicings that theoretically shouldn't work because they clutter up the sound. Try hitting your elbow on a piano and see what comes out! Then he's got all these chord voicings that just sort of sit. It sounds like they aren't leading anywhere, and that creates a sense of unease. His songs have a calm sort of tension to them, which I understand is the way he was personally. He was a very calm guy, but emotional stuff was hard for him and he held a lot inside."

Marsland has found it more challenging to deconstruct some of Carl's songs than those of his brothers. "Brian and Dennis musically were somewhat orthodox," he says. "Dennis' stuff is all pretty logical. The structures are kind of strange, but chords he uses — they're more complicated than your garden-variety pop — but they're basically minor sevenths and things like that. They're pretty easy if you're trained. Brian is much harder, but a lot of what makes his distinctive thing happen is he's got bass notes and chords that don't usually go together. But Carl does stuff on the piano I just couldn't believe. I finally figured out 'Long Promised Road' once I realized he was taking certain shapes from the chord and moving them around. It wasn't just 'I've got my fingers here.' It's 'Now I'm moving this up and down the keyboard,' or 'I'm just going to move one note here.' He's got this untrained approach that creates a sound I've never heard anybody else do, and then he layers this murky production style on top of it."

And that style is Carl's all the way. He played nearly every instrument on the muscular "Long Promised Road," displaying how fully formed his talent had become. Blending organ textures, innovative percussion and Moog synthesizer effects — some devised by engineer Stephen Desper[2] — the soulfully rocking number showed Carl able to adapt the group's sound for the new decade, incorporating group vocal backgrounds that were both fresh and familiar. The song was expected to help reverse the group's fortunes and spark interest in *Surf's Up*, but, released as a single in May 1971, it merely prolonged the group's longest drought to date as its fifth consecutive 45 to miss *Billboard*'s Hot 100.

But as it turned out, "Long Promised Road" was just one of several highlights on the new LP, which appeared late that summer. Other cuts revealed an awakened social consciousness from the group, touching on political, ecological and spiritual themes. It is an uncharacteristically brooding Beach Boys record, from the dark Don Quixote–like cover painting on in. The songs live in the shadows of *Sunflower*'s sunny positivity, apparent right from Alan and Mike's opening "Don't Go Near the Water," in which the ocean playfully extolled in *Sunflower*'s closing grooves has been reduced to an industrially poisoned bubble bath. The *Sunflower* leftover "Take a Load Off Your Feet" by Alan, Brian and Alan's friend Gary Winfrey is the record's only lighthearted moment, but it still looked to connect with hippies over a shared sandal fetish.

Some critics dismissed all this as trendiness, but for many listeners it worked. The album was pivotal in the band's bid for a comeback, garnering some strong reviews — it was voted 12th best album of 1971 in *Village Voice*'s famed Pazz & Jop Critics Poll — and good sales, its #29 U.S. chart peak being the group's highest since *Wild Honey*. (It went to #15 in the U.K.) Encouraged by this success, Brother/Reprise rereleased "Long Promised Road" in October. This time it made the charts, but only as far as #89 in the U.S., its lyrics likely too obscure for AM radio.

Surf's Up was the first Beach Boys album Marsland bought. "My entry point to The Beach Boys was the '70s music," he says. "I was drawn to the lush but grainy vocal tone and the darker, more ambivalent soundscape those records have. I got into the music of Dennis and Carl first, and then into Brian's, which is opposite to the way most people do it."

In the mid-'90s, Marsland founded L.A. pop-punk band Cockeyed Ghost, which released several acclaimed albums before disbanding early in the new millennium. He then formed a new band with singer-songwriter-guitarist Evie Sands, whose storied career includes singing the original versions of "Angel of the Morning" and "I Can't Let

Go" in the mid-'60s. At their first gig they did "Long Promised Road," leading into "Antarctica Starts Here," a 1973 number by John Cale (whose Beach Boys admiration was confirmed in his Brian tribute "Mr. Wilson"). "They're virtually the same song," Marsland notes. The Chaos Band built a reputation for its prolific repertoire of cover songs, which it often grouped into theme nights. Marsland came up with the idea of performing the Carl and Dennis songbook, in the process recruiting Beach Boys archivist and hobbyist musician Alan Boyd, who would sing lead on "Long Promised Road."

"I told the band, 'The music's great and no one's ever going to do it. The Beach Boys are never going to do it.' We knew the stuff could be done,'" he recalls. This caught the attention of Alan Jardine, who joined the band at several shows. They continued to hone the Carl and Dennis material onstage, and then, after three months of intense rehearsals, mounted a performance for the *Long Promised Road* album, which was recorded by Brian's engineer Mark Linett and mixed by former Beach

Boys engineer Earle Mankey. Having Boyd involved led to the group getting access to Dennis' beautiful "Wouldn't It Be Nice to Live Again," a *Surf's Up* outtake about which fans had long speculated but never heard. Sands' interpretation of the ballad is the high point of the superb disc, which sheds light on some of The Beach Boys' overlooked gems and includes a welcome smattering of originals by Marsland, Sands and Boyd.

With *Surf's Up*, The Beach Boys embarked on a fascinating and underrated phase in their career. The band had become a democracy, and Carl its benevolent leader. The group continued to forge ahead artistically until the audience requests for the old hits became too loud to ignore. Marsland regards the group's later backward-looking direction as a tragedy. "The Beach Boys could have been such an interesting band in the later years if they had just committed to doing more mature material," Marsland says. "But I like the idea of taking The Beach Boys' lessons and applying them elsewhere. It's one of my motivators as a musician and songwriter."

Cameron Crowe on...
FEEL FLOWS

Written by: Carl Wilson and Jack Rieley
Lead vocal: Carl Wilson
Produced by: Carl Wilson
Recorded: July 29, 1971
Released: August 30, 1971, on *Surf's Up*

Carl and Jack Rieley followed up their "Long Promised Road" collaboration with the powerfully atmospheric *Surf's Up* cut "Feel Flows." Continuing in a spiritual vein, Rieley penned impressionistic lyrics seemingly about the soul overcoming real-world sorrow. Whether it was poetry or "wacked out meandering" — as *Village Voice* critic Robert Christgau panned[1] — Rieley's alliterative lines are wonderfully musical and delivered with conviction by Carl.

Most remarkable is Carl's production. The recording features an eerie forward echo on his vocal and an organ part run through a Moog synthesizer and then played back simultaneously with the original part. He also applied a variable-speed oscillator to the piano track for an out-of-tune sound[2] and laid down a menacing guitar break. He added a left-handed bass part so tricky that touring player Ed Carter had to read the notes when performing it live.[3] Noted jazz musician Charles Lloyd, a Transcendental Meditation practitioner who played with the band throughout the decade, added flute and saxophone — the finishing touches to a stylistic tour de force that displayed a level of creativity not heard from the group since *Smile*.

With its jazzy solos and mystical aura, the

Carl, Mike and Billy Hinsche. In the early 1970s, Carl was taking the reins onstage and in the studio. [© Ed Roach]

number is unique in The Beach Boys' canon. It's great stoner music that sits comfortably on the soundtrack of Cameron Crowe's acclaimed movie *Almost Famous* alongside contemporary songs by The Allman Brothers Band, Led Zeppelin and Lynyrd Skynyrd. Released in 2000, writer-director Crowe's autobiographical film dramatizes his experiences as a teenage *Rolling Stone* correspondent in the 1970s. He uses the song twice: over the closing credits and in a scene where protagonist William Miller (played by Patrick Fugit) meets band hanger-on Penny Lane (Kate Hudson) after conducting a backstage interview with a fictitious rock group. In one evening, William has experienced his big professional break and meets a girl who will have a profound effect on him. With emotions running high, the inclusion of "Feel Flows" feels just right.

"To me, this song is about the human experience — the giddy high-highs and the aching low-lows and all those glorious spots in between," says Crowe, who won an Academy Award for his screenplay.

"Feel Flows" is similarly admired by Nancy Wilson, the Heart guitarist who scored the film and who was married to Crowe at the time. In an August 2007 interview in *The Believer*, she explains that she and Crowe rediscovered the song while assembling the soundtrack. *Surf's Up* was, rather shockingly, out of print on CD at the time, so Wilson had to dig up a vinyl copy in the basement of her sister Ann, Heart's lead singer. The version in the movie was copied directly from vinyl, crackles and all.[4]

The tune got new life from exposure in the film and inclusion on its Grammy Award–winning soundtrack. Omitted from The Beach Boys' 1993 boxed set, it would pop up on the 2007 compilation *The Warmth of the Sun*, sequel to the group's *Sounds of Summer* greatest-hits collection.

The Beach Boys figure in another one of the film's key scenes after William's sister Anita (Zooey Deschanel), no longer able to live under the same roof with their overbearing mother Elaine (Frances McDormand), hits the road with her boyfriend. Her parting instruction to her little brother is to "look under your bed — it'll set you free." There he finds a bag of classic rock records, including The Rolling Stones' *Big Hits (High Tide and Green Grass)*, *Led Zeppelin II* and Jimi Hendrix's *Axis: Bold as Love*. But The Beach Boys get pride of placement: *Pet Sounds* is at the top of the pile.

"Every time I'm lucky enough to make a movie I always end up pressing a copy of *Pet Sounds* into all the actors' hands, and I just end up babbling and saying, 'Here's what it feels like to live; here's what it feels like to grow up. Let's try for this feeling,'" Crowe told the crowd at *An All-Star Tribute to Brian Wilson*. "That's the magic of *Pet Sounds* — even more than the greatest rock album, *Pet Sounds* may just be the greatest rock 'feeling.'"

For this book, Crowe considered selecting as his favorite Beach Boys song the *Pet Sounds* cut "Caroline, No," which in the 1970s Carl performed in a mellow, jazzier live version that appears on *The Beach Boys in Concert*.

Another song candidate for Crowe would have been "Good Vibrations," which he used to underscore a disorienting chase sequence in the surreal thriller *Vanilla Sky* starring Tom Cruise. But no.

"A big part of me wants to pick 'Caroline, No' as their quintessential song, but the fact that Carl sings 'Feel Flows' makes it a kind of distant cousin to that wonderful earlier song," he explains. "'Feel Flows' has the happy/sad greatness that defines the group and the timelessness that allows The Beach Boys to tower over any attempt to classify them as simple poster boys for the California experience. It is the essence of the fulfilled promise of The Beach Boys and everything Brian envisioned for their creative journey."

David Leaf on ...
'Til I Die

Written by: Brian Wilson
Lead vocals: Brian with group
Produced by: Brian Wilson and Carl Wilson
Recorded: August 15, 1970, July 30, 1971
Released: August 30, 1971, on *Surf's Up* and October 11, 1971, as B-side to "Long Promised Road"

The inspiration for one of Brian's most personal songs came as he reflected on his personal anguish, the vastness of the universe and his place in it. "I was thinking to myself, 'In the universe I'm so small that it's [absurd],' he told his biographer and friend David Leaf in the latter's documentary *Beautiful Dreamer: Brian Wilson and the Story of Smile*. "I went to the piano and I said, 'What are some ways that I can express being small?'"

According to author Keith Badman, Brian recorded a solo piano demo for "'Til I Die" in November 1969.[1] The lyrics, which Brian wrote alone, are sparse but moving. He casts himself as a series of objects helpless in the face of natural forces beyond his control. In summer 1970, Brian recorded and mixed the track, featuring vibes, a churchlike organ, heartbeat bass, a delicate synthesizer and a drum machine that coalesce to recreate the ocean's ebb and flow. Reportedly at least one band member did not respond well to the downbeat message. Brian was stung by the negative reaction and put the song on the shelf,[2] although it stayed in contention for the *Surf's Up* album.

But the objection to the lyrics remained. According to author Peter Ames Carlin, by the time the album sessions ramped up in summer '71, Brian had tried tweaking the words to give the song a more positive feel. However, the rest of the band conceded that simply didn't work,[3] so they reverted to Brian's original lyrics. They sing a group vocal on three short verses, the first pair punctuated with solo lines sung by Brian that get to the heart of the matter. There is no proper chorus, and after the third verse the song transitions to a vocal tag that takes up more than one-third of the running time, repeating through the fade. This structure makes the song seem deceptively simple, but it all serves Brian's fatalistic message, which is: this is how insignificant I feel and this is how it always will be. The multipart vocal arrangement combined with the music's chord and rhythm changes stunningly evoke the enormity of oceans, valleys and emotional chasms. Blessed are we that Brian stayed the course, because, paired with the title track of *Surf's Up*, the LP closes on a peerless high.

The song was immediately cited as a standout, and its reputation has grown. A 1998 *Mojo* poll surveying a panel of high-profile fans voted it Brian's all-time greatest song, and in a 2004 Canadian TV interview with CBC news anchor Peter Mansbridge, Brian named it one of the five best Beach Boys songs he ever wrote. Reverence for it could be heard in 2010 in the instrumentation of American indie duo Beach House's "Walk in the Park" and in a heavily electronic cover produced by Van Dyke Parks for Lightspeed Champion.

But in the case of David Leaf, you could say the song changed his life.

As a teenager in New Rochelle, New York, Leaf was a Beach Boys fan with a couple of their 45s in his collection. As a 15-year-old he saw them perform a November 21, 1967, gig at the Westchester County Center in White Plains, New York. "It was a very exciting night. They were great. Their singing was amazing, but what I remember most vividly about their show was how short it was," he recalls. "When their set ended and everyone stood up to leave, I thought it was intermission."

In fall 1971, Leaf was a junior at George Washington University in Washington, D.C., and was shopping at Record City when he noticed The Beach Boys on the cover of *Rolling Stone*. He picked up that October 28 issue and was enthralled by the landmark two-part profile "The Beach Boys: A California Saga" by Tom Nolan with David Felton. With *Surf's Up* peaking on the charts and concerts starting to generate buzz, the time was right for a band reappraisal, and the piece didn't shy away from The Beach Boys' darker corners, including inner-group tensions, Brian's eccentricity, Murry and the collapse of *Smile*, which was driving fan speculation again with the emergence of "Surf's Up."

Leaf bought the album to hear that unearthed song, which to him miraculously exceeded its mighty legend. He remembers also being deeply moved by the track that preceded it. "From the first time I heard ''Til I Die' it went right to my heart," he recalls. "For a new song to be able to stand up to 'Surf's Up' was and remains almost inconceivable."

The song is Brian's ultimate statement of existential angst, or, as Leaf calls it, an even more revealing "In My Room." "The harmonies, melody and vocals are beautiful, and Brian's lyric is heartbreaking," he says. "I love The Beach Boys' up-tempo stuff, but the ballads are the songs I connect with. I tend to focus on the more adventurous compositions, arrangements and productions or the ones where the lyric, regardless of who wrote it, seems to come right from Brian's soul."

More of a sports writer, Leaf was so moved by the music and the *Rolling Stone* piece that he reviewed *Surf's Up* for his college paper, *The Hatchet*. He saw the group in concert again on November 7, 1971, at Georgetown University — a show that demonstrated how much both the band and the music industry had changed. "Unlike the concert I had seen four years previously, this time they came out, played about an hour, took an intermission, came back and played another 40–50 minutes and then came out and did encore after encore after encore," he recalls.

He and the friend who accompanied him shared a memorable encounter outside after the show. "I turned around and standing right there was Mike Love, whom I started peppering with questions," Leaf recalls. "Mike said something like, 'One of these days I'm going to write a book and answer all those questions.'" As it turns out, Leaf would beat him to the punch.

Leaf moved to California in fall 1975, one of his ambitions being to write a biography of Brian. Two years later, after having made connections in The Beach Boys organization, he launched the *Pet Sounds* fanzine focusing on the group's music. That led to a book deal with Grosset & Dunlap. *The Beach Boys and the California Myth* hit the shelves in fall

1978, and Leaf would update it in the mid-'80s. Although long out-of-print and succeeded by other bios about Brian and the group, its shadow looms over them all. What one takes away from it is that Brian's artistic voice had been stifled and mishandled, whether at the hands of record companies or the monster he had created in The Beach Boys. Some take issue with the Brian-centric take on the group's history, but it is that unwavering point of view that makes the book so compelling.

In 1986, Leaf co-wrote the group's silver anniversary TV special *The Beach Boys: 25 Years Together*, and a couple of years later he was hired by Warner Bros. as a consultant on Brian's debut solo album, churning out perhaps the most verbose press kit in rock history. Then, in 1990, when Capitol released The Beach Boys' 1960s albums on CD, Leaf wrote the extensive liner notes. As interest in the band rose yet again, Capitol assembled the five-disc career-spanning 1993 boxed set *Good Vibrations: Thirty Years of The Beach Boys*, and Leaf was contracted not only to write the accompanying booklet, but also to hash out the musical content with engineer Mark Linett and Brian's songwriting collaborator Andy Paley. Leaf recalls suggesting sequencing

"'Til I Die" at the end of the third disc after "Surf's Up," reversing the order from the original album. In 1997, Capitol followed up with the Grammy-nominated four-disc box *The Pet Sounds Sessions*, which Leaf co-produced with Linett and for which he contributed two historical booklets.

The vaults remained open beyond Leaf's involvement. The 1998 soundtrack to Alan Boyd's *Endless Harmony* documentary includes a previously bootlegged alternate version of "'Til I Die" mixed by Stephen Desper. It begins with a run-through of just the musical track, building one instrument at a time, followed by another pass that includes the vocals. This dramatic presentation brings clarity to the song's various elements, and Brian would later perform this version in concert and include it on *Live at the Roxy Theatre*.

Leaf, meanwhile, was seasoned in TV specials and documentary filmmaking by the time he wrote and produced the 2001 concert special *An All-Star Tribute to Brian Wilson*, filmed at Radio City Music Hall. This was followed by the 2004 Grammy-nominated *Beautiful Dreamer*, which is a remarkable companion piece to the *Brian Wilson Presents Smile* album. For Leaf, making the doc was a fitting coda to his history with the group.

"I sometimes think about the confluence of events: in the fall of '71, I heard "Til I Die' and 'Surf's Up,' read the *Rolling Stone* story and saw the group in concert — and then, 33 years later, the studio version of *Brian Wilson Presents Smile* is released, Brian plays *Smile* at Carnegie Hall and Walt Disney Concert Hall and *Beautiful Dreamer* premieres. In terms of life and art coming full circle, it's not going to get much better than that."

BRUCE JOHNSTON ON...
DISNEY GIRLS (1957)

Written by: Bruce Johnston
Lead vocal: Bruce Johnston
Produced by: Bruce Johnston
Recorded: June 3, July 23, 1971
Released: August 30, 1971, on *Surf's Up*

The group may not have landed a hit single in the U.S. in a couple of years, but its live appearances were garnering favorable reviews, starting with a set at the Big Sur Folk Festival in October 1970, followed the next month by a four-night residency at Los Angeles' Whisky a Go Go featuring rare appearances by Brian the first two evenings. These paved the way for a sold-out gig at New York's Carnegie Hall on February 24, 1971, where the band performed a hefty 27-song set favoring recent material. Two months later, they shared the stage with the Grateful Dead — avatars of hipness — at the Fillmore East, followed by a weekend performance at a Washington May Day anti-war rally before a reported 500,000 spectators. These legendary concerts marked a turnaround in the band's popularity at home. Word was getting around: The Beach Boys were cool after all.

Looking out in the crowds at the band's East Coast dates that spring, Bruce noticed a difference — not only were the audiences mostly getting larger, but also there was a sizable contingent of young wannabe hippies.

"I started seeing kids in the audience — precocious 15-year-olds — who just couldn't wait to smoke some marijuana in front of the band, most likely thinking we thought it was cool," Bruce recalls. "They waited until we would come out onstage before lighting up, and I thought, 'This is really dumb.' Here I am — 13 to 14 years older than a lot of them, with a little bit of my possibly emerging maturity — thinking I should write a song about what was going on in my semi-innocent high school teen years. The drug world is never such a great idea, and sadly, I had a front-row seat observing it have a horrible effect on some of the guys in the band. 'Disney Girls' was my very subtle anti-drug song. I'm a real conservative guy. I've never done drugs in my life. On the other hand, a glass of Château Lafite Rothschild Pauillac 1959 now and then just might hit the spot."

The wistful ballad "Disney Girls (1957)" never directly addresses drugs, the Vietnam War or the turbulent times America was going through, but it does look back longingly at a simpler era and the more innocent pleasures of lemonade, Patti Page's "Old Cape Cod" and, of course, the swell kind of girl one might see on *The Mickey Mouse Club*. Bruce had composed the song before the band went on tour, but initially had a different concept for the lyrics.

"My original thought on the song was very pretentious," he admits. "It was about a lost love. It was something that wasn't happening to me. I was just making it up. And I thought, 'Why don't I write something that is really me?' I thought I should write a song about what things were like when I was the same age as these kids at our concerts having their first journey in drugs."

Bruce recalls the basic track being recorded by Stephen Desper in Brian's 16-track living-room studio with Bruce playing upright piano, Ed Carter on acoustic guitar and Dennis Dragon on drums that were echoed and delayed in the final mix. Kathy Dragon added flute, Carter added electric guitar with a phased wah-wah effect and Bruce played the bass part on a late-'60s Moog synthesizer. ("The Moog was in the booth and filled up the whole room!" he says.) He also performed the mandolin intro that establishes the song's nostalgic mood.

No other Beach Boy participated in the instrumental session, but Bruce later double-tracked background vocals featuring himself, Mike, Alan, Carl and Brian. "Brian was great," Bruce says. "He 'got it' vocally. He also 'got' the chord changes. There's the

Bruce in the late '60s proves Dennis wasn't the only one who surfed.
[© Cyril Maitland, Courtesy Bruce Johnston]

bridge, which is really difficult to sing. It's very Four Freshmen and he was into it. That was a nice tip of the hat from the band to me to sing on my song and not question my vocal parts. The background vocals took about three hours to record one evening, with breaks to go to Brian's kitchen and raid his huge Traulsen refrigerator. We'd get food, mess around and then get back to recording." (Bruce says he doesn't recall why Dennis wasn't present. He was possibly off with Daryl Dragon recording material for a proposed solo album on the heels of his U.K.-only solo single "Sound of Free.")

The finished "Disney Girls" harks back to the Great American Songbook and is itself a candidate for "modern standard" status. Following its appearance on the *Surf's Up* album in August 1971, Bruce joined several high-profile artists in recording covers of the tune, including Cass Elliott on her self-titled 1972 album, Art Garfunkel on his 1975 platinum-seller *Breakaway* and crooner Jack Jones on 1977's *The Full Life*. It got even more exposure from Captain & Tennille's rendition on their 1975 smash LP *Love Will Keep Us Together* and the duo's subsequent best-of collections. Bruce would record a stripped-down version for his 1977 solo album *Going Public*. In 2011, a version recorded in the 1980s by Doris Day, mother of his best friend Terry Melcher, appeared on Day's album *My Heart*, on which Bruce wrote or co-wrote five tracks.

In retrospect, "Disney Girls" could have made a strong Beach Boys single. While the group's biggest hits have been its fast songs, the cut is an undeniable crowd-pleaser. But working against its chances was the lack of chart success a year previous for the Bruce-penned ballad "Tears in the Morning" (except in The Netherlands, where it reached #6). As it stands, "Disney Girls" is a highlight of *Surf's Up*, displaying Bruce's knack for tapping into Brian's well of melancholy while providing a sophisticated lyric. To this day, the song is often misidentified as Brian's, which can only

be taken as a compliment. In an interview with Timothy White, Brian spoke of his admiration for Bruce's composition, commenting, "I thought it was marvelous the way he wrote the harmonies and chords."[1]

Despite the commercial and critical success of *Surf's Up*, the LP has never totally sat right with Bruce, who regards it as the work not of a band, but of various individuals. "I always thought it received more acclaim than it deserved, as though it was one unified thought, but it really wasn't," he says. "We had just made such a connected album with *Sunflower* — with the band still young and in sync — and then we're getting all the band's solo songs organized to patch together the *Surf's Up* album. It's like a repository for a lot of our solo things, where we lent out our voices to whoever was doing the lead. But it was great to see everyone show up with some very interesting music."

To Bruce, one of the essential Beach Boys elements absent from the record is any collaboration between Brian and Mike, who had teamed up on stellar *Sunflower* tracks "Add Some Music to Your Day," "All I Wanna Do" and "Cool, Cool Water." "I am as much a fan of Mike Love as I am of Brian Wilson," he says.

Of Brian's two new compositions on *Surf's Up*, the bizarre but beautiful "A Day in the Life of a Tree" features an unexpected croaking lead vocal from Jack Rieley, who also wrote the words. "That's a very odd but wonderful track," Bruce notes. "Jack's not a singer, but he is actually the right voice for the song. He even sounds like an ancient tree. I don't know if that belongs on *Surf's Up*, but I thought it was fantastic." Bruce's favorite track on the album is Brian's "'Til I Die." "I would like to write those backing vocals out and put them in a book for music students — that's how good those wonderful parts are," he says.

He recalls how quickly Brian worked, even on such intricate arrangements. "If something was wrong, he would stop singing, run over and fix it at the piano," Bruce says. "He would think in front of you and recalculate the vocal parts. I hate to say this — because it's been repeated so many times — but Brian is such a genius. Send him back in time and he would be Rachmaninoff or Tchaikovsky. Maybe Rachmaninoff would write something at the piano and then orchestrate it so you would hear it symphonically. Well, that's what Brian did, but he went beyond that in terms of also being able to write and record the vocal arrangement and then sing the lead."

As it turned out, *Surf's Up* would be the last Beach Boys album of the decade graced by a Bruce composition. Despite some happy times making the LP, tensions were rife within The Beach Boys organization — so much so that when finalizing the track lineup, Dennis' contributions (likely "4th of July" and "Wouldn't It Be Nice to Live Again") were pulled. By 1972, after Carl had brought Ricky Fataar and Blondie Chaplin into the group, the stage was getting pretty crowded, and in April that year Bruce left the band by what a press release described as "mutual consent." His departure indeed seemed amicable, as he would guest at Beach Boys shows in the ensuing years and return to the fold before the decade was out.

When the group first asked Bruce to join in 1965, it got much more than a concert stand-in for Brian. It got a rounded musician whose recording career predated its own. A prolific session player and producer, he had recorded Beach Boys–like solo albums (1963's *Surfin' Round the World* and *Surfers' Pajama Party*) and collaborated with Melcher both as Bruce & Terry and on The Rip Chords. Then, as a Beach Boy, he would co-produce the single "Bluebirds over the Mountain" and contribute the lushly produced numbers "The Nearest Faraway Place," "Deirdre" and "Tears in the Morning."

After leaving the group in 1972, he picked up his multifaceted career, forming the Equinox record company with Melcher and even signing Brian, although little would come of that. He produced artists Barry Mann and David Cassidy and did vocal arrangements and sang backgrounds on Elton John's "Don't Let the Sun Go Down on Me" and Pink Floyd's *The Wall*. Most memorably, he penned the ballad "I Write the Songs," which was covered by Barry Manilow in 1975 and became a monster schmaltz classic, topping the *Billboard* charts, selling millions worldwide and netting Bruce the Grammy Award for Song of the Year. (Some people believe the lyrics are about Brian, but Bruce says flat-out they're not.) In 1978, when things began to go awry for The Beach Boys as they recorded *L.A. (Light Album)*, they invited him back to produce, and he has remained ever since.

Considering that by 2012 he had logged more years as an active Beach Boy than anyone except Mike — with whom he performed 120 or more shows per year — Bruce remains modest about his contribution. "I'm much smarter than I am talented. I know where to stand; I know where to be," he says. He adds that "Brian Wilson is a brilliant soul — perhaps the finest creative talent I could've worked with in 10 lifetimes. He is the music man, always has been. Can you imagine that here I am in this great band and I got in early enough to be part of it? I took a ride while he drove."

BLONDIE CHAPLIN ON...
SAIL ON SAILOR

Written by: Brian Wilson, Tandyn Almer, Van Dyke
Parks, Jack Rieley and Raymond Kennedy
Lead vocal: Blondie Chaplin
Produced by: Carl Wilson
Recorded: November 28–30, 1972
Released: January 8, 1973, on *Holland*
and as a single January 29, 1973, March 10, 1975
Chart peak: U.S. #49

Despite the success of *Surf's Up*, The Beach
Boys hit a creative dry spell in the latter half
of 1971. If Brian was in the studio at all, it
was mostly for sessions with Marilyn and
Diane for the *Spring* album. Bruce would
soon be gone, and Dennis focused on a solo
album. Following Dennis' hand injury, his seat
behind the drum kit was filled for most of the
next three years by Ricky Fataar from South
African band The Flame, which had opened
for The Beach Boys a year earlier. Before long
The Flame's lead singer and guitarist Blondie
Chaplin also joined The Beach Boys.

Terence William Chaplin was nicknamed
"Blondie" for his soccer-playing style, which
resembled that of South African footballer
Blondie Campbell. Known originally as "The
Flames" — the "s" was dropped in the U.S. to
avoid confusion with James Brown's Famous
Flames — the band was rounded out by
Fataar's brothers Steve on guitar and Edries
(a.k.a. "Brother") on bass. The black R&B
combo from Durban topped the 1968 charts
at home with a cover of Jerry Butler's "For
Your Precious Love."

"We had a gold record, but they could not
figure out how to present us with the equivalent of a Grammy or even what category to

put us in within the Apartheid system, as all the nominees were white," Blondie recalls. "We would still like an award like that, but SARI, the South African Recording Industry, turned a blind eye and offered a cold heart. We used to call it the 'Sorry Awards.'"

The group's local success allowed them to save up enough money to relocate to England, which seemed to them a musical Mecca since South African radio was flooded with British Invasion music, in part because of the two nations' Commonwealth connection. Blondie, just 16 at the time, describes the move as traumatic. "We weren't used to going out of the country. You get shell-shocked. It's a new country, new people. You're very young and you miss home. But we did okay. We just hung in there. The first few months we didn't know where we were or what we were doing, but we got into it," he says.

The group settled in the suburb of North Harrow and got gigs where they could until a June 1969 performance at London's Blaises club provided their big break. Blondie recalls Carl and Mike dropping in at the trendy night spot after a pair of Beach Boys shows at north London's Astoria Theatre.[1] (Beach Boys percussionist/drummer Mike Kowalski also remembers being at Blaises that night.) Carl was impressed enough by the group to offer them a contract with Brother Records. For The Flames, this meant "next stop: California" and more uprooting.

"It's all foreign when you come out of a place that's completely iron-fisted," Blondie says. "In America, they were at the tail end of flower power and 'make love, not war' and all the shit that was happening, and we just thought, 'Oh boy, this is different.'"

Carl was credited as producer on *The Flame*, the band's first and only U.S. album release, cut at Brian's home studio. The record — which fuses rock, R&B, country and prog elements — documents an ambitious young band eager to experiment. The album came out in March 1971 and, even after a shout-out from Paul McCartney, died at record stores despite minor chart action for the single "See the Light" (U.S. #95). The Flame nevertheless recorded a follow-up album in late 1971, but due partly to internal problems it never saw release.[2] "We didn't get a fair shake to stay together, but that has a lot to do with us. And after a while The Beach Boys didn't know what to do with us, either. The band just broke apart," Blondie explains.

The worst part was that while Ricky had a new gig with The Beach Boys, the prospects for Ricky's brothers and Blondie were not so promising, and they returned to South Africa. "That was a massive, depressing shock to be back," Blondie recalls. But he was there for only a couple of months. Carl and Jack Rieley, seeing The Beach Boys were in need of a shake-up, realized Blondie had much to offer and invited him to tour with the band.

"Of course I wanted to do it, because I didn't want to stay in South Africa under the Apartheid system anymore and I thought I was going nowhere fast," Blondie recalls. It wasn't long before he and Ricky were promoted to official-member status, announced at a February 1972 press conference in London.[3] The new lineup meant the lily-white Beach Boys were now integrated.

Blondie's Gibson Les Paul Goldtop added a third guitar behind Carl and Alan, and onstage he played bass on "Heroes and Villains" and "Surf's Up." His most notable gift, however, was his voice. Although he could handle the high register Brian had occupied, his vocals didn't so much fill a void in the harmony blend as add a whole new dimension. He even took over Carl's lead on "Wild Honey," bringing out the song's rockier edges and steering it closer to the R&B feel that was originally intended.

Carl also encouraged Ricky and Blondie to write songs for the group. Their first two Beach Boys compositions appeared on the next album, *Carl and the Passions — "So Tough."* (The title references a group name Brian, Carl and Mike used in the early days.) The LP was rushed to completion and released on May 15. The piano on their groovy cut "Here She Comes" sounds like Traffic and the harmonies are in the Crosby, Stills and Nash vein. Some fans griped that although the number felt contemporary for 1972, it lacked any connection to the group's classic sound. Blondie sings the lead, as he does on the pair's other contribution, the pleasing country-inflected ballad "Hold On Dear Brother," to which Ricky adds haunting steel guitar.

The extent of Brian's official studio credits on the album is his co-production with Carl on the funky "You Need a Mess of Help to Stand Alone" (a writing collaboration with Rieley), but he also reportedly showed up to work on his two other compositions. He sings on the R&B stomper "Marcella" (lyrics again by Rieley) and arranged the gospel-flavored

"He Come Down," on which he plays keyboards and sings backgrounds.[4] The latter, co-written by Alan and Mike, is a paean to Transcendental Meditation that gains credibility from Blondie's pleading vocal part. "We'd see Brian occasionally, but most of the time I couldn't tell you where he was or what he was doing," Blondie says. The album impressed neither record buyers nor critics in its day. It made it only as far as #50 in the U.S. — despite being packaged along with a reissue of *Pet Sounds* — and #25 in the U.K. But it stands today as a soulful and original entry in the group's catalog.

"They were experimenting," Blondie reflects. "You're either awake or you're sleeping. For me — not because I was involved — that was one of their better times. They were trying to unshackle whatever the 'Beach Boys' name was. They always did traditional stuff live, but on the recordings things seemed to open up a bit, which is good."

Before the group finished *"So Tough,"* Carl and Rieley made a surprising decision to move the band's base to the Netherlands for their forthcoming European tour, with plans of sticking around to record the next album, aptly titled *Holland*. The clean and serene countryside seemed perfectly conducive to creativity, and the group remembered appreciative Dutch audiences from its 1970 tour and a prize for *Surf's Up* at the Edison Awards, the country's version of the Grammys. The fish-out-of-water approach inspired the Rolling Stones to record *Exile on Main St.* in the south of France, so why not?

It sounded romantic, but the logistics involved were of a military scale — and nearly as expensive. Housing had to be secured for the group and its hefty entourage. Blondie and his girlfriend (and later wife), Linda, along with Carl and his family, were set up in the village of Hilversum, 19 miles outside of Amsterdam, where they were later joined by Brian, who resisted making the trip as long as possible.

To ensure the group 24/7 studio access, engineer Steve Moffitt was charged with building a state-of-the-art mixing console at the group's new Santa Monica studio, disassembling it, shipping it and all the other gear to the Netherlands and then reassembling it in a barn in Baambrugge that would be painstakingly converted into a studio. The console's installation brought with it all manner of electrical and soundproofing problems. "There were wires everywhere you looked. There was a train station close by, and when a train went by, it would rumble and stop the recordings for a few minutes, and we'd start up again," Blondie recalls. "There was so much to work on getting the studio together and getting Brian over there that there was a lot of down time. It was a bit of a three-month vacation."

Blondie found the band cliquish. He and Ricky remained closest to Carl, who had brought them over to California, where they still resided more than 40 years later. "Mike and Al were in their own meditation camp. They seemed to have more in common with each other," he notes. While Blondie dabbled in meditation, he didn't take to it significantly. "I just like to play music and sing and look around the world," he says. "That's my meditation."

Blondie and Ricky contributed two new songs, including "We Got Love," an upbeat tune with anti-Apartheid overtones, and "Leaving This Town," produced by Ricky, who plays an impressive Moog synthesizer solo. It is movingly sung by Blondie, who easily related to its theme of the weariness of life on the road. Elsewhere on the album, Carl collaborated with Rieley on "The Trader," an ambitious epic about Old World imperialism observed through the perspective of both conqueror and conquered, while the experimental "Steamboat" by Dennis and Rieley is a period travelogue that name-checks steamboat innovator Robert Fulton and uses the sound of a chugging engine to carry its rhythm.

The album's centerpiece is the three-part "California Saga" by Alan and Mike, which evokes the rugged mountains and cool, clear water in the titular state's northern region and incorporates passages from Robinson Jeffers' poem "The Beaks of Eagles." Being away from home so long inspired Alan to write the climactic "California" segment, which announced the end of the Holland excursion with the opening line "On my way to sunny Californ-i-a," sung by Brian, who was otherwise a minor presence at the group's sessions. Instead, he became fixated on creating a musical fantasy inspired by Randy Newman's *Sail Away* and which would be narrated by Rieley. There was no room on the album for the unusual 12-minute piece, titled "Mount Vernon and Fairway (A Fairy Tale)," so it was issued on a bonus EP.

After all the toil overseas, the group came home for some North American concert dates and to put the finishing touches on the album. They were then mortified to hear that Warner

Dennis and Blondie onstage at SUNY Binghamton, May 12, 1973. The former Flame singer/guitarist brought a soulful new dimension to The Beach Boys' vocals. [© Ed Roach]

Bros. was rejecting the record for lack of a radio song. Van Dyke Parks, then a Warner Bros. staffer, saw a solution in a song he had worked on with Brian called "Sail on Sailor."

The tune has a murky history. In Parks' telling, he contributed musical intervals, chords and lyrics — many of which were ultimately discarded. Brian, in his memoir, recounts seeking further input from his inner circle of party friends,[5] including "Along Comes Mary" writer Tandyn Almer and Ray Kennedy, who would later sing the tune with KGB, a short-lived group that also featured guitarist Mike Bloomfield, drummer Carmine Appice and bassist Ric Grech. This bluesy version contains Kennedy's completely different lyrics about a down-and-out, coked-up gospel singer.

Engineer Stephen Desper has spoken of a Beach Boys version that was nearly finished by late 1971[6] — before he left the group's employ — and featured Carl on lead vocals. Whatever the case, Rieley rewrote the words, which in their final state lean heavier on seafaring imagery as symbols of life's travails, fitting nicely alongside the nautical themes of "Steamboat," "California Saga" and "The Trader."

"It's almost like a blues shuffle. I remember it as something Van Dyke and Brian started, and then there was a whole lot of chipping in from a whole lot of people," recalls Blondie, who provided the eventual lead vocal. Despite its many cooks, the song seems to make a statement about Brian and his personal struggles, but Blondie could also connect with lines that brought back memories of his journey to England as a teenager.

He remembers cutting the track in Los Angeles in November 1972. Brian wasn't around for these sessions at Village Recorders,[7] but phoned in some suggestions to Carl, who produced the track. "I played bass, Ricky played drums and Carl played

piano. That was the basic track. And then I got a chance to sing it, which I wasn't expecting. I guess they just thought that the timbre of Dennis' voice wasn't right, and Carl gave it a shot a couple of times. What you hear is the second take of me singing it. It has so many words to get around to make it flow into the melody. That drove me nuts," he says. Blondie's yearning vocal, which betrays frustrations stewing since his Apartheid-era childhood, was a complete departure for a Beach Boys radio song, but the group's backing harmonies — aided by Gerry Beckley of group America, touring player Billy Hinsche and guitarist Tony Martin Jr. — keep it anchored in their oeuvre.

The addition of the new number convinced Warner Bros. to green light *Holland*, although "We Got Love" had to be sacrificed. "Sail on Sailor" was released as a U.S. single in February 1973, and although it peaked at only #79, it did get the group some FM radio play. (In the U.K., Alan's "California Saga: California" was chosen as the lead single, likely because Alan's "Cotton Fields" had been the band's last hit there. With "Sail on Sailor" on the B-side, it reached #37.) The single proved durable enough that two years later, following the success of *Endless Summer*, it was reissued in the U.S. in the absence of any other new material from the group save for "Child of Winter (Christmas Song)." This time it made it to #49. "Sail on Sailor" would come to be admired by other artists including Genesis, which used the song's piano-driven rhythm as the basis for its 1980 hit "Misunderstanding."[8] Ray Charles covered the song masterfully on the TV special *The Beach Boys: 25 Years Together*, and Martin Scorsese brought the original back in the spotlight on the soundtrack to his Oscar-winning 2006 picture *The Departed*.

Holland was generally well received by the rock press, its biggest kudos coming from *Rolling Stone*, which named it one of the five best albums of 1973.[9] Sales were modest, however, with chart peaks of #36 in the U.S. and #20 in the U.K. The band followed up with relentless touring throughout the U.S. One of the more interesting features of these shows was the decision to close with a cover of The Rolling Stones' "Jumpin' Jack Flash," with Mike prancing about à la Mick Jagger. "Mike wanted to do that, which I thought was a different choice for him, but it ended up going over very well," Blondie recalls. It's a song Blondie has since played many times in his more recent role as a Rolling Stones supporting player, where he has chipped in guitar, percussion and backup vocals.

The high quality of Beach Boys concerts in this era is documented on *The Beach Boys in Concert*, which, reflecting growing interest in the live act, climbed to #25 in America. No doubt the exorbitant cost of the Netherlands adventure had necessitated the accelerated tour schedule and record release. And if somebody had to play fall guy for the Dutch misstep, Rieley fit the bill. He decided to stay behind in the land of windmills to continue to administer Beach Boys business, which seemed anything but practical. In the fall, Carl returned to Holland to fire him, and Rieley's post was taken over by Mike's brother Stephen, previously the band's assistant manager. That would prove a fateful development for Blondie.

One of Blondie's favorite places to play was New York's Madison Square Garden, but it's also where his stint as a Beach Boy came to a sudden end after a show on December 19, 1973. "It had been a long tour," he recalls. "I complained to [Stephen] about some tickets. People close to me were put in the nosebleed

section, so I wasn't too thrilled about that."
Walking back to the dressing room, he and
Stephen got into an altercation and punches
flew. "After that I just said, 'Fuck it, I'm not
working with these guys anymore.' A lot of
people thought I was nuts, but I still stand by
that decision and I don't feel nuts at all."

At subsequent shows, Billy Hinsche took
over the lead on "Sail on Sailor" and Fataar
stuck around for another year until after
Dennis returned to the drum kit. Soon the
band reverted to its classic lineup and began
coasting on past glories. "They should have
nurtured that middle period of *"So Tough"*
and *Holland*. I think the public would have
come back around and things would have tak-
en off the right way," Blondie reflects. "I don't
think they focused enough on making new
songs. They should have utilized what they
had with Ricky and me, which was just starting. But they just didn't let it take hold longer.
It's almost like things stopped after that."

What didn't stop was Chaplin's association with musical royalty. He went on to play
with a reformed version of The Band, blues
man Paul Butterfield, The New York Dolls'
David Johansen, The Byrds' Gene Clark,
Bonnie Raitt and the Stones. He released a self-
titled solo album in 1977, followed nearly 30
years later by the well-received *Between Us*.
Along the way he has sung "Sail on Sailor" at
many solo shows.

"I'm completely at ease with what I've
done, so if people want me to do the song, I
do it," Blondie says. "I'll take the recognition,
because it's rock 'n' roll history."

JIM GUERCIO ON ...
GOOD TIMIN'

Written by: Brian Wilson and Carl Wilson

Lead vocal: Carl Wilson

Produced by: Bruce Johnston, The Beach Boys and Jim Guercio

Recorded: November 4, 1974, December 13, 1978

Released: March 16, 1979, on *L.A. (Light Album)* and as a single April 17, 1979

Chart peak: U.S. #40

In 1973, the group found itself creatively adrift again, having done precious little in the studio to follow up *Holland*. In June, the Wilson brothers and cousin Mike had to cope with Murry's death from a heart attack at age 55. Dennis, whose focus had shifted from a potential solo career back to band business, wanted to turn things around, so he flew out to Colorado to call on old friend Jim Guercio.

James William Guercio was a classically trained musician who had played bass for Chad & Jeremy on a 1966 Beach Boys tour, where he struck up a friendship with Dennis and Carl. Soon afterwards he became manager-producer of The Buckinghams, indulging his penchant for horn-based sounds and helping them become America's top band of 1967. He went on to play guitar for Frank Zappa's Mothers of Invention and later, as a Columbia staffer, produced the second, self-titled LP for Blood, Sweat & Tears, which would sell more than 4 million copies in the U.S. and win the Grammy for album of the year.

His most lasting success came with the similarly brassy Chicago, which ruled the U.S. charts throughout the '70s, scoring 11 consecutive Guercio-produced platinum albums — five of them number ones. And if this wasn't enough, the bespectacled Renaissance man had a parallel motion-picture career, having produced, directed and scored the well-reviewed 1973 cop movie *Electra Glide in Blue* starring Robert Blake.

Never enjoying the music scenes in Los Angeles and New York, Guercio paid $2 million for a 3,000-acre property in Colorado's Rocky Mountains called Caribou Ranch, where he built a state-of-the-art recording studio in a converted barn.[1] It became the hottest place to record, hosting the likes of Elton John, Rod Stewart, Billy Joel and Earth, Wind & Fire. Set on running things his way, he also launched the Caribou Records label and management company.

He had the Midas touch, and Dennis thought The Beach Boys could use some of it. Following their meeting, Guercio flew to Seattle to check out the band in action at the 2,800-seat Paramount Theater, where they performed cuts mostly from their recent, moderate-selling releases. "They weren't playing many of the old songs," Guercio recalls. "They were really not making any money. I went back to Santa Monica with Carl and I said to them, 'If you guys listen to me, we'll be a big success in one year. You've got to let

Carl and I run the band.' And I pulled out all the old Beach Boys material. I said, 'You guys gotta trust me — we're going to do every old hit you ever did.'"

Guercio also served as a link between the group and Chicago, helping the bands realize the benefits of cross-pollination. When The Beach Boys were around for a Denver Coliseum gig, Chicago singer-bassist Peter Cetera, a huge fan of the band, invited Alan, Carl and Dennis up to Caribou to add harmonies to Chicago's "Wishing You Were Here,"[2] which topped *Billboard*'s Adult Contemporary chart.

The Beach Boys bought into Guercio's oldies concept, and soon the likes of "In My Room," "Little Deuce Coupe" and "Catch a Wave" crept onto the setlist. Blondie's departure had left a hole onstage, so Guercio, who admits he was "kind of bored with Chicago," took over bass duties when available, while Ed Carter could alternate between bass and guitar. The crackerjack touring band in 1974 was rounded out by multi-instrumentalist Billy Hinsche, Carli Muñoz and Ron Altbach on keyboards, and Bobby Figueroa on percussion and drums. With new manager Stephen Love minding the fort, Guercio ran the road show, putting the band through a grueling schedule.

"I said, 'Book every college in the United States. They're going to associate The Beach Boys and all the old music with homecoming and the spring prom,'" Guercio explains. "We made no money. We were making about $5,000 a night, and then by the spring it had generated huge word of mouth."

Sunny beaches and early '60s adolescent pursuits were as good a place as any to escape the lingering Vietnam War, stagflation, Watergate and President Richard Nixon's impending resignation. George Lucas' *American Graffiti*, set in 1962 and featuring "Surfin' Safari" and "All Summer Long" on its soundtrack, tapped into that hunger for nostalgia and became a sleeper box office smash. Meanwhile, Capitol Records, which had let its Beach Boys titles fall out of circulation, figured it was sitting on a potential goldmine, and on June 24 released *Endless Summer*, a two-record compilation of the band's best 1962–1965 recordings.

As the collection made its chart ascent, The Beach Boys played its revised show in front of massive crowds as the opener for Crosby, Stills, Nash & Young's groundbreaking outdoor stadium tour. Meanwhile, the group's sound was all over the radio again

with Carl, Bruce — who was still out of The Beach Boys — Billy Hinsche and Captain & Tennille singing backgrounds on Elton John's U.S. #2 hit "Don't Let the Sun Go Down on Me," providing further evidence of The Beach Boys' influence on new pop stars.

Unlikely as it was, this exposure helped propel *Endless Summer* all the way to the top of the U.S. charts by October, making it the group's second #1 album, following the 1964 concert record. The triple-platinum seller remained on the charts until 1978 and proved to be the defining release in the band's career. American record buyers had given up on worrying about whether or not The Beach Boys were hip and embraced the timelessness of their music. And there was a whole new generation of listeners out there who never had that hang-up in the first place.

All that was missing was an album of new material, and Guercio believed he could get one out of the band with Brian's involvement. In late fall, Dennis brought Brian to Caribou Ranch, where he stayed in the main house that had been previously occupied by the likes of Elton John and John Lennon. But as with the Holland expedition, Brian may have come along in body, but not quite in spirit. Guercio remembers, "From the day he got here, he said, 'I want to go home.'"

A handful of tracks were worked on at Caribou, the most notable being "Good Timin'," a pretty ballad written by Brian and Carl that recaptured the harmonic purity of "Surfer Girl." When Brian did get down to work on the track, he played keyboards, with Dennis on drums, Guercio on bass and Carl manning the board. But Brian's creative process had little flow.

"It was hard to get Brian's attention and focus," Guercio says. "Once he had a lock on a melody or a progression he would repeat it, but he might not have a chorus. We got a pretty good track but it wasn't a complete song. And then Brian said, 'Well, that's it. I did it, Jim. I'm done. Let's go to dinner.' So we walked up from the studio to the mess hall, and a few minutes later Brian came in with a suitcase and said, 'Okay, I'm ready to go. I want to go to the airport.' And I got up and walked over and said, 'Brian, we can't leave tonight.' And he'd go, 'Okay,' and sit down and eat. This happened four nights in a row. So we'd go back to the studio and he would say, 'I don't know if I can play it again.' It was a very traumatic period for him. This was a big thing to get Brian out of Bel Air."

Since Brian had laid down only one minute of the song, Guercio had to dupe Brian's keyboard part and string together sections to build the basic full-length track. Despite the music's quality — and the fact the band could have used a hit — it languished in the vaults for several years.

Other songs the band worked on around this time include, oddly, a rendition of "The Battle Hymn of the Republic," an early version of "Ding Dang," Dennis' "River Song," and "Child of Winter (Christmas Song)." It didn't add up to an album, and for the next year the group turned its attention back to its growing tour business. Their concerts had become such a big deal that they landed 1974 "band of the year" honors from *Rolling Stone* without having released an album of new material in two years.

Ahead of the summer of '75, Capitol, eager to keep riding the wave, released a best-of sequel to *Endless Summer* entitled *Spirit of America*, which peaked at #8 in the U.S. Meanwhile, as a recession-plagued industry geared up for the concert season, Guercio brought his two bands together on the same bill. The plan was for The Beach Boys to open for Chicago. (The concept had been given a dry run when the groups played together on Dick Clark's *New Year's Rockin' Eve* special that had rung in the year.) When Chicago would finish its set, The Beach Boys would join them on Chicago's "Wishing You Were Here," "Saturday in the Park" and "Feelin' Stronger Every Day," as well as "California Girls," "Fun, Fun, Fun" and "Jumpin' Jack Flash."

Despite Chicago's chart dominance at the time, The Beach Boys showed what they could do in front of a live audience with their unassailable catalog. "The Beach Boys, playing more than 1,000 miles from an ocean, stole the show," wrote *Rolling Stone*'s Eliot Wald of a date at Kansas' Arrowhead Stadium.[3] *Village Voice* critic Robert Christgau, reviewing the second of four sold-out Madison Square Garden shows, called The Beach Boys "a revelation, as beautiful as all the fools who compared them to Madrigal singers have always claimed them to be." Chicago, he added, was "tolerable."[4]

Billed as the Beachago tour, it put Guercio, who was still playing bass for The Beach Boys, in an awkward spot. "I loved The Beach Boys music and I actually wanted to blow Chicago off the stage, and we did," he says. "Here's Chicago with all these #1 records and The Beach Boys without a new record. There were huge fights with Chicago screaming and yelling at me. And I said, 'The only people responsible for getting blown off the stage by the opening act are you, so grow up.'"

Despite whatever professional rivalries may have existed between The Beach Boys and Chicago, there was plenty of friendship as well. But there was also a growing point of contention: Dennis' new romance with actress/model Karen Lamm, Chicago keyboardist Robert Lamm's ex-wife whom Dennis had met the previous October.[5] (Dennis had divorced second wife Barbara, with whom he had sons Michael and Carl, in 1974.) Guercio says that just as plans were developing to take the hugely successful tour international, the whole endeavor was scotched after Dennis and Karen married on May 21, 1976. It would take until 1989 for the Beachago concept to be revived for a North American tour.

Guercio, who would return to producing Chicago records up until and including 1977's *Chicago XI*, was relieved of his managerial duties with The Beach Boys, because, according to author Steven Gaines, some members felt Caribou was getting too big a cut of the concert revenue.[6] Nonetheless, Guercio remained interested in The Beach Boys — especially in their studio potential. He persuaded CBS Records, which distributed his Caribou label, to sign the band to an $8.5 million deal — including a $2 million advance[7] — in the process snatching them away from CBS' dreaded rival Warner Bros. He also secured a three-record solo deal for Dennis and would produce *Carl Wilson*, the first of Carl's two solo albums.

Dennis' *Pacific Ocean Blue* was released on the Caribou label in September 1977, followed in 1979 by *L.A. (Light Album)*, The Beach Boys' first album for CBS. It's no surprise "Good Timin'" would finally appear on Guercio's first LP with the group. He wanted to complete the track and oversee its mix but was busy in pre-production on the Steve McQueen Western *Tom Horn*, a directing gig that ultimately didn't pan out. The task of finishing the song fell to Bruce, whom The Beach Boys had invited back into the fold to produce the *L.A.* sessions.

The released version of "Good Timin'" features Carl singing the spare and moving lyrics about simple folks coming together to celebrate life. What really lifts it to the heavens, though, are the gorgeous double-tracked harmonies featuring Carl and Bruce covering four parts with a reported assist from Bobby Figueroa.[8] The second single off *L.A.*, it would make it — just — into the top 40.

In 1981, Guercio put together a two-record compilation including "Good Timin'" and the rest of the best of the group's 1970–1980 output, which became possible when he took over Warner Bros.' Beach Boys catalog. The resulting album, *Ten Years of Harmony*, is an interesting collection but was met with indifference, reaching only #156 in the U.S. and soon going out of print. Within a few years, Guercio would see all his Beach Boys titles vanish from store shelves — collateral damage, he claims, in a feud with notoriously difficult CBS president Walter Yetnikoff.

That experience, combined with a 1985 fire at Caribou Ranch that destroyed the studio control room, prompted Guercio's exit from the music biz. It would take the ghost of a Beach Boy to bring him back. He spearheaded the 2008 *Pacific Ocean Blue* reissue that also includes tracks from Dennis' never-completed follow-up album *Bambu*, and had plans to release a collection called *Tornado* — the title of Dennis' projected third LP — which he says would include "some recorded tracks Dennis never finished, some remixes of *POB* and some unreleased *POB*." Guercio also was drawn back into the film industry as executive producer on *The Drummer*, a planned biopic about Dennis.

And he can reflect on his participation on "Good Timin'" and the key role he played in The Beach Boys amazing mid-'70s comeback, which charted them on a whole new course. At the root of all his efforts was always his love for the music. "Brian's stuff was unique harmonically and structurally and I enjoyed playing it," he says. "I thought it was the most representative American music of the 20th century."

EARLE MANKEY ON...
IT'S OK

Written by: Brian Wilson and Mike Love
Lead vocal: Mike Love with Dennis Wilson
Produced by: Brian Wilson
Recorded: Fall 1974, March 1976
Released: July 5, 1976, on *15 Big Ones*
and as a single August 9, 1976
Chart peak: U.S. #29

In the mid-'70s, The Beach Boys set up Brother Studio so group members could record whenever they had the urge. For Brian, though, the thought of entering a studio and trying to recapture the old magic remained a frightening proposition. It was a period marked by his cocaine consumption, dramatic weight gain and artistic inertia. His brothers, on the other hand, eagerly took advantage.

"Dennis and Carl were recording all day long, coming back and working again and again on songs," recalls Earle Mankey, Brother Studio engineer. "There weren't really comments about what a recording would be for. I assumed because they were The Beach Boys, it would get released. But all through that time we wondered, 'Is Brian going to show up or not?' It was like that for a year or two."

Mankey had studied electronic engineering at UCLA and played guitar in gonzo band Halfnelson, which mutated into cult favorite Sparks. But he preferred a behind-the-scenes role and left in 1972. Soon afterwards he had a gig helping finish construction on The Beach Boys' new custom-designed recording console — the same unit that would be shipped overseas for the *Holland* recordings. "When they brought it back, they dropped it off the airplane onto the tarmac, which didn't do it any good," Mankey says. "They said, 'We gotta get somebody over here to put this thing back together.' I pretty much spent most of my time at their studio for the next few years."

Working under Steve Moffitt, Mankey did much of the group's hands-on engineering, adapting to the Wilson brothers' respective work hours. None were early risers, but Carl would be first in the studio, while Dennis tended to work through the night. It was all fine by Mankey. "I really loved The Beach Boys. I knew their history and I could grill them about old sessions they'd done. I was happy as a clam," he says.

One of the sessions Brian did show up for, likely in late fall 1974, was for "It's OK," a funky, upbeat song he and Mike had written that took a philosophical stance towards summertime fun: life is fleeting, so enjoy it while you can. The session was made especially memorable by the participation of Roy Wood, the big-haired British prog-rock pioneer who cofounded The Move and Electric Light Orchestra and who was at the time leading the band Wizzard. The setup was arranged by Mankey's friend John Mendelsohn, the former Sparks drummer who became a noted

Rolling Stone critic. Wood adored Brian, and for Mankey it was a once-in-a-lifetime opportunity to work with two of his idols together.

The session began uncommonly early — meaning late morning/early afternoon — and it was all Mankey could do to keep up with the two eccentric legends. Wood and his Wizzard mates Mike Burney and Nick Pentelow, also present, were credited only for playing saxophones on "It's OK,"[1] but the engineer recalls that they worked on several tracks.

"They just went frantically from song to song and part to part, putting things on all these tracks," Mankey recalls. "I'd run to the library and put up a song and they'd work on it. Roy was fast and played it all. On one song he would do the drums, one song he'd do the saxophone, one song he'd do bass or guitar. After about the third or fourth thing they were working on, Brian, who obviously didn't have a clue who Roy was, finally said, 'Uh, what's your instrument?' But Roy was just tickled pink to be doing anything with Brian."

As the session went on, Wood decided to take things up a notch. "He said, 'Let's get some rocket fuel!' and he pulled out a flask of something," Mankey says. "It didn't seem to slow him down. He was pretty manic. I doubt

As Brian tentatively returned to active duty at Brother Studio, Carl helped build tracks for a new album. [© Ed Roach]

Brian was drunk, because we were always very careful about not allowing Brian to have any drugs or alcohol. By the end of the day, the session kind of dribbled apart. It was an exciting thing for me — and a disappointing thing when they rushed through all of these songs and I couldn't tell for sure if they'd actually

gotten anything."

Still, it was a rare burst of creativity for Brian at that time. Marilyn was nearing her limit with his depressive behavior, and in late 1975 hired Hollywood psychotherapist Dr. Eugene Landy to help him return to overall health. Landy, whose clientele included actor

Richard Harris, harbored showbiz aspirations, and as a young man had discovered jazz guitarist George Benson. A 1976 *Rolling Stone* piece stated that he had done PR for various record labels,[2] but his later claim of having co-produced Barry McGuire's "Eve of Destruction" was adamantly refuted by P.F. Sloan, the song's composer.[3]

Landy's approach, which he called "milieu therapy," was to monitor Brian 24 hours a day. Under his instruction, Marilyn rid the Bellagio house of all drugs, cigarettes, alcohol and fatty foods, and he put Brian on a strict regimen of daily exercise. His fees were exorbitant — ballooning to $20,000 per month — but when Brian shed 40 pounds,[4] it seemed like things were on the right track. Landy even argued that he should be entitled to a percentage of Brian's earnings.[5]

"I can't think of anybody who ever had anything good to say about Landy," Mankey says. "But on the other hand, Brian *was* in the studio working. He otherwise might have just floated around forever. I'd heard Landy say, 'Brian's farther gone than you guys know, and to get him to function will take a big part of my life.' So there might've been more there than we know."

Meanwhile, The Beach Boys, who were now selling out arenas across the country, hadn't capitalized with a new LP in three years. And most concertgoers were paying to hear songs off *Endless Summer*, all of which had been produced by Brian. So the key ingredient needed on the next album, all believed, was to have Brian in charge. Sessions got underway in early 1976 on what would be Brian's first solo production of a Beach Boys album since *Pet Sounds*. And if that seemed a dubious enough plan given Brian's recent state, here was the kicker: he would also tour with them for the first time since 1964.

There had been talk of making a double-album, consisting of one record of new material and one of oldies covers, but the LP ultimately was a one-platter affair titled *15 Big Ones* — a nod to both the band's 15th anniversary and the number of tracks contained therein. There were eight oldies cuts, focusing on the kind of R&B and doo-wop on which the guys grew up. "I don't know who decided to do the old songs, but I imagine it was Brian because that would probably be the easiest, laziest thing that he could possibly do," Mankey says with a laugh. Combining oldies such as "Palisades Park" and "A Casual Look" with some Brian originals would, hopefully, approximate the flavor of the group's early records.

To ease Brian back into the producer's chair, a session for "Blueberry Hill" was arranged with many of his favorite players from his 1960s heyday, including Hal Blaine, Ray Pohlman, Steve Douglas, Jay Migliori, Julius Wechter, Tommy Tedesco, Carl Fortina and old face Bruce Johnston.

"The place was jammed," Mankey recalls. "We started getting mikes together and figuring out how to get monitoring for everybody, and Brian comes in and says, 'All right, let's go!' and they started playing. We barely got the tape recorder turned on. We were still setting up. You can hear by the way the musicians play that they were still working it out. Then the song finishes and Brian says, 'That was great, guys! Let's call it a wrap.' Brian saw a thousand guys, got intimidated and just wanted to leave."

One way Brian kept some of the other sessions more intimate was by playing various parts himself on Moog and Arp synthesizers. The use of these instruments would lend *15 Big Ones* an uncharacteristically electronic sheen and signal a new sonic direction for Brian. "It was a discovery for him that he could fake the string parts on a synth and not have to worry about anything else," Mankey says. "He was in there to play the part and get out."

By this point, the group had evolved into two clear factions, as the sessions would demonstrate. Carl and Dennis helped Brian build the tracks, and then Mike and Alan showed up to add just their vocal parts. "All the people at the studio were always wishing Brian could come in and were feeling sorry for him," Mankey recalls. "'Oh Brian, can't we help you do a better job? Brian, we love you — let's do some more work.' But Mike and Al would come in and we'd play things back for them Brian had done and they'd just make faces. They just thought it was crap. They'd show up and say it was terrible."

Alan's lone writing contribution on the album is the catchy "Susie Cincinnati," which had already served as the B-side to "Add Some Music to Your Day" while Mike's "Everyone's in Love with You" — a love song to the Maharishi — marked his second solo composition on a Beach Boys record. Given the ever-present tension between Dennis and Mike, it was surprising to hear Dennis in a radio interview praising Mike's tune as "the most beautiful song I've ever heard." On that count, Mankey suggests that perhaps Dennis "had something to drink and he was feeling magnanimous." The album was completed in spring 1976, and Mankey, credited as engineer on five tracks, says he felt "a little bit embarrassed" by it. "It was just a total cacophonous disaster when it happened. Now it just sounds like a messy record," he adds.

Nonetheless, it satisfied America's pent-up demand for new music from its again-favorite sons. The lead single, a busy, synthed-out arrangement of Chuck Berry's "Rock and Roll Music," went all the way to #5 in the U.S. after a May release, making it the group's biggest U.S. hit since "Good Vibrations." The LP followed on July 5 with the nation buzzing on its bicentennial high and reached #8 in the U.S., remaining on the charts for the rest of the year despite mixed reviews.

One of the highlights is "It's OK," which the group dug up and fleshed out with strong harmonies. Dennis provides a memorable bass-vocal "Yeah!" and sings an irresistible tag, while lead vocalist Mike is — as Bruce said in a promo podcast for the 2007 compilation *The Warmth of the Sun* — "at his nasal finest." In the same podcast, Mike cites the song as a favorite for its positivity, while

Brian cryptically comments that it "doesn't bring back real pleasant memories," although he does express fondness for the bass line he played on the Moog, as well as Mike's lyrics and the fade.[6]

"It's OK" was released as a single in August — curiously sped up from the album version — and reached #29 in America. Mike griped that it would have done better had it been released earlier in the summer,[7] but it was nonetheless the group's highest-charting original song in the U.S. for the entire decade. (That is, unless you count the movie theme song "Almost Summer," co-written by Alan, Brian and Mike and recorded by Mike's side group Celebration. It peaked at #28 in 1978.)

Also that month, NBC aired the one-hour special *The Beach Boys* produced by *Saturday Night Live*'s Lorne Michaels and best remembered for a skit in which *SNL*'s John Belushi and Dan Aykroyd, dressed as highway patrolmen, burst in on Brian in his bedroom and charge him with "failing to surf." They escort him to the beach and direct him to mount a surfboard, on which he lies before being pummeled by waves. In November, Brian appeared solo on *Saturday Night Live*, playing an awkward rendition of "Good Vibrations" in a room full of sand. It was all part of a massive "Brian Is Back" campaign spearheaded by Stephen Love. There were cover stories in *People* and *Rolling Stone* and a Brian interview on *The Mike Douglas Show*. If the focus was on his reclusive behavior and drug abuse and the fact that relations within the group were not so harmonious, well, there's no such thing as bad publicity.

Mankey, who worked for the band until the sale of Brother Studio in 1978, points out that even if Brian seemed at odds with it all, his record-making skills were essentially intact. "He struck me as having plenty of control, but he didn't want to be doing what *you* wanted to be doing. I never got the feeling that he could be in the studio and not know what to do or what to say to somebody if he had to say it. He was good at that," Mankey says.

And, as it turns out, he was just getting warmed up.

PETER AMES CARLIN ON...
JOHNNY CARSON

Written by: Brian Wilson
Lead vocal: Mike Love and Carl Wilson
Produced by: Brian Wilson
Recorded: November 10, 1976
Released: April 11, 1977, on *The Beach Boys Love You*

If part of the point of *15 Big Ones* was to reacclimate Brian with the studio, artistically it paid off. In late fall 1976, he recorded enough original tracks for the next album and then some. Earle Mankey recalls Brian adhering to a more disciplined regimen. He would come down to Brother Studio every morning at 10 or 11 and work until early afternoon. Landy was employing a carrot-and-stick approach. As Brother Studio manager Trisha Campo recounts in Peter Ames Carlin's *Catch a Wave: The Rise, Fall & Redemption of The Beach Boys' Brian Wilson*, Landy would have one of his lackeys hovering over Brian with a baseball bat, as if to say, "Write songs or else!"[1] But, according to Mankey, if Brian did as he was told, he got one joint — a guilty pleasure Landy allowed.

Sitting at the piano at Brother, Brian would sing about whatever crossed his mind. After staring at a stained-glass window of the stars he came up with "Solar System."[2] In several other compositions he looked to revive the adolescent perspective of the pre–*Pet Sounds* era, writing about roller skating, classroom crushes and dealing with your girlfriend's folks. But having The Beach Boys, now grizzled rock stars, sing these teenage ditties made the tunes a little creepy. Nonetheless, these are the themes Brian imagined fans wanted. The fast — and presumed fun — songs would occupy side one of the next album, *The Beach Boys Love You*, while on the second side a more adult point of view would be reflected in the nocturnal longings of "The Night Was So Young" and in the parental affection of "I Wanna Pick You Up."

Of course, Brian was no ordinary adult. Carlin, in an interview with this author, calls the record "a tour through the cracked funhouse mirror of Brian's imagination. He's got this weird story he wants to tell — a suspended-animation story about this young, rich pop star who essentially has been on the bench for 10 years, living in his own world and who has to some degree lost his connection to reality."

It was the closest any Beach Boys album came to being a Brian solo record. He is credited with the words and music on all cuts except the co-writes "Let Us Go on This Way" (with Mike), the 1970 *Sunflower* outtake "Good Time" (with Alan) and "Ding Dang" (with Roger McGuinn). He expediently plays nearly all the parts himself, leaning even heavier on the buzzing, honking, gurgling, bleeping

Moog synthesizer than he did on *15 Big Ones*. Electronic textures define the record's oddball sound, which is miles removed from the organic, orchestral feel of old. Brian even handled much of the drumming, building tracks on a simple hit of the floor tom and snare. "This guy whose life was built for a very particular kind of music is now throwing up stuff that says, 'Ladies and gentlemen, I don't give a shit' — except for the fact that he can't help but write really interesting songs," says Carlin, a former writer for *People* and *The Oregonian* and author of *Paul McCartney: A Life*.

Dennis participated in some of the tracking, as did Carl, who is also credited as "mixdown producer." Mike and Alan again were rarely around, but everyone ended up singing several leads. Billy Hinsche was tapped to sing "Honkin' Down the Highway" but recalls getting into a dispute with Landy, who then convinced Brian to scrap his vocal. Alan would rerecord it for the released version. Alan's intact voice, along with those of Carl and Mike, provide a welcome respite from Brian's and Dennis' leads, which are in places just as strained as they had been on the previous album.

"It's strange how Brian's voice is so rough and bad on that record. This is a guy who years earlier would stop takes because he didn't think the background 'ooo's' had enough emotion. Now he's singing in this gravelly, messed-up baritone and often slightly off-key. It's the behavior of a very different kind of person, and in some ways it almost feels like a suicidal gesture," says Carlin. The author remembers eagerly picking up the album as an eighth grader. "I was at the height of my excitement created by *15 Big Ones* and the joyous sense of Brian being back," he continues. "This was his big return — all original songs; a complete Brian production. And you listen to it and you were like, '*What the hell is this?*' It's so different."

Everything about the album was peculiar, starting with the title. Reportedly, Brian had wanted to call it *Brian Loves You*[3] as a thank-you to fans for their support. The change to *The Beach Boys Love You* echoed a dedication on the inner sleeve from Carl, Dennis, Mike and Alan that begins "To Brian whom we love with all our hearts . . ." Dean Torrence lobbied to have the record titled *Cowabunga*, a term that had been Chief Thunderthud's catch-all exclamation on *Howdy Doody*. It was hardly authentic Native American, but it tied into both the cover — which Torrence designed

to look like a Navajo rug — and the Brother Records' logo based on Cyrus Dallin's Native American statue *Appeal to the Great Spirit*. The expression was also adopted by surfers as a yell of exhilaration, and as such captures the LP's sometimes joyful abandon.

Members of the group have attributed the album's ultimate lack of sales to apathetic promotion by Warner Bros., which was aware the band was jumping ship to CBS. In a 2009 *Record Collector* interview, Alan points even to the record jacket, which has an unusual matte finish. "Everything about that thing is homemade. . . . They didn't spend a penny on *Love You*. . . . They used real cheap cardboard," he said.[4] But according to Torrence, a paper of above-average cost was used to simulate a stitched texture. Featuring the album title in colored squares, the cover inadvertently suggests a Lite-Brite toy, which suits the childlike wonder of the record's contents.

Warner Bros. certainly showed apathy by not issuing a preview single to build anticipation around the LP. "Honkin' Down the Highway" was released seven weeks after *The Beach Boys Love You* hit stores, and after the album had plummeted to #108 on the U.S. charts from its #53 peak. (It made it to #28 in the U.K.) "Honkin'" is tremendously goofy and catchy rock 'n' roll, but missed the charts altogether. If Warner Bros. had wanted to really get people talking, it might have instead chosen "Johnny Carson," Carlin's favorite cut on the album. "It's a fascinating piece of work," he says of the song. "It stops you dead. And it takes something to make people look at each other and go, 'What the fuck? What is this? What is this about?'"

What — or rather, who — it's about is exactly what the title says: John William "Johnny" Carson, king of American late-night TV — then 51 and halfway through his remarkable 30-year run as host of *The Tonight Show*. "Brian is musing on how masculine Johnny is, how charming and how he can just go and go and kick ass," Carlin notes. "He's like the surfer of the airwaves, the king of the beach. He won't stop. He can't stop. He's just such a winner." Not unlike Brian for a stretch in the '60s.

Who else but Brian would have even *thought* to write a song about Johnny Carson? Those who find it beyond the pale are missing Brian's dry sense of humor, underlined by Mike's lead vocal delivery. Since the beginning, Brian displayed a comical eye for unlikely subject matter — how about "Chug-a-Lug," that ode to root beer off *Surfin' Safari*, or the *Smile* numbers "Vega-Tables" and "Wind Chimes"?

The music in "Johnny Carson" is as unique as the words — a Wall of Sound built on synths, organ and piano. Carlin remembers a DJ spinning it on FM station OK 102 and a half in his Seattle hometown. "I remember he said, 'Here's a song from the new Beach Boys record that I really love. What really knocks me out is that organ solo,'" Carlin recalls. "So I'm listening and thinking, 'Organ solo? What organ solo?' And then I realize it's that part at the end — it's like three notes: 'dun, dun, dun, dun, ba ba da bum!' It's simple, but there's something really anthemic and powerful about it, too. It's yet another herald for our man Johnny."

Carlin feels the entire track is put together with great purpose. "Brian is doing something really interesting musically," he says. "The rhythm — the way he uses the synths and drums — sounds like a factory. It sounds like serious work is being done. It's got this crunch and grind and those hooting synthesizers. It sounds like machinery moving, and he's singing this tune about Carson — the longtime, hugely successful, completely unbeatable host of *The Tonight Show*."

In a 1979 *Rolling Stone* interview, Timothy White asked Carson if he had heard the song. The TV host was either humbled by the tribute or as baffled as many others. "Sure I heard it," he replied. "Someone sent it over to the office. I don't think it was a big seller. I think they just did it for the fun of it. It was *not* a work of art."[5]

For some, neither is *The Beach Boys Love You*. For casual listeners, it's way too idiosyncratic, while some fans have a hard time with the rough-and-ready vocals and production. To them, Carlin observes, "It's Brian being lazy, nobody caring enough to make the record what it ought to have been, and the other guys letting him get by with what are essentially pretty chintzy demos." But it found immediate champions among highly esteemed critics including *Circus*' Lester Bangs, *Creem*'s Mitchell Cohen, *NME*'s Nick Kent, *Village Voice*'s Robert Christgau and *Rolling Stone*'s Billy Altman. "Godmother of Punk" Patti Smith was moved to pen a poetic response in *Hit Parader*. To them, a great Beach Boys record didn't need high-minded lyrics or a chamber orchestra. It just needed Brian's

unbridled creativity, and this was the first Beach Boys project that offered that through and through since *Smile* went down. Brian has on several occasions referred to the album as his favorite.

After years of prog-rock and overproduced AM cheese, some welcomed the record's rawness as an almost punk-rock statement and now see it as a progenitor of new wave. Carlin lines up with these supporters. "It was hard to get into at first, but it's kind of funky. The songs have a rough-edged charm of their own. When I get into listening to the record, I *really* get into listening to it," he says.

For all those who got into it, the LP promised Brian was indeed back and that the future looked bright. But after it stiffed commercially, his level of engagement would decline again, as would his physical and mental condition. The group had fired Landy before 1976 was out, fed up with his salary and the way he had assumed the role of Brian's unofficial manager and tried to run group meetings. That left Brian's physical rehabilitation to Mike's brother Stan Love, a 6'9" former Los Angeles Laker, and Rocky Pamplin, a former Canadian Football League player and *Playgirl* model.

Brian composed eight of the dozen songs

on the 1978 follow-up *M.I.U. Album*, but was credited as "executive producer" while Alan and keyboardist Ron Altbach assumed the producers' chairs. The record took a critical drubbing, matching *Sunflower*'s humiliating #151 U.S. chart performance and becoming the group's first studio album to miss the U.K. charts since the Christmas record in 1964. The following year saw the release of *L.A. (Light Album)*, produced by Bruce, which sold better (U.S. #100, U.K. #32) and spun off singles including a disco-fied version of *Wild Honey*'s

"Here Comes the Night" (U.S. #44, U.K. #37), "Good Timin'" (U.S. #40) and "Lady Lynda" (U.K. #6), Alan's Bach-inspired ode to his then-wife, Lynda Sperry.

"*The Beach Boys Love You* was the last time the group really let Brian take the reins," Carlin says. "After that it was 'We don't trust you; *we're* going to do *this*; you have too much control and too many copyrights; you're out of your head.' On *L.A.* there are some songs I really like. From there, the soup gets really thin."

BILLY HINSCHE ON . . .
FAREWELL MY FRIEND

Written by: Dennis Wilson
Lead vocal: Dennis Wilson
Produced by: Dennis Wilson and Gregg Jakobson
Recorded: April–May 1976
Released: September 1977 on *Pacific Ocean Blue*

As Dennis' writing and production skills matured throughout the '70s, landing a couple of his songs on Beach Boys albums had become an insufficient outlet. By early 1976, as *15 Big Ones* turned into a nearly all-Brian affair, the time finally had come for Dennis to branch out, and he and co-producer Gregg Jakobson got started on *Pacific Ocean Blue*, the first solo LP by a Beach Boy.

One of the cuts, the heartfelt ballad "Farewell My Friend," is a tribute to the late Otto "Pop" Hinsche, father of Billy Hinsche. In a 1977 interview in the *Pet Sounds* fanzine, Dennis told David Leaf that when Murry had died four years earlier, "Pop saved my life in a way."[1] Billy explains that Dennis was close to Pop even when Murry was alive. "They just clicked," he says. "They had their own private world together. They'd just have fun and share stuff. Dennis had a relationship with my dad that I didn't have. It wasn't so much a father-and-son relationship as it was a pal relationship."

Dennis often cruised around with Pop, who was more than 50 years his elder. One day, Dennis brought him to the high-end Battaglia shoe store on Rodeo Drive. "Dennis wanted to get Pop a pair of shoes," Billy recalls. "The store owner came over and Dennis decided to have some fun. He told him, 'Look at my friend — look how old he is. Why don't you just *give* him a pair of shoes?' So the guy gave my dad a really expensive pair of shoes. They both laughed about it later."

Pop was born in Hoboken, New Jersey, in 1893 and later moved to the Philippines, where he was sent to a civilian POW camp during the Japanese occupation in World War II. He later owned a popular supper club in Manila, but during the Korean War returned to the U.S. to avoid the risk of another incarceration. He settled his family in Beverly Hills, where young Billy attended the Good Shepherd Catholic School alongside the progeny of many Hollywood celebrities. There Billy met Dean "Dino" Paul Martin, the son of Dean Martin, and Desi Arnaz Jr., the son of Desi Arnaz and Lucille Ball. The three formed bubblegum rock band Dino, Desi & Billy, which went on to make numerous mid-'60s TV appearances and scored the top 30 hits "I'm a Fool" and "Not the Lovin' Kind."

The Hinsches would become part of The Beach Boys family. The first point of intersection came in 1965, when Dino, Desi & Billy performed at The Beach Boys' Summer Spectacular at the Hollywood Bowl. The two groups met at sound check, where Billy, who had just turned 14, bonded with Carl over their 360/12 Fireglo guitars. Dino, Desi & Billy opened for The Beach Boys at several more gigs over the next couple of years, including some on a pair of trips to Honolulu. In Waikiki, Bruce took Billy and Desi surfing, marking the first and last time Billy got on a surfboard.

Coincidentally, Billy's older sister Annie had a friend who was dating Bruce in '65 and accompanied her to the Los Angeles airport to greet The Beach Boys, who were returning from a tour. Carl met Annie and was immediately smitten. They were soon dating, and around Christmas time 19-year-old Carl proposed to 16-year-old Annie. By February, they were married. Carl, like Brian, was serious about his emotions from an early age. "He had a great sense of humor, but he was serious about most things," Billy says of his former brother-in-law.

Annie and Billy were present for the recording of *Beach Boys' Party!* album, on which Billy contributed harmonica to "Mountain of Love." He continued guesting on the group's records while Pop tried to persuade Brian to write a song for Dino, Desi &

Billy. Brian came through with "Lady Love," an upbeat number with a yearning lyric that became one of the trio's final singles. "I made a few suggestions. Brian was very generous in giving me a writer's credit. It was a thrill," Billy says.

In 1969, an even more thrilling opportunity presented itself. According to Billy, there was talk of Bruce leaving the band long before it actually happened. He recalls Mike, Brian, Carl, Dennis and Beach Boys manager Nick Grillo coming to the Hinsche home, where Billy still lived with his parents, and inviting him to officially join the group. (Alan didn't take part in such decisions since he did not become a band shareholder until 1973.[2])

"I said yes, but then Nick and my dad had a powwow," recalls Billy, who was crushed when his parents kiboshed the offer. "This would have been a major step for me to leave my group and to not continue with my education. My parents didn't have the opportunity to get a higher education and they wanted me to have that. My sister married at an early age and so it fell on my shoulders. That was heartbreaking. I cried myself to sleep that night."

Shortly after Billy's dream of becoming a Beach Boy was dashed, Dino, Desi & Billy

disbanded and he went off to study at UCLA, majoring in motion pictures and television. He joined The Beach Boys onstage when his studies permitted, playing guitar and keyboards and taking on Brian's harmony parts. He can be heard singing the high end on "Surfin' U.S.A.," "Fun, Fun, Fun" and other tracks on *The Beach Boys in Concert*. He came along with the group for *Holland* — he sings backgrounds on "Funky Pretty" — and afterwards played bass on a couple of tours. One of his most treasured credits is singing backgrounds on Elton John's "Don't Let the Sun Go Down on Me," for which he says he is "eternally grateful" to Bruce, the song's vocal arranger, for including him.

Back at school, he began working with an early mobile video recorder called a Portapak and brought it along to document the group's U.S. tours from April to June 1974. Three decades later, he stumbled upon the reel-to-reel tapes in his garage, and set about editing the material into several DVD projects. *Dennis Wilson Forever* combines footage of the drummer and new interviews Billy conducted with some of those who knew him best, while *1974: On the Road with The Beach Boys* features grainy behind-the-scenes video of the

Co-producer Gregg Jakobson (left) kept Dennis focused enough to complete his solo album *Pacific Ocean Blue*.
[Courtesy Gregg Jakobson]

band touring just as they were climbing back to the top.

What we see of Dennis in *1974* is most revealing. At one point he commandeers the camera and has a willing young woman privately pose for him. Billy includes just a short clip and treats the image with an x-ray effect to hide the woman's identity. Billy calls it the "casting couch scene." "It's just so funny to me," he says. "Dennis says to her, 'I've hardly ever done this before.' Give me a break."

"He was a complex person," Billy says of

Dennis. "He could be a clown. He was there to make you laugh. You don't see the tender side of Dennis all the time. You're more likely to see the ebullient, enthusiastic, flamboyant, extroverted side. But the depth of his emotions is reflected in all that great cross-genre music that he wrote."

One emotional song Dennis took to singing at mid-1970s concerts was "You Are So Beautiful," which had been a #5 U.S. hit for Joe Cocker. Fans may have wondered why Dennis, who had written a number of great ballads himself, would be so drawn to performing somebody else's composition — this one credited to funk artist and legendary keyboardist Billy Preston along with Bruce Fisher. Part of the reason, Billy explains, is that Dennis was actually involved in the iconic tune's creation. It happened at the West Hollywood condo of America's Gerry Beckley, where a group of buddies ended up after a night at the Rainbow Bar and Grill on the Sunset Strip.

"Billy Preston was at the piano playing this beautiful song," Billy recalls. "There were some lyrics and melodies being sung, and out of the corner of my ear and the corner of my eye I witnessed Dennis and Billy working on it and Dennis singing his heart out. I don't know

how much of it Billy had already written, and I don't know how much Dennis brought to the party. Maybe it was just his interpretation of the song. Later Dennis said to me, 'Well, you know, I helped write that song.'" At shows, Billy Hinsche played piano as Dennis serenaded the audience with the number, stirring them before the finale. "The crowd always went wild for Dennis, but particularly when he did that song," Billy says. The only officially released version of Dennis performing the tune is on *Good Timin': Live at Knebworth England 1980*.

In 1974, after Billy finished his schooling, he became a full-time Beach Boys touring player, taking the lead vocal on gems "I'm Waiting for the Day" and "Sail on Sailor." His voice can also be heard in backgrounds on *Pacific Ocean Blue*. One night around the time of those sessions, while Pop was in the hospital, Dennis was driving around Westwood in his Porsche when part of one of his teeth fell out. "He took that as a sign that something was wrong with Pop and that he needed to go see him, which he did," Billy recalls. "Later he called me from the UCLA Medical Center and told me Pop had died in his arms. It was late at night. He was the only person with him."

A few nights later, Dennis came into Brother Studio, sat intently at the piano and worked out the words and melody to "Farewell My Friend," which built on an existing track called "Hawaiian Dream."[3] He recorded the vocal immediately.[4] The lyric could hardly be simpler, consisting of only 28 different words, but Dennis' delivery — both mourning and celebratory — is deeply moving. The track, floating on piano, marimbas and steel guitar, is understated and beautiful. Most arresting is an electronic effect that evokes the sound of tropical birds and, symbolically, the soul taking flight. The Hawaiian vibe is appropriate, as Pop loved the islands, where he vacationed regularly with his family. Billy says he also hears the Philippines in the music.

Pacific Ocean Blue was in stores by September 1977, earning strong reviews and peaking at #96 on *Billboard*. The centerpiece is opener "River Song," a plea for nature over city living, put over with Brian-like symphonic grandeur and gospel flavor courtesy of the Double Rock Baptist Choir. Dennis' voice is raspy after years of drugs, booze and cigarettes. It's not pretty, but it adds plenty of lived-in emotion to the ballads "Moonshine" and "Thoughts of You," both about the

dissolution of his rocky marriage to Karen Lamm. The melancholy love songs, rich harmonies and exotic instrumentation are classic Beach Boys, but given a 1970s spin.

That November, *Rolling Stone* reported that Mike had fired most of The Beach Boys' touring band, Billy included.[5] "It was about lifestyle," Billy explains. "He wanted a band that was all meditators. As much as possible, he wanted a crew that was also all meditators. I don't think he ever got that."

Carl and Annie, who had sons Jonah and Justyn, divorced in 1980 but Carl and Billy remained close. "It was Carl's way that somehow he made it okay, and I made it okay," says Billy, who joined Carl's tour in support of his self-titled solo album the following year. After Carl reunited with The Beach Boys in 1982, Billy soon also came back. It wasn't an altogether happy return, however, as Dennis died soon thereafter. "Farewell My Friend," the song Dennis wrote in memory of Billy's father, was, at Lamm's suggestion, played at his own funeral.

The 2008 rerelease of *Pacific Ocean Blue*, which had been out-of-print for 17 years, was a top 10 seller for online retailer Amazon in the U.S. and Canada, and reached #16 in the

U.K. and #5 in Norway. *Rolling Stone, Mojo* and *Uncut* banded together to crown the album "re-issue of the year." A quarter-century after his death, the bad-boy Beach Boy finally received the recognition that proved elusive for most of his short, turbulent life.

Billy played with The Beach Boys until 1995 and later assumed the role of musical director in Alan's band. He sat in with Mike's Beach Boys and also toured extensively with Brian. He released subsequent DVD documentaries about The Beach Boys, including *Carl Wilson — Here and Now* and the tour film *24 Hours*. The thing that prevented him from becoming an official Beach Boy — his university film training — led to a new role. "It makes sense to me now, although it didn't at the time," he says. "Carl and Dennis are no longer with us, yet I have them forever young on film and video. I guess it's just part of my destiny to bring these films to the public and keep their memory alive."

Randy Bachman on...
Keepin' The Summer Alive

Written by: Carl Wilson and Randy Bachman
Lead vocal: Carl Wilson
Produced by: Carl Wilson and Bruce Johnston
Recorded: August 27–29, 1979, and various dates
October 1979–February 1980
Released: March 17, 1980, on *Keepin' the Summer Alive*

As the '70s drew to a close, there were problems in Beach Boys land. When it came time to record the next album, Brian could not take the lead. He was going through even harder times than usual after his marriage crumbled. As Marilyn explained in a 1991 *Rolling Stone* interview, when she saw Brian's behavior — marked by a return of substance abuse — as detrimental to their children's well-being, she finally said, "I've had it," and the couple divorced.[1] Dennis, meanwhile, barely participated in the new sessions, reportedly due to his aversion to the new material and his ongoing grudge match with some members of the group. The band was losing its way in the studio and would release only two albums of new material in the 1980s, compared to eight the decade before.

The first of those '80s releases, *Keepin' the Summer Alive*, was on the whole competent, but offered few highlights. With production credited to Bruce, it suffers from both its hodgepodge construction — having been assembled at no fewer than four studios — and a glossy but flat sound. It stalled at #75 in the U.S. and #54 in the U.K.

The lament "Goin' On" from Brian and Mike was tapped as the first single, climbing no higher than #83 in the U.S. Elsewhere on the LP, the band returns to the Chuck Berry well once again with Alan singing a rendition of "School Day (Ring! Ring! Goes the Bell)." Alan also contributes the ecologically minded "Santa Ana Winds," which loses some of the charm from a 1978 demo with different lyrics. The band even digs back 10 years to revive the outtake "When Girls Get Together," which boasts an interesting orchestral Brian production but is presented in a poor remix. Bruce's ballad closer "Endless Harmony" provides a corny account of the group's history but boasts excellent harmony vocals in the tag and grew in stature after Alan Boyd borrowed the title for his 1998 documentary.

Among the better songs are a pair co-written by Carl and Randy Bachman, guitar legend and founding member of The Guess Who and Bachman-Turner Overdrive. In 1979, Bachman's new band Ironhorse opened for The Beach Boys on a U.S. tour, after which Carl invited him up to Caribou Ranch to co-write some songs. "Carl said to Brian, 'I'm going to write with Randy. Do you want to come?' And Brian said, 'You know, I can't write anymore' and just shrugged it off. So I went with Carl and we wrote four or five really

good songs," Bachman recalls. Their collaboration yielded the two numbers for *Keepin' the Summer Alive* — the title track and "Livin' with a Heartache" — as well as an homage to "Don't Worry Baby" called "What's Your Hurry, Darlin'?" (which Ironhorse recorded), "The Very First Time in My Life," "Something Better," "Ace" and "California Nights."[2]

"Keepin' the Summer Alive" was Bachman's idea — a harmless slice of fun in the sun that recalls the early Beach Boys hits he grooved to when he and Chad Allan were trying to get The Guess Who off the ground. It also pretty much sums up The Beach Boys' philosophy at this point, both on record and onstage. As Bachman explains, the opening line was inspired by his frigid Canadian hometown. "Everything's closed in Winnipeg in the winter," says the axman. "Then the snow melts, and May 1st all the ice cream places open and you call it 'ice cream weather' and you drive up and down Main Street and you get a milkshake at Dairy Queen."

Bachman recalls providing the title, first verse and a hook, while "Carl changed a whole bunch of other lyrics and came up with a really great bass part." The song begins with a classic Mike bass-vocal segment pulled from The Beach Boys' cover of "Louie, Louie" off *Shut Down Volume 2*, but sung with the chord progression reversed. "We were just goofing around, having fun," Bachman says. "The Beach Boys music was all about fun, and that's what I was trying to put in the songwriting with Carl."

Although satisfied with the composition, Bachman was disappointed with the version the Beach Boys ultimately released, which softened the demo he and Carl had produced at Bachman's studio in Lynden, Washington. "I had power guitars and scorching, distorted Hammond B-3 organ under it and heavy drums," he explains. "It was a massive power hit like 'Louie Louie' with rockin' AC/DC guitars. It was BTO meets The Beach Boys."

He would bring the demo's instrumental track to his later group Union and lay down vocals with bandmate Frank Ludwig for their 1981 album *On Strike*. (This rendition is titled "Keep the Summer Alive.") He still hoped to get his hands on the tapes of The Beach Boys' vocals, which he wanted to sync to the original track. "I could make it a new Beach Boys anthem," he says. "They did really good stuff vocally. It just didn't have the balls. The Beach Boys are always light musically, and I'm heavy."

Alan plays rhythm guitar at Monmouth Park Racetrack in Monmouth, New Jersey, on July 12, 1979.
[© Neil ShoenHolz]

A version closer to what Bachman had envisioned belatedly emerged on The Beach Boys' 2002 DVD and CD releases of *Good Timin: Live at Knebworth England 1980*. The concert film had been relegated to the vault for more than two decades, even though the group's performances are sharp. In the live setting, "Keepin' the Summer Alive" rocks harder than anything the band had done since at

Mike relished his frontman role following The Beach Boys' mid-'70s resurgence. [© Neil ShoenHolz]

least "Marcella." If they could have found the same energy in the studio, the song perhaps would have brought them a much-needed hit.

The country ballad "Livin' with a Heartache" became the album's second single and failed to chart. The catchy but familiar tune would have fared better in a more organic arrangement, but is instead given the adult-contemporary treatment. The harmony-filled "Ace," another attempt to recreate the good

old sunny days, was intended for the album but never got beyond the demo stage.

Bachman recounts that Carl asked him to produce and play on the album tracks, while Brian was so impressed by the songs written at Caribou that he wanted to try writing with Bachman as well. Bachman feels that had he accepted those requests, he may have gone on to join the band full time. But the timing was bad, as he had just gotten custody of his six children in a divorce. (One of his sons, 11-year-old Tal, would record the smash single "She's So High" 20 years later.) "I had to go and look after my kids," the elder Bachman says. "I was Mr. Mom for three years and I couldn't leave the house."

With Bachman out, Carl looked elsewhere for someone to play the solo on "Keepin' the Summer Alive" and recruited Joe Walsh, who would soon be out of a gig following the breakup of The Eagles. Bachman feels that had he assumed the producer's chair, he could have helped The Beach Boys find their way. "The Beach Boys would have gotten heavier," he says. "They probably would have hired Joe Walsh to play with them full-time, and/or they would have hired me to play with them. I even kind of looked like them. They had beards and they were kind of chubby guys. They weren't Mr. Six-pack. Putting me and Joe in there along with a solid drummer and all their vocals would have been the most incredible band in the world next to The Beatles — heavy power guitars and cool solos."

It would have been a dream come true for Bachman, who, back in the early days of The Guess Who, would try to learn the guitar intros to Beach Boys hits and sing Brian's high part when his band played "I Get Around" and "California Girls" at dances. After his group broke out later in the decade with Burton Cummings singing hits like "These Eyes" and "Laughing," Bachman found himself and his mates opening for his musical idols. He would again share the bill with The Beach Boys as part of BTO, which provided the immortal '70s rock anthems "You Ain't Seen Nothin' Yet" and "Takin' Care of Business," on which, he says, he tries to sing like Mike. He left BTO in 1977 and started Ironhorse a couple of years later, when he got the call from Carl to join The Beach Boys for some East Coast dates.

Bachman and his Ironhorse mates were backstage at their first gig with The Beach Boys when their dressing-room door was kicked in, revealing Dennis and new girlfriend Christine McVie of Fleetwood Mac. (Dennis had reconciled with and remarried Karen Lamm the year before, but their relationship ended after he met McVie.[3]) "In comes Dennis with a beard and long hair looking like Animal from *The Muppet Show*, and he has Christine with him and they're both blasted on something and he comes in raging," Bachman says. "And we're backing up, and he goes, 'I'm

Dennis Wilson.' And I go, 'Yeah, hi, Dennis,' and he says, 'I just wanted to welcome you to the tour, man.' What a welcome! And he gave us all a hug and went out. He was a nice guy but a little zoomed out on whatever he was on at the time."

Of all the group members, Bachman was closest to the far mellower Carl. Not that the youngest Wilson brother didn't have his own problems — he was also going through a divorce and was wrestling with drugs and alcohol — but Bachman remembers him as "a very gentle soul, a very spiritual guy." That side came out when the pair recorded in Washington. Bachman was about to start playing, when Carl asked if he could light a candle. "Then he puts his hands together and says, 'Oh, Great Spirit of Music, we are together as two souls and we ask for your guidance that we make some good music together.' I really loved Carl like a brother. We intuitively understood each other," Bachman says.

Bachman may have gotten to see his rock 'n' roll heroes up close, warts and all, but that never diminished his admiration for their music. "I did dozens and dozens of dates with them, and every time I would be done, I'd go change my clothes, sit at the side, watch them play and relive my youth," he says. "I enjoyed every single concert they put on."

STEVE LEVINE ON...
GETCHA BACK

Written by: Mike Love and Terry Melcher
Lead vocals: Mike Love and Brian Wilson
Produced by: Steve Levine
Recorded: November 1984, January 1985
Released: May 8, 1985
Chart peak: U.S. #26
Appears on *The Beach Boys*

In the early '80s, Dennis and Brian were hurtling towards life-threatening personal crises. Dennis' drug and alcohol consumption was out of control. He couldn't be counted on to show up at gigs, and when he did, his playing was erratic. The situation irked Mike and Carl, both of whom would find satisfaction working on solo records. Mike would have further reason to be irked when Dennis, after the dissolution of his relationship with Christine McVie, married and had a son, Gage, with Mike's alleged illegitimate daughter Shawn Love. Their marriage was short-lived. Carl hit the road with his own band in spring 1981 and was out of The Beach Boys for the next year. If the rest of the group wanted to be sure of at least one Wilson onstage, they looked to Brian. And he may have showed up in body — one which maxed out at a reported 340 pounds — but mostly he just sat at his piano, smoking and drinking Diet Coke and not singing much.

Carl, Marilyn and Beach Boys management were so concerned about Brian's well-being that they did the hitherto unthinkable and rehired Eugene Landy. They still didn't like his fees or his manner, but Landy was the only person who'd had any success treating

Brian. In January 1983, the therapist and his small army of helpers whisked Brian to a private compound in Hawaii and submitted him to a rigorous program of detoxification, exercise and healthy eating that got him to slim down to 250 pounds.[1] The consensus was that he saved Brian's life.

Meanwhile, Dennis' unhealthy habits had become all too evident in his bloated, once-handsome face, and rehab clinics weren't helping. On December 28, 1983, Dennis, by then homeless, was hanging out with friend Bill Oster and others on Oster's boat in Marina del Rey, near where Dennis docked his beloved yacht *Harmony* before being forced to sell it. Dennis swigged copious amounts of vodka that day and dove into the 58° waters looking for personal items he had thrown overboard years earlier. Eventually, he didn't resurface. His body was recovered one hour later.[2]

January and early February Beach Boys shows were either rescheduled or canceled[3] while the surviving members mourned. Then the wheels of the touring machine began to turn again, minus the one who had embodied the group's very spirit. There was also the matter of a long-overdue new record. Brian had only partially returned to active duty,

joining the band for occasional shows[4] — so who would take the helm? Bruce, who had produced the previous two LPs, believed he saw the answer in his friend Steve Levine.

Levine was on top of the pop world after producing three platinum LPs for Culture Club, but he never forgot the role Bruce had played in his career. They first worked together at London's CBS Studios on the 1977 *Checkpoint* album Bruce was producing for British popsters Sailor. Bruce appreciated that Levine — then a teenaged trainee tape-op — understood the new MCI in-line mixing console and shifted him to the engineer's chair. Afterwards, Bruce told Levine he should be a producer and brought him to L.A. for various projects. All these years later, Levine was more than happy to work with Bruce and The Beach Boys.

"They wanted to make an '80s album with the latest technology I was using with Culture Club and many other bands," Levine explains. That would include the Fairlight CMI sampling computer — which cost £40,000 in 1980s currency — two £100,000 Sony PCM-3324 digital multi-recorders and a £20,000 Sony 1610 digital audio processor for mixing.

Gone was the need for a live studio band, and — with the odd exception — the group would no longer gather around one microphone to sing the harmonies. Each musical and vocal part would be individually recorded and overdubbed, allowing for unprecedented control in the mixing stage. And there was no need to find a drummer to replace Dennis since most of the beats would be programmed. In fact, many of the other instrumental parts also would be played on synthesizers.

Basic backing tracks were begun at London's Red Bus Recording Studios in June 1984 before the project moved to Santa Monica's Westlake facility in the fall. Levine found the band "really out of kilter." By now the group was on autopilot, cranking out the old hits at casinos, baseball stadiums and amusement parks, often with cheerleaders as an onstage distraction. "They hadn't been in the studio together for quite a while and they were very rusty. They needed to get back on the treadmill and do some work," Levine says.

For him, making the album was a combination of "highs and extreme lows." The defining event came a few days in at Westlake, after Brian had laid down a weak vocal. "It was just awful," the producer recalls. "He walked in the control room and everyone's going, 'Hey, great, Bri, really great.' Everyone

was so unbelievably patronizing. And Brian says to me, 'What do you think, Steve?' And I said, 'Do you want an honest answer? It's shit. You need some singing lessons,' at which point everyone in the room took a deep breath and Brian stormed out."

The room cleared and Levine believed his critique had just earned him his walking papers. He returned the next morning to pack up, when the phone rang. It was Tom Hulett, who had replaced Stephen Love as Beach Boys manager years earlier. "Brian's not coming to the studio today," Hulett told a contrite Levine. "Do you know where he is? He's having some singing lessons. Thank you."

One person who didn't appreciate Levine's candidness, however, was Landy, who thought the producer had overstepped his bounds and proceeded to speak to him only through a go-between. Landy also created problems by imposing his creative ideas on the Brian compositions "I'm So Lonely" and "It's Just a Matter of Time." He was initially given a third credit on Alan and Brian's "Crack at Your Love," but that was later removed.

Digital recording was new to the band — as was an outside producer — and this led to clashes over approach. After a particularly a sudden, Brian drove up, unaccompanied by either Landy or Landy's assistant Carlos Booker. Brian got out of the car, approached Levine and asked what was wrong. The producer burst into tears. "I'm trying so hard to make this record as good as you guys want it to be, but Al just doesn't understand the technology," he told Brian.

Brian put his arm around Levine and said, "Don't worry about it. I've had it with them all the time. I spend weeks on things and they come to the studio for five minutes and dismiss everything."

Levine had Brian's sympathy, and relations with the rest of the band turned the corner after he joined them for a one-off gig at the Arizona State Fair. They also came to appreciate how he was making them sound on record. "I think those are some of the best vocals they've ever sung — some of the backgrounds in particular," Levine says. "This is pre-Auto-Tune. It is tracked, but there is no faking."

One of the eventual album's highlights is "Getcha Back," a nostalgic number written by Mike and Terry Melcher. The lyrics, about a guy looking to rekindle a lost love, were definitely from another era. The track has touches of Motown and Phil Spector and a melody

Producer Steve Levine found a surprisingly supportive shoulder from Brian while recording the 1985 album *The Beach Boys*.
[© Greg Laney, Courtesy Steve Levine]

heated exchange with Alan, Levine retreated to the parking lot behind the L.A. studio. (Levine says Alan later apologized for the incident.) Here he was, a chart-topping producer a long way from home, enduring a rough ride from these rock 'n' roll veterans. All of reminiscent of Bruce Springsteen's "Hungry Heart," which Mike would also later record.

Mike seemed to be always running off making some personal appearance or another, but he spent extra time making sure the track was good, cranking up the nasality on his lead vocal to sound half his age and adding trademark bass-vocal parts. Meanwhile, Brian's singing lessons evidently paid off, as he contributes an impressive, eight-times-tracked falsetto backing that could have been lifted from a mid-'60s Beach Boys classic.

Melcher, who would play a major role on the group's next few records, played the basic keyboard part on a Kurzweil K250, while Julian Lindsay, the album's musical arranger, played other parts on the same sampler. Adding organic sounds were John Alder on guitar, Steve Grainger on baritone sax and Graham Broad on percussion. The song's fat, echoing drum intro was recorded at the Century City Club + Spa. Carl and Levine had visited the club and were amazed by the reverb in the racquetball court. "I thought, 'If I'm going to have that Holland-Dozier-Holland sound, why don't I do it with the big hair and shoulder pads of the '80s? Instead of it being a tiny back room at Motown, I'll go to the Century

City racquetball court!'" Levine recalls. He returned to the club with some portable gear to record percussion samples triggered from a customized AMS delay line/pitch shifter.

Levine actually enlisted one of Motown's top stars on the album. Just as the L.A. sessions were winding down, a representative for Stevie Wonder called Levine out of the blue to see if he could help the R&B legend sort out a technical issue with a drum machine. Levine could hardly believe it when he found himself in the house of another one of his musical idols. He was able to quickly remedy the gear problem, and then boldly asked Wonder if he might have a song for The Beach Boys to record. The musician offered up the upbeat "I Do Love You," even agreeing to play on it. He came down to the studio to program the drums and lay down bass, electric piano, his signature harmonica and a guide vocal that was replaced with Carl's lead.

The LP boasts other A-list guest stars. "Boy George" O'Dowd and Roy Hay, Levine's mates from Culture Club, contributed the song "Passing Friend," with Hay recording nearly all the instrumentation. Ringo Starr came in to play drums and timpani on Alan and Brian's "California Calling," while Thin

Music arranger Julian Lindsay helps set up Carl with a keyboard at Westlake Audio in West Hollywood.
[© Steve Levine]

Lizzy guitarist Gary Moore lent his substantial chops to Carl's "Maybe I Don't Know" and Bruce's ballad "She Believes in Love Again."

Bruce and Alan joined Levine in London in early 1985 for vocal overdubbing before everybody reconvened in L.A. in March for mixing. After Levine played a finished mix to the band, each member had his say, which sent him back to the drawing board. "We settled on a democratic process where it was Carl, me and Bruce doing the mix and then everyone would approve it and we would move on to the next song. It was a slow process," Levine explains.

"Getcha Back" was released that May as

a single, supported by an amusing video about a nerdy guy who tries to reunite with his childhood sweetheart. The American public's appetite for Beach Boys music was high again, as evidenced by David Lee Roth's "California Girls" cover charting at #3 two months earlier. "Getcha Back" made it to #26 on the Hot 100 (and #2 on the Adult Contemporary chart) — higher than any original Beach Boys song since "Do It Again." A second single, Carl's "It's Gettin' Late," scraped onto the charts at #82. It was one of five tracks on the album sung by Carl, who is in fine form and who contributed the standout slow number "Where I Belong."

The LP arrived in June simply titled *The Beach Boys* and bearing a back-cover message to Dennis: "This album is dedicated to the memory of our beloved brother, cousin and friend." Reviews were varied. *Rolling Stone* found the record "pleasantly innocuous, undemanding and mildly enjoyable."[5]

The biggest champion was *Billboard* editor and Beach Boys biographer Timothy White, who went so far as to call it "nearly as strong *Sunflower*, the banners of its felicity being the harmonies, which had rarely been more smartly and adroitly lush."[6]

The final Beach Boys album for Caribou Records, it peaked at #52 in the U.S. one week after the band played before a global TV audience of two billion at the Live Aid fundraising concert at Philadelphia's JFK Stadium. (The album reached #60 in the U.K.) Despite being the best LP chart performance since *15 Big Ones*, it was disappointing given the care taken.

"I wish it had sold in greater numbers," Levine says. "I'm immensely proud of it. We were trying to make an album with the timestamp of the '80s and I think it achieves that. Everyone contributed in every single way the best they could."

RUSS TITELMAN ON...
LOVE AND MERCY

Written by: Brian Wilson
Lead vocal: Brian Wilson
Produced by: Brian Wilson and Russ Titelman
Recorded: various dates April 1987–March 1988
Released: July 1, 1988
Appears on *Brian Wilson*

For Brian, the 1985 album *The Beach Boys* was a warm-up for another comeback. By the next year, he wanted to do a solo record. Or, as he would tell *Bay Area Music* interviewer Jerry McCulley, "Eugene Landy, my executive producer, told me that he would like to do a solo album with me, that he'd like to help produce it."[1] Brian's memoir — quite apparently written through Landy's filter — claims that embarking on the project was a ploy to lure the other Beach Boys into working with him again,[2] but it was really more about Brian expressing himself creatively and, in no small measure, about Landy's own ambitions.

A friend of Brian's suggested he reunite with old collaborator Gary Usher, and they worked together for nearly a year on a batch of songs before Usher was ultimately edged out by a jealous and suspicious Landy,[3] who was on the lookout for a big record deal.

In January 1987, Brian, looking remarkably trim and poised, inducted songwriters Jerry Leiber and Mike Stoller into the Rock and Roll Hall of Fame. Seymour Stein, president of both Sire Records and the hall foundation, was so impressed with Brian that he floated a two-record solo deal on the spot. As it had been a decade since Brian had last produced an album, Stein figured Brian could use a supervising collaborator and tapped producer and Beach Boys aficionado Andy Paley for the role.

Stein visited Brian on the West Coast to hear his stockpile of unproduced compositions,[4] and it was the simple, prayer-like "Love and Mercy" that sealed the deal. Inspired by the Hal David/Burt Bacharach tune "What the World Needs Now Is Love,"[5] it commands attention right from the opening line. The subsequent verses envision a tumultuous world and all the lonely people who inhabit it. But if The Beatles' "Eleanor Rigby" simply wonders where they all belong, Brian offers them a musical benediction. He explained he was trying to "bring some spiritual love to people."[6]

Paley evaluated songs Brian had already written and eventually collaborated on new ones. Brian's comeback was so important to Sire that Lenny Waronker, president of parent Warner Bros. Records, also got hands-on. He suggested a suite on an Old West theme à la "Heroes and Villains," and even proposed the title "Rio Grande." Meanwhile, Stein asked Russ Titelman — a Grammy Award–winning producer who had worked with Steve Winwood, James Taylor and Randy Newman — to co-produce some tracks.

As a young songwriter in the mid-'60s, Titelman had met Brian at the offices of Screen Gems, where Brian visited producer/manager Lou Adler. They struck up a friendship and ended up co-writing the gems "Sherry, She Needs Me" (a.k.a. "Sandy, She Needs Me") and "Guess I'm Dumb." Brian recorded a track for the former in 1965, but never finished The Beach Boys' vocals. He recorded a full version in 1976, but it did not see release. The latter song, originally intended for The Beach Boys, was a commercially unsuccessful single for Glen Campbell.

Titelman was excited to work with Brian again, and as part of the deal they would take another stab at "Sherry, She Needs Me." Listening to the album's tracks-in-progress, he thought Brian and Paley made a strong team. "What they had done already was very good," Titelman says. "Andy did an amazing job on that record. Without Andy, it's very possible it never would have been made."

As for "Love and Mercy," which he calls "an anthem about forgiveness and compassion," it was love at first listen. "It's so heartbreakingly beautiful," he says. He adds that he contributed a line but did not take a writer's credit.

The album would be recorded at a dozen or so different studios. One theory for all the moving about is that Landy didn't want Brian getting too comfortable with any outsiders. The sessions with Titelman got underway in June 1987 at The Hit Factory in New York.[7] The producer saw his role as facilitating whatever Brian wanted to do. "I understood him very well creatively and knew all his records backwards and forwards," Titelman says. "The job was to create an atmosphere in the studio that would nurture his creativity and allow him to go do stuff and keep him focused."

Titelman had attended a couple of Brian sessions in the '60s and recalled that Brian "had the arrangements in his head. He knew what he wanted and what to tell people to do." And nearly a quarter-century later, despite all Brian had been through, he says little had changed. "It was the old Brian — full of creative ideas and doing beautiful vocal harmony stuff. It was a thrill to watch these things come out of his head. I would say, 'Okay, go ahead,' and he would lay down his part, double it, lay down another part and double it. And all of a sudden there would be this beautiful thing there."

There was only one problem: Landy, who had secured an executive producer credit and believed that entitled him to call the shots. Much to Titelman's consternation, Landy assigned assistant Kevin Leslie to watch over Brian in the studio at all times, and Landy constantly called in to see what track Brian was working on, often directing him to change course for no apparent reason. "He kept Brian off guard all the time. He kept interrupting the creative flow and it was unbelievably frustrating," Titelman says. "I started to go out of my mind. It was so chaotic and unpleasant that it became rather untenable. Brian would have been a lot happier left to his own devices and without Landy's interruption. We would've had a much easier time and probably it would have come out a little different."

"Sherry, She Needs Me," logged this time as "Terri, She Needs Me,"[8] became a casualty of the chaos. "We cut a track and then Landy intervened and we never finished it. Because of him it got the kibosh," Titelman says.

Brian had gotten a crash course in the latest synthesizer technology on the Steve Levine Beach Boys project, and fully embraced it on the new album, contributing samples, sound effects, keyboards and percussion.

Eugene Landy (right) helped Brian get back into good physical shape, but he was forced to surrender his therapy license for, among other charges, treating Brian while being in a business relationship with him. He seemed more interested in the business side, anyway. [© Getty Images/Kevin Winter]

on backgrounds for the upbeat "Walkin' the Line," which hailed from the Usher sessions and got a rewrite by The Dream Academy's Nick Laird-Clowes. ELO's Jeff Lynne brought "Let It Shine" to the table and co-produced the track, while Lindsey Buckingham co-wrote and co-produced the fitness-oriented "He Couldn't Get His Poor Old Body to Move," which ended up on the B-side of "Love and Mercy." *Rolling Stone* reported that Bob Dylan, Van Dyke Parks and Harry Nilsson also discussed potential collaborations.[9] John Sebastian tried co-writing with Brian, but says the endeavor was thwarted by Landy, who, along with his girlfriend Alexandra Morgan, tried to impose their own "dreary lyrics" on the music.

Brian and Titelman relocated to Los Angeles' A&M Studios to mix their co-productions, which also included "Melt Away," "Baby Let Your Hair Grow Long," "Little Children" and "Night Time." Most of the mixing was handled by Hugh Padgham, known for his work with Peter Gabriel and The Police. After Titelman moved on, Landy attempted an album remix with Brian, although, as Titelman says, "Lenny Waronker was in there doing his best to retain what we

Programmer Michael Bernard was also heavily involved on a number of tracks. High-profile artists also participated, including Cars guitarist Elliot Easton, jazz keyboardist Philippe Saisse and singer Christopher Cross. Terence Trent D'Arby joined Titelman did. It pretty much sounds the way the original mix sounded."

Work on the album dragged on for more than a year, taking four times longer than *Pet Sounds*. The final bill was reported at an astronomical $1 million. While Sire allowed Brian and his collaborators time to perfect the tracks, Titelman adds, "There were overages because of the insanity of Dr. Landy."

By then, steps were underway to stop the insanity. In February 1988, the California Board of Medical Quality Assurance accused Landy of inappropriately entering a business relationship with Brian while treating him, of financially exploiting Brian and illegally prescribing him medication. Landy surrendered his therapy license, but was preoccupied with his would-be music career anyway. He fought for songwriting credits on the album — scoring five for him and three for Morgan — while trying to have others' names removed. But when Warner Bros. issued a deluxe CD version in 2000, Landy's and Morgan's credits had been taken out.

"Love and Mercy" was tapped as the preview single and opener of the album, simply titled *Brian Wilson*. The LP drew some glowing reviews, including four stars from *Rolling Stone*, which called it "a delightful, engaging pop masterpiece"[10] and named Brian comeback artist of the year. Some find the reliance on synthesizers and drum machines dated even for its time. But while "Night Time" and "Let It Shine" veer towards the ordinary, the rest is pure Brian — heartfelt in its balance of wonder and wisdom. The vocal arrangements are at times overwhelming, the changes startling. It ranks among Brian's most ambitious works, recalling past glories without recycling them.

An emboldened Titelman even nicknamed the record "*Pet Sounds '88.*" "I was hoping it would be," he says. "It was an attempt at returning to that pure sense of creativity and beauty." The results were certainly more than even the most diehard fan could have hoped for. Unfortunately the album didn't take the world by storm, rising no higher than #54 in the U.S. and not charting in the U.K. There was plenty of ink surrounding Brian's return, but Landy's behind-the-scenes shenanigans stole the spotlight. The lack of a video for "Love and Mercy" likely also hurt, and the single missed the charts. But more than anything, it seemed the Beach Boys' name still overshadowed that of any of its members, even Brian's.

Despite the commercial disappointment, "Love and Mercy" remains special to Brian. He reinterpreted it in more organic fashion for 1995's *I Just Wasn't Made for These Times*, and years later would close his shows with a simplified version to send the crowd home, with, as he would say, "a nice little love message." He spread that same musical message at benefits following the 2004 Indian Ocean tsunami and Hurricane Katrina. And he's not the only one who has blessed his audience with the tune. For one, Wilco front man Jeff Tweedy has done a country rendition with the band collective Golden Smog.

On a more personal level, "Love and Mercy" helped launch Brian's solo career, and Titelman looks back on it fondly. "It showed that Brian still was there as an amazing force in American popular music," he says. "I was proud that I could be someone who could help him reenter the arena and do great work."

MIKE LOVE ON . . .
KOKOMO

Written by: John Phillips, Mike Love, Terry Melcher
and Scott McKenzie
Lead vocal: Mike Love and Carl Wilson
Produced by: Terry Melcher
Recorded: March 22, April 5–6, 1988
Released: July 18, 1988
Chart peak: U.S. #1, U.K. #25
Appears on *Cocktail* (soundtrack) and *Still Cruisin'*

While Brian was wrapping up his solo album in spring 1988, the rest of The Beach Boys were in another studio working on a little movie assignment.

Filmmaker Roger Donaldson asked the group to come up with a song for his feature *Cocktail*. The romantic drama would star Tom Cruise — red-hot after *Top Gun* and *The Color of Money* — as a New York business student who becomes a hotshot bartender and goes to ply his trade in Jamaica, where he falls for an American artist played by Elisabeth Shue, whose performance in *Adventures in Babysitting* had made her a star. It couldn't miss.

Terry Melcher, who had produced the band's 1986 chart single "Rock 'n' Roll to the Rescue" (U.S. #68) and a cover of The Mamas & the Papas' "California Dreamin'" (U.S. #57), believed he had a suitably tropical number for them. It came from none other than Papa John Phillips, who was trying to relaunch his dormant band with old friend Scott McKenzie, best known for singing Phillips' Summer of Love anthem "San Francisco (Be Sure to Wear Flowers in Your Hair)." The pair had co-written "Kokomo," an easy-listening recollection of a Caribbean getaway with a former love. (There is a Kokomo, Indiana, but the song's locale doesn't actually exist.) It had a solid melody and clever verses, but it wasn't rock 'n' roll.

Calling Dr. Love, purveyor of hooks. "I said, 'Wow, this is really nice but it needs something to groove to,' so I reached back into some of my influences," Mike recalls. That would be primarily the '50s R&B of "Smokey Joe's Café" by The Robins, precursors of The Coasters. "The rhythm of the chorus is somewhat similar. It influenced my thinking on 'Kokomo' — not in terms of melody, but in the groove and the beat," Mike notes.

Mike — Mr. Positivity — changed the tense from past to present/future, thereby transforming a wistful memory into an anticipated romantic rendezvous. While the verses in the two versions sound alike, the original song's chorus is completely different. (The demo of which saw release on the 2010 John Phillips collection *Many Mamas, Many Papas*.) Mike rewrote it, coming up with the most indelible section, in which the narrator lists off Caribbean locales and begs the woman to go with him.

Melcher then tacked on a memorable part for Carl to sing. (Carl was in a singing mood; he had recently married old friend Gina Martin, daughter of Dean Martin.) The record wrings these hooks for all they're worth. Mike sings the chorus right out of the gate, and the original verses are streamlined so the group can return to the chorus as quickly as possible. The chorus is sung five times throughout the song, so the listener can't escape it. It's a case study in the difference between a languishing demo and a smash hit.

While Melcher and engineer Keith Wechsler recorded the instrumental tracks, Mike was on the phone with them reciting the new chorus to make sure everything conformed. Among the musicians present were slide guitar great Ry Cooder, legendary session player Jim Keltner (who programmed the drums) and touring Beach Boys guitarist Jeffrey Foskett. Steel drums add Caribbean spice, while old collaborator Van Dyke Parks, whose presence is surprising, plays accordion and contributed to the vocal arrangement.[1] One wouldn't imagine the song to be his cup of tea, or that relations between him and Mike would be anything but frosty after their legendary confrontation over Parks' *Smile* lyrics.

"I always thought he was a brilliant musician and a really neat guy," Mike counters. "I don't think there is any animosity whatsoever from either side. I made up a term called 'acid alliteration' to describe the type of lyrics he was doing on *Smile*. My perspective on lyrics is they ought to connect with ordinary mortals who aren't under the influence of anything in particular other than life. There are other schools of thought on that. Lewis Carroll was whacked out of his mind and he wrote some outrageous stuff such as *Alice in Wonderland*, which is very psychedelic. I thought some of the lyrics Van Dyke came up with were extremely clever and interesting, but as far as it translating into a hit record [I didn't think they would work]. Believe me; I harbor no animosity towards anyone who wrote lyrics with Brian other than myself."

The trippiest lyric Mike came up with on "Kokomo" is about getting a "contact high." "You can get a high from drugs or alcohol, but you can also get high on romance. The endorphins can really start to flow if you're in a romantic place with somebody you're in love with or attracted to," Mike says. He'll stick with the romantic highs, thank you. "I didn't appreciate how LSD made some people act," he adds. "It's just like alcohol. Some people can have a little bit of alcohol and be fine and other people can have a bit of alcohol and it ruins their life. And when you see your cousins become addicted and impair themselves and affect their lives and everyone around them, I absolutely did have an aversion to all that. That's led me to becoming more appreciative of learning Transcendental Meditation from Maharishi, and I meditate to this day every day. You're able to gain some deep rest and clarity without the negative side effects of drugs or alcohol."

Mike introduced a new dimension to his voice on "Kokomo." "Most of my lead vocals on all those hit singles in the '60s happen to be in that tenor range. On 'Kokomo,' it's more laid-back and mellow," he explains. Alan and Bruce add to the harmony blend.

More remarkable than who was involved in the sessions is who wasn't: Brian, whose hurt over the exclusion is evident in an interview 10 years later in the *Endless Harmony* documentary. According to Brian's memoir, the other Beach Boys did not give him enough of a heads-up about a vocal session, informing him about it at the last second while he was busy recording his solo album, thereby ensuring he wouldn't be able to attend.[2] Available session-date information does not substantiate this claim, however. Mike insists there was no intention to leave out Brian.

"Dr. Landy wouldn't let Brian sing on it unless Landy was a producer and co-writer, and Terry Melcher didn't really feel he needed Landy since he had produced some #1 records," Mike says dryly. "It was pathetic of Landy to do that, but he controlled Brian completely at that time." In the group's quest to make sure the Latin world didn't miss out, it re-recorded the song in Spanish ("Bermuda, Bahamas — vámonos mañana") and this time Brian got to sing on the chorus.

Upon hearing the "Kokomo" demo, Disney — which was releasing *Cocktail* through its Touchstone Pictures division — gave the song the green light. The demo was solid enough that instead of re-recording it, the group simply sweetened it until they had a releasable master. Mike recalls that when director Donaldson heard it, he said, "This is the best song you've done since 'Good Vibrations.'" That sentiment would soon be shared.

On July 18 — with Brian's "Love and Mercy" floundering in the marketplace — Elektra Records released the "Kokomo" 45 backed with the Little Richard oldie "Tutti Frutti." Eleven days later, *Cocktail* opened to a $12 million box office,[3] providing the song with a strong launch pad. But its climb would be long and slow — and astonishing.

A video was produced that cut between clips from the movie and the band lip-synching the tune on the beach at Walt Disney World's new Grand Floridian Resort in front of an adoring crowd including the requisite bikini-clad babes. Other elements purely for optics include John Stamos on steel drums and Mike handling the saxophone solo, which on the record is played by Joel Peskin. Boosted by MTV's video airplay, the record finally entered the *Billboard* charts on September 24.[4] With temperatures getting nippier, record buyers tried to keep the summer alive by picking up the 45 in droves. Its momentum unstoppable, the single surprised everyone — not least of all, the band — when, on November 5, it brought them their fourth U.S. #1 and first since "Good Vibrations" 22 years earlier. It was their first single to even crack the top 10 in America in all that time except for their 1976 cover of "Rock and Roll Music." It would become their best-selling U.S. 7". In Australia it also topped the charts and helped send the *Cocktail* soundtrack album to #1. It was less popular in the U.K., however, making it only as far as #25.

In 1988, The Beach Boys became the first group to win the Award of Merit at the American Music Awards. Many were stunned by the new slender look of Brian (second from left). [© AP Photo/Reed Saxon]

Mike sees the song's success lying large-ly in its built-in multigenerational appeal. "'Pretty mama' could be a child literally thinking his mama is pretty, or it could be this senior citizen saying, 'Let's get in the RV and go down to Florida,' or the young guy who's checking out the chick," says Mike, who married Jacqueline Piesen in 1994. "No mat ter what age a person in the audience is, they'll sing along with that chorus. It's probably the biggest sing-along song we have, and we have some big ones."

Despite Grammy and Golden Globe nomi-nations, the hit does have its detractors, riding as it does that fine line between what *Village Voice*'s Robert Christgau once described as "catchy-seductive" and "catchy-annoying." *Blender* magazine awarded it the ignominious distinction of being the "worst song to have sex to," while blogger DJ Funktual writes, "It makes me wanna grab a baby boomer with a lame-ass Jimmy Buffett shirt by the back of the neck and stick him face first in the sand."[5]

Some Brian fans don't like it because he's not on it. The A&E Biography documentary *Brian Wilson: A Beach Boys Tale* claims Mike privately bragged about topping the charts without his cousin's involvement, but Mike refutes this. "It wasn't a sense of pride," he says. "Obviously we were happy we had a #1 record, but it was sad that Brian was under the influence of Landy to the extent that he couldn't even record with us."

While the song appeared on the *Cocktail* soundtrack along with Bobby McFerrin's monster hit "Don't Worry, Be Happy," there was the matter of making it available on a Beach Boys LP. Sensing a short-term opportunity, Capitol signed the group to a one-off album deal and released the LP *Still Cruisin'*, which compiles "Kokomo" along with other songs the group had contributed to recent movies, including the record's title track from *Lethal Weapon 2*, "Make It Big" from *Troop Beverly Hills* and even classic '60s hits that had popped up in films. The LP is rounded out by the band's 1987 cover of The Surfaris' "Wipe Out" done with hip-hop act The Fat Boys — a surprising #12 U.S. and #2 U.K. hit — the flop single "Somewhere Near Japan" and some new songs. The disc is no longer in print, but it sold well at the time and by 2003 had achieved platinum status.

Love it or hate it, "Kokomo" remains pervasive in mainstream culture. In fall '88 the group performed it on an episode of Stamos' *Full House*, and it has subsequently appeared in less reverent forms on comedy series including *Friends*, *The Simpsons*, *Saturday Night Live*, *Scrubs*, *How I Met Your Mother*, *Family Guy* and *American Dad*.[6] And who could forget Kermit the Frog's spirited rendition with the rest of the Muppets on the 1993 LP *Muppet Beach Party*? Never one to let a successful idea alone, Mike recorded "Santa's Goin' to Kokomo" for the 2009 charity album *Hope for the Holidays*.

For The Beach Boys, well entrenched as an oldies act by the late '80s, the song garnered a whole new generation of listeners. The kid who dug it upon its release was a thirtysomething fan in 2012. "It increased the appeal of the group to a broader audience. Even today, teenagers and even preteens sing it along with us in concert," Mike notes.

Half a century in, The Beach Boys' front man continued to rule as rock's ultimate road warrior. Having passed 70, he was still singing and clowning his way through 120 or more shows per year around the world with no signs of shutting down. And it's a guarantee that concertgoers would hear "Kokomo"

— and many would find themselves joining in.

"It's remarkable that going on 50 years our songs are so well-appreciated," Mike says. "It's very heartwarming how people *won't* say, 'Why do you keep doing it? Don't you ever think of retiring?' Why would you not want to see people by the thousands happy, knowing that you had a hand in creating the songs they enjoy so much? It's both altruistic and egotistic. For the performer, it's a good feeling, and for the public it's quite evident that they have a great time experiencing The Beach Boys."

Don Was on ...
STILL I DREAM OF IT

Written by: Brian Wilson
Lead vocal: Brian Wilson
Produced by: Brian Wilson
Recorded: 1976
Released: August 15, 1995, on *I Just Wasn't Made for These Times*

Despite the artistic success of Brian's first solo album, the headlines he made in the years that followed were mostly about his controversial relationship with Eugene Landy.

Having surrendered his California therapy license in March 1989, Landy could no longer treat Brian, but it hardly slowed down their business association. They had a corporate partnership titled Brains and Genius in which they split all publishing, recording, film and book revenue, and according to witnesses, Landy also became the chief beneficiary in Brian's will.[1]

Carnie and Wendy believed Landy was blocking them from their father. Brian's often dubious autobiography, which he is credited with having written with *People* magazine scribe Todd Gold, offers a different spin, claiming Landy took steps to try to reunite Brian with his daughters, but either Brian would choose to not return their calls, or Marilyn would block initiatives such as having the girls sing backup on Brian's single "Let's Go to Heaven in My Car."[2] Landy is also said to have put the brakes on Brian's budding romance with Melinda Ledbetter, an ex-model and car salesperson Brian had met when she sold him a Cadillac.

Despite Brian's messy personal life, his musical legend continued to spread. It was around this time that producer Don Was fell under Brian's spell. At the time, Was, part of satirical R&B combo Was (Not Was), was producing the album *Serious Fun* for The Knack. Doug Fieger, The Knack's lead singer and Was' high-school friend, slipped him recordings from the famed *Smile* sessions.

"I was obsessed with the bootlegs," Was recalls with a laugh. "That's all I could listen to. It was actually a fatal mistake for The Knack, because I should have been listening to their rough mixes and making their album better." Was went on to display his own knack for reinvigorating the recording careers of iconic performers including Bonnie Raitt, Bob Dylan and The Rolling Stones by putting them back in touch with their musical roots.

It was in the midst of his *Smile* fixation that Was ran into Brian and Landy at a party for the AIDS benefit album *Red Hot + Blue*. "I might have scared Brian with my enthusiasm, but Landy picked up on it and invited me around to the studio," Was says. Brains and Genius were soliciting outside opinion on *Sweet Insanity*, Brian's would-be sophomore LP. Sire Records ultimately refused to release it, reportedly on account of lyrics by Landy and Alexandra Morgan that sounded like therapy-session excerpts.

"Somebody needed to get Brian out of there. That was pretty clear," Was recollects of Brian's situation with Landy. "He was alternately really out of it and incredibly lucid and perceptive. You could see that he was medicated and there were times his eyes rolled back into his head. At the same time, he would sit at the piano and play things and say things that showed he was incredibly present. Your first instinct would be to run for the hills because it was a weird scene, but there was something about Brian — a spark alive in him — that made me keep going back."

Meanwhile, there was renewed interest in Beach Boys history. In April 1990, ABC aired the dramatic TV movie *Summer Dreams: The Story of The Beach Boys*, and the following month, Capitol rolled out the 1960s Beach Boys albums on CD. With the group's profile riding high, Brian, reportedly goaded by Landy,[3] launched a $100 million lawsuit against A&M Records, Almo/Irving Music and law firm Mitchell Silverberg & Knupp over the 1969 sale of his publishing rights, alleging that he was mentally incompetent when he allowed Murry to proceed with the deal.[4]

Landy's hold over Brian had become too much for Brian's family to bear. In May, Brian's former caretaker Stan Love — with the backing of Carl, Audree, Wendy and Carnie[5] — spearheaded legal action to have Landy removed from Brian's life and himself be appointed Brian's conservator. In the end, the courts forced Landy and Brian to terminate all professional connections beginning in 1992, and Landy would not be able to contact Brian in any way. Los Angeles attorney Jerome S. Billet was agreed upon as Brian's conservator, and for the first time since Landy had reentered his life in 1983, Brian was a free man.

Landy would get in several parting shots at Brian's bandmates and family in Brian's memoir. Brian joined Was and a backing band for a book-launch concert at writer Gold's house, during which they played Beach Boys songs as well as "Be My Baby" and "Proud Mary." Brian also did "Rhapsody in Blue," and according to Rolling Stone, Landy, weeks ahead of his departure from Brian's life, shouted for Brian to sing the words to the tune, which is widely known to be an instrumental.[6]

While the book incited lawsuits from Mike, Carl and Audree, Brian got some good news from the courts in June 1992 when he was awarded $10 million in the matter of his lost publishing rights. The very next month, Mike turned around and sued Brian for a portion of that, claiming that he had not received his fair share of royalties for songs he had co-written, and that he had not been credited for another 30-plus songs for which he had penned lyrics. In December 1994 — after a trial that saw Brian, Mike, Alan and Bruce take the stand — Mike won his case and was awarded $5 million and a share of future royalties.[7]

Relations between Brian and the band — and in fact, among most of the guys — were strained. Brian did not participate in the 1992 self-released Beach Boys album *Summer in Paradise*, the first collection of all-new group material in seven years, and Carl and Alan showed up only to chip in vocals. The record, leaning heavily on nostalgia and programmed parts, was produced by Lanny Cordola, Gary Griffin, Terry Melcher and John Stamos and executive produced by Mike. Critics trashed it and it would be the only Beach Boys studio LP to miss the American charts altogether.

Meanwhile, Brian was finally getting the right psychiatric care. According to Peter Ames

Carlin, Brian had been wrongly diagnosed and treated for schizophrenia, and his new doctors determined that he was in fact mildly manic-depressive with a schizo-affective disorder. They prescribed the proper medication,[8] much to the relief of insiders who believed the drug cocktail Landy had fed Brian posed a serious health risk.[9]

Was helped bolster Brian's confidence with some small-scale live shows. They teamed up for a gig at a Mandeville Canyon estate for the Elizabeth Glaser Pediatric AIDS Foundation, taking the stage following Jackson Browne before a crowd that included former President Ronald Reagan and children lining the first 10 rows. "We did a couple of songs, including 'California Girls,' in a very uninspired way. At one point Brian said, 'Hell, I sure fucked that up!' Parents were coming to grab their kids," Was recounts with a laugh. "Then he went into 'Love and Mercy' and he gave a performance that was so transcendental that I stopped playing in the middle. It was so powerful and focused. That was the greatest thing I've ever been onstage for. And I walked up to him after and said, 'Wow, man, how did that happen?' And he said, 'Well, I was just watching the sun go down over the hillside there and I felt God.'"

Was gained Brian's trust and they decided to take their collaboration into the studio. Was started a record company called Karambolage and signed Brian. He was so inspired by what he'd seen Brian do onstage that he wanted to also make a movie about him. *I Just Wasn't Made for These Times* was originally intended to capture more of these revelatory performances, but ended up being a more straightforward documentary. It features plenty of talk from Brian, who is in a philosophical and mostly upbeat mood. By his side throughout much of the film is Melinda, with whom he reconnected following Landy's departure and married by the time the film started doing the festival rounds in spring 1995.

In one remarkable scene, Brian, Carl and 77-year-old Audree gather at the piano to sing "In My Room" and "God Only Knows." Such family sing-alongs were impossible in the era of Landy and lawsuits. Sadly, within three years of the film's shooting, both Audree and Carl — unaware of the cancer growing inside him — would be gone.

Woven into the movie's narrative are scenes of Brian and session players and singers miming newly recorded versions of gems ranging from "The Warmth of the Sun" to "Melt

Away," while Wendy and Carnie, with whom he had reconciled, assist him on a peppy run-through of "Do It Again." Was saw the film as a key component in re-launching Brian's recording career. "The thought was before we make an album, let's get all the *National Enquirer* stuff out of the way. Let's cleanse the palate and start fresh with why this guy is so great, and to do that he had to play those songs," he explains.

The film's stripped-down soundtrack album is a treat for fans and made it to #59 on the U.K. charts. Included is a home demo of the ballad "Still I Dream of It," which Brian recorded during his mid-'70s comeback. The song was intended for *Adult Child*, which Brian had recorded to follow up *The Beach Boys Love You*. The finished version and three other tracks feature big-band arrangements courtesy of Dick Reynolds. Apparently Brian wrote some of the songs with outside vocalists in mind — perhaps Stevie Wonder or even Frank Sinatra, who is name-checked in the mournful "It's Over Now." It wasn't exactly what fans would expect from The Beach Boys. Stan Love told Peter Ames Carlin that, upon hearing the songs, Mike blurted out to Brian, "What the fuck are you doing?"[10]

Yet "Still I Dream of It" is one of Brian's most personal statements, and the demo, in which he sings in ravaged voice alone at the piano, is particularly direct. As the song opens, Brian relates that he's exhausted after a tough day and all he wants is dinner. His mind then wanders to the dream of a new romance — a clear indication that his marriage to Marilyn was deteriorating.

"I think that demo is one of his greatest records," Was says. "It's a gut-wrenching vocal performance and really represents where he was at that time. It's the guy from *Pet Sounds* grown-up. Sometimes he's innocent and yet he's a really deep thinker, and that's embodied in the song. He's telling you things that are so mundane, and yet by the time the chorus comes around, he's jumping to some of the most profound issues about life. It's very Buddhist — love being like a dream that's linked to the stars. You walk away with the conclusion that the mundane is connected to the divine — there's no separation between smelling the food down the hall and being in heaven. That's pretty amazing coming from a guy everyone thinks is catatonic in bed. If you really want to know about Brian Wilson, it's all there in that song."

The version later recorded for *Adult Child* is far more polished than the demo, featuring a smoother Brian vocal and an undulating synthesizer imbuing a cosmic quality. It was kept from public ears until its 1993 release on the boxed set *Good Vibrations: Thirty Years of The Beach Boys*, which set in motion a critical reevaluation of the band. The question, fans wondered, was could the guys get it together again in the studio?

Brian surprised Was when he told him he indeed wanted to make a new record with The Beach Boys. He wanted Was involved and asked the producer if he would approach the other guys about it. A week later, Was flew down to San Diego to catch up with the rest of the guys, who were performing at a Padres game. They spoke in a motel opposite Jack Murphy Stadium, Was explaining that Brian wanted to make music like in the old days, laying down the instrumental tracks then having them come in and sing. "They were a little cynical, but they didn't hesitate," Was recalls. "They were like, 'Come on, let's do it!'"

Brian had already amassed an impressive batch of new songs co-written with Andy Paley. The group was able to put aside recent conflicts and legal maneuvers and gather at Was' house to sift through the material several weeks later and select a couple of songs to test the waters. "The first day we had a full band there and Brian went around the room and told everyone what to play and cut the tracks. He was confident," Was says. "And then the next day The Beach Boys came in and did all the vocal parts. Everybody got along and it was a lovely couple of days. There wasn't a tense moment and the results were pretty good."

The first of the songs, "Soul Searchin'," is an enjoyable slice of old-school New Orleans R&B featuring a strong lead vocal from Carl. (It would be covered by Solomon Burke on the soul legend's 2002 *Don't Give Up on Me* LP.) "You're Still a Mystery," meanwhile, is classic Brian — the kind of economical composition that would have been at home on *Smiley Smile* or *Wild Honey*. But despite these encouraging tracks, work on the proposed album ended there. It may have had to do with Carl's cancer diagnosis, but Was also accepts some of the blame.

"We did the cuts and lived with them for a month," he recalls. "Then I went to Brian's house and told him, 'This shows that a great Beach Boys record could be made, but I think you could write better songs. Let's do better songs and finish this record.' He said, 'Yeah, I agree with you.' And then Carl was sick and it just never happened. The situation never came up again and I had to live with my role in stopping the momentum. Maybe I should have just kept the momentum going instead of worrying about making a worthy successor to *Pet Sounds*."

Following Carl's death and the splintering of the band in 1998, there would be no new Beach Boys record through the first decade of the new millennium. But Brian would prove he still had plenty of new music in him.

Darian Sahanaja on ...

MRS. O'LEARY'S COW

Written by: Brian Wilson
Produced by: Brian Wilson
Recorded: April 16–17, 2004
Released: September 28, 2004,
on *Brian Wilson Presents Smile*

Brian's emergence as a solo touring artist was unexpected to say the least. The wheels were set in motion after he recorded his 1998 album *Imagination* — a project that saw him and Melinda temporarily relocate to St. Charles, Illinois, to be near co-producer Joe Thomas. Brian, with Melinda's encouragement, decided to embark on a mini-tour to drum up interest in the forthcoming release.

A band was assembled featuring local Chicago players Scott Bennett (keyboards), Bob Lizik (bass), Todd Sucherman (drums), Paul Von Mertens (woodwinds) and Taylor Mills (vocals). Adding the requisite California component were former Beach Boys touring guitarist Jeffrey Foskett and the entire L.A. indie band The Wondermints, consisting of Darian Sahanaja (keyboards), Nick Walusko (guitar), Mike D'Amico (percussions/drums) and Probyn Gregory (guitar and horns). Not only were they skilled singers and instrumentalists, but on the whole they were young musicians who worshipped Brian. In fact, Sahanaja, Walusko and Gregory had originally come together out of their shared obsession with Brian's more experimental work. It was at the 1994 tribute-to-Brian show in Santa Monica where Brian, hanging out backstage, first heard

The Wondermints play one of his songs. Their performance reportedly prompted him to prophetically remark, "If I'd had those guys in '67, I could have taken *Smile* out on the road!"[1]

The proficiency of Brian's new band made possible the 2000 North American *Pet Sounds Symphonic Tour*. It was beyond the wildest dreams of longtime fans to see Brian alive and well and leading a complete performance of his classic album. He had never been a front man and relied on an Autocue prompter to feed him the lyrics as he sat at a keyboard he would play only occasionally. He seemed ill-at-ease at some of the early shows, but by the time he and his band were sharing the bill on a 2001 tour with Paul Simon, he had grown noticeably more comfortable. And if all this wasn't enough good news for fans, Brian started giving off positive vibrations about revisiting *Smile*.

At a Christmas party in 2000 at Bennett's house, Brian sat at the piano and, to everyone's surprise, played "Heroes and Villains."[2] While he had been onstage for Beach Boys performances of the number during his late '70s comeback, he usually shied away from even discussing anything related to *Smile*. That impromptu run-through for family and

friends, then, was a crucial first step. Three months later he sang it again, this time before a rapturous crowd for the TNT special *An All-Star Tribute to Brian Wilson*. The set opener "Our Prayer" by the Boys Choir of Harlem and a stunning rendition of "Surf's Up" by Vince Gill, David Crosby and Jimmy Webb gave further nods to *Smile*. That summer, Brian and band did spot-on versions of "Prayer" and "Heroes" on *Late Night with Conan O'Brien*.

Sahanaja recalls further seeds being planted in January 2002 when the band was at London's Royal Festival Hall recording performances for the CD and DVD releases of *Brian Wilson Presents Pet Sounds Live*. He was among those chatting over lunch with Brian, Melinda and show promoter Glenn Max. "Glenn was going on about how it was all turning out so well, and he said, 'How are we ever going to top this?' And somebody said, 'The only thing that could ever top this is to do music from *Smile*.' But at the time it was like, 'Ha ha — yeah, right,'" Sahanaja recalls.

The band continued to work sporadically on Brian's *Gettin' in Over My Head* album, and in summer 2003, Sahanaja, who was out on the road with the band Heart, received the astonishing news that they were actually going to tackle *Smile*, the non-appearance of which had been a millstone around Brian's 61-year-old neck ever since 1967.

"I was back with Brian in the fall and I remember feeling really nervous about it, because the times I did have contact with him over the summer, he was not that into it. There's always the question of whether you're forcing Brian to do something he doesn't want to do," Sahanaja says. "But in the end, do you want a Brian Wilson who just sits at home, lazy, watching TV, or should you try to put a spark under him and get him going to the point where it is a productive, positive thing for him?"

Sahanaja became the project's musical "secretary," which, he explains, meant "allowing Brian to be free in whatever role he wanted to take and perhaps not do a lot of the grunt work." Sahanaja's first task was to load his computer with the *Smile* cuts that had seen official release as well as those on the collectors' circuit. He then presented the material to Brian, who would gauge which songs to include and try to recall the intent of the unfinished tracks. Sahanaja was also given access to the original multi-track recordings, which enabled him and Brian to isolate instrumental parts and figure out how sections had been built. Sahanaja approached it all with great sensitivity.

"I knew there were a lot of people who were very familiar with this stuff, and for most of them even touching *Smile* was sacrilege," he explains. Even the *New York Times* weighed in, running an editorial by Verlyn Klinkenborg arguing that "those old essential voices" of the mid-'60s Beach Boys could never be emulated.[3] "I was of that same mindset, but then gradually Brian started getting into it," Sahanaja continues. "He knew he had to do it, similar to the way he has to run laps to keep in shape. It's almost as though by getting through it, he'll have what it takes to survive the next challenge."

And there was much to get through. At this point, all involved were thinking only in terms of playing *Smile* music live. They had already performed several of the cornerstone tracks, but what were they to do with those pieces that existed only as snippets, such as "Barnyard" and "I'm in Great Shape"? How would they all fit in? "I would ask, 'How did you come up with this song?' And Brian would say, 'That was part of "Heroes and Villains,"' and it kept going on and on,"

Sahanaja recalls. Three separate movements began to emerge: one set in pioneer times and tracking westward American expansion; one about childhood innocence; and another that was originally to include a four-part suite titled "The Elements" evoking air, water, fire and earth. This affirmed long-held beliefs of how *Smile* was to be structured, but Sahanaja doubts Brian and lyricist Van Dyke Parks had ever finalized their plans.

"I imagine that back in the day all sorts of ideas were flying around," he says. "Brian would be on some sort of health kick or they'd be on an ecological kick and they'd say, 'This could be our "air" song,' and 'this could be part of "The Elements,"'" and then the next day, they'd be on to something completely different."

As shown in the documentary *Beautiful Dreamer: Brian Wilson and the Story of Smile*, Brian called up Parks to help decipher a word on an old handwritten lyric sheet for the track "Do You Like Worms" (which would be renamed "Roll Plymouth Rock"). Not only did Parks help fill in some blanks, but he came on board to contribute new lyrics for tracks that were unfinished or originally meant to be instrumentals. As Brian and Parks picked up on *Smile* where they had left off all those years before, Sahanaja happily sat back and let the old masters find their way, piping in mainly to suggest how things could be best presented onstage.

The most infamous section of "The Elements" was the instrumental fire segment, properly titled "Mrs. O'Leary's Cow" after the bovine that, according to legend, knocked over the lantern that started the Great Chicago Fire of 1871. Brian recorded the original track on November 28, 1966, meshing the humor and menace that was to define *Smile*. Opening with a cacophony of toy whistles evoking cartoon firemen scrambling to the scene of a blaze, it then becomes fierce and droning, riding Carol Kaye's hypnotic, determined bass line as sirens blare and strings dance like scorching flames. It may as well have been called "Wilson's Inferno."

"I was feeling unhappy so I thought that 'fire' tape would express the crazy, weird thoughts I was going through," Brian says in *Beautiful Dreamer*. And he was not the only haunted participant. The atypically jolting drums, conjuring up the sound of a burning wall crashing to the ground, are played by Jim Gordon, the 21-year-old protégé of Hal Blaine

Darian Sahanaja was vital in helping Brian sequence the various musical segments on *Brian Wilson Presents Smile*. [© Amy Rodrigue, Courtesy Darian Sahanaja]

who went on to be a member of Derek and the Dominos. He was also an undiagnosed paranoid schizophrenic, and in 1983 obeyed voices in his head that told him to kill his 72-year-old mother with a hammer and a butcher's knife.[4]

The notoriety of "Mrs. O'Leary's Cow" was born in Jules Siegel's 1967 *Cheetah*

article. Siegel, who attended the recording session, described Brian setting the mood by passing around plastic fireman's helmets to everyone in the studio. Brian also had a janitor start a fire in a trash bin for some atmospheric smoke — an effect "not conducive to breathing" according to onlooker Danny

Hutton in *Beautiful Dreamer*. This was all just innocent whimsy, but Brian's behavior would become more troubling. According to Siegel, days after the record was finished, a building across the street from the Gold Star studio burned down, and, according to Brian, there was an unusually high number of conflagrations in Los Angeles shortly thereafter. In an increasingly paranoid state, Brian believed his fire music had somehow set those blazes, and he hid the master. "That would have been a really bad vibration to let out on the world," he told Siegel. He claimed to have destroyed those tapes, which wasn't true, and in ensuing interviews he would cite the scary "fire" track as one of the main reasons *Smile* was not released.

So Sahanaja was understandably trepidatious before playing back the 1966 recording to an anxious Brian. "I said, 'I know this track has some bad history with you, but I think it could be really cool with Nick on the fuzz guitar, strange strings, big tom toms and timpani.' And you could see him lighting up. He said, 'Yeah! Yeah!' He gets excited when things are going in a positive direction," Sahanaja says.

As they went over the chords, Brian suddenly began humming the wordless melody to "Fall Breaks and Back to Winter (W. Woodpecker Symphony)," a spooky number on *Smiley Smile*. Fans had long noted similarities between the two tracks, and Brian acknowledged to Sahanaja that they shared the same harmony part.

Brian's band was nervous about him showing up at their first rehearsals of the track. *Beautiful Dreamer* reveals that in Brian's lowest moments during the new *Smile* sessions he experienced a return of the auditory hallucinations that had plagued him intermittently since his first LSD trip in 1965. "He was in a transition of showing up to one rehearsal and then not showing up for the next one, or he'd show up and just stay for a little while," Sahanaja says. "But he was slowly growing accustomed to what we were doing. We would run the songs down and he would stare at certain band members as they played, zoning in on the sound." Luckily Brian wasn't around for the "Mrs. O'Leary's Cow" rehearsal when, like a bad omen, the electricity went out. It might have convinced him the song was cursed after all.

Sahanaja figured Brian wanted no hand in redoing the wild string arrangement. "I think that's the part that spooked him the most. I told him I'd deal with it," he says. To bring *Smile*'s orchestrations to life, Sahanaja reached out to Stockholm Strings 'N' Horns, a young eight-player ensemble that had toured behind Arthur Lee and Love for performances of the *Forever Changes* album — another high point of 1960s pop, although one that did make it to stores. "I had them listen to the original *Smile* recordings for reference," Sahanaja explains. "The music wasn't written out, per se. It was more about describing 'this is what you're going to do.' There's a certain counterpoint going on with cellos going downwards while the violins go upwards."

The *Smile* tour was set to open with a six-night engagement beginning February 20, 2004, back at Royal Festival Hall — ground zero for Brian Wilson appreciation. (By this point there had been a lineup change in the band, with Sucherman and D'Amico replaced by percussionist Nelson Bragg and drummer Jim Hines.) The anticipation in the audience and onstage was overwhelming. "So much of this was tied into Brian overcoming his demons — 'Mrs. O'Leary's Cow' being the epitome of that," Sahanaja recalls. "I was really nervous, thinking, 'Will all of this have been worth it? Will it be fulfilling for him?'"

The band opened with a 20-song set of Beach Boys numbers and a couple of tunes off the forthcoming *Gettin' in Over My Head*.[5] Then, after intermission, Brian, following some anxious backstage reflection, joined his players onstage to a standing ovation from a crowd aware it was about to see the making of pop music history. The singer-musicians launched into the soaring a cappella of "Our Prayer," and *Smile* finally lived outside the fevered imaginations of long-waiting fans. When it came time for "Mrs. O'Leary's Cow," the Stockholm players donned toy fire helmets in a playful nod to the past, while lighting effects created faux flames. "It was a really cool thing to play live. We were always waiting for that section of the show, because it was heavy. It was rockin'," Sahanaja says.

That first performance of *Smile* was met with a reported 10-minute standing ovation from the 2,900 in attendance. "I remember looking over at Brian and seeing so much weight lifted from him. And after the show he said, 'I did it! We did it!'" Sahanaja says.

They played 10 more *Smile* dates throughout the U.K. and Europe before coming home to record a studio version. By then they had the material down pat, and the principal recording took only five days in April. Mark Linett and Sahanaja took charge of mixing and overdubbing throughout the spring.

The new album, properly titled *Brian Wilson Presents Smile*, was released through Nonesuch Records on September 28, debuting on the *Billboard* charts at #13, the highest-ever entry for a Beach Boys–related album. In the U.K., it reached #7 and gold status. Thirty-eight years of publicity had helped — as, of course, did the album's contents. *Smile* 2004 not only met near-impossible expectations, but exceeded them. The band's renditions of known tracks such as "Cabin Essence" and "Surf's Up" stand up next to the originals, while the newly completed numbers are a revelation. Brian's voice may not be what it was when he was 24, but the album does feature his most impassioned singing in years.

Reviews were universally ecstatic. Robert Christgau, who had pooh-poohed the *Smile* myth for decades, awarded the record five stars in *Rolling Stone* and named it album of the year in *The Village Voice*, while *NME* effused that "*Smile* stands up with any of the great music of the 20th century." At the Grammy Awards, the record lost out for best pop vocal album to *Genius Loves Company* — the sentimental favorite awarded posthumously to Ray Charles — but "Mrs. O'Leary's Cow" won for rock instrumental performance. It remains Brian's only Grammy win outside of The Beach Boys' 2001 lifetime achievement award — ironic given it's a non-vocal number in Brian's vocal-heavy oeuvre, and a track to which he's had a historical aversion.

It had been a long, painful labor before *Smile* finally saw the light of day. The happiest moment had come months earlier when the mix was finished and Brian and Melinda came to Linett's studio to hear the entire album.

"Mark had burned a CD copy, and when it was done, he handed it to Brian and Brian was so thrilled: 'Oh wow — it's done! It's done!'" Sahanaja recalls Brian saying as he pressed the CD to his chest. "He said, 'I'm going to hold this dear to my heart.' He was trembling. That moment was a big one for me, too, because he was so proud of it. He could finally say he completed something that had been haunting him for decades."

MIDNIGHT'S ANOTHER DAY

Written by: Brian Wilson and Scott Bennett
Lead vocal: Brian Wilson
Produced by: Brian Wilson and Scott Bennett
Recorded: April 2008
Released: September 2, 2008, on *That Lucky Old Sun*

Brian Wilson Presents Smile would have made a fitting finale to Brian's storied career. After facing the last thing he had left to prove — and triumphing so absolutely — he could have walked off into the California sun and enjoyed his adopted children Daria, Delanie and Dylan and five grandchildren, and nobody would have blamed him. Instead, it merely marked the close of one creative chapter and the beginning of another new and exciting one.

But first there were several accolades coming his way. As part of the Grammy Awards in February 2005, the National Academy of Recording Arts and Sciences named him its MusiCares person of the year for his artistic and philanthropic accomplishments and threw a tribute concert headlined by Red Hot Chili Peppers and Jeff Beck. Brian's charitable side was on display in July when he performed in Berlin as part of the international Live 8 benefit concerts, watched by an estimated TV audience of three billion.

In May, The Beach Boys Historic Landmark was unveiled on the Hawthorne site of the Wilson brothers' childhood home, which had been demolished for a freeway. Brian attended the ceremony along with Alan and David Marks. Back at the studio, Brian and his band were busy on the holiday LP *What I Really Want for Christmas*. After *Smile*, it was a breezy project, and turned out to be at least as much fun as *The Beach Boys' Christmas Album*.

Brian was saddened the following March to learn that Eugene Landy, who had been suffering from lung cancer, died of pneumonia in Honolulu, age 71. Carnie recalled her dad phoning to say, "Dr. Landy died today. I know a lot of people didn't like him, but I loved him." As his own personal tribute, Brian came over to her house to record the Doris Day song "My Secret Love" with her and her husband, Rob.

A happier occasion came in June 2006, when Brian, Alan, David, Mike and Bruce put conflicts aside to attend a Capitol Records celebration of the double-platinum success of *Sounds of Summer*, the greatest-hits compilation that had supplanted *Endless Summer* in the digital age. It was the first sign a band reunion could be possible. But for now, Brian had other plans. That summer, he phoned his band member Scott Bennett out of the blue and asked if he could come over to Bennett's home studio to record — of all things — a cover of Sheena Easton's "Morning Train

(Nine to Five)." Instead, when Brian got there, Bennett recalls, "He sat down at my grand piano and said, 'I've just started this other song. Maybe you can help me with the words.'" It was a *Friends*-type composition called "Ever Strong," which has not seen release, but, as Bennett says, "We had a good time knocking that out and making a quick demo."

Brian may have been testing the waters with Bennett, who first worked with him as a session guitarist on the 1998 *Imagination* album. He recalls that at that time Brian "was very out of it. He came to the session and looked comatose in the chair." Now, a more active Brian was dropping by Bennett's apartment every day to record covers and new songs, with Bennett mostly providing the words, playing the other instruments around Brian's keyboards and engineering the sessions. Brian's selection of Bennett as a collaborator was typically instinctual. Bennett suggests that since he wasn't quite a Beach Boys obsessive, he could offer Brian a fresh outlook. He adds, "I'm very fast and Brian's very impatient. We were finding that in two or three hours Brian could leave my house with a CD of a decent demo."

Songs such as "Forever She'll Be My Surfer

Girl" and "Good Kind of Love" were upbeat, lightweight fare, which spoke to Brian's post-*Smile* mood. His creative approach varied. "On some stuff he would really dictate what he wanted," Bennett explains. "On 'Mexican Girl,' he put down the keyboard part and a quick guide vocal and said, 'Now put on a bunch of percussion, some Spanish guitars and anything you feel and I'll come back tomorrow and see what you've got.' The next day, after I had worked long and hard on it, he was floored. He said, 'This thing is stacked!'"

After a month, they had stockpiled a dozen and a half songs, never discussing what would become of them. "If Brian wanted to pop around and be creative, I wasn't going to make it some official thing. I wanted Brian to feel like we were just doing it for fun," Bennett says. The songs came in handy, however, when London's Southbank Centre approached Brian with an offer. The facility looked to make a splash with the fall 2007 reopening of its renovated Royal Festival Hall and asked Brian if he could return with a brand-new song cycle à la *Smile*. "I had to take all these song ideas and try to make a conceptual thing out of it," Bennett recalls.

As a press release proclaimed, the song cycle was assembled as Brian's "autobiographical travelogue" of Southern California — his love letter to L.A. To imbue the project with some of *Smile*'s luster, Van Dyke Parks was invited on board and penned a series of spoken-word vignettes of scenes and characters in the City of Angels. The songs by Brian and Bennett were divided into five movements linked by Parks' narratives. Parks also contributed the ecologically minded lyrics for the song "Live Let Live." "I tried to get Van Dyke more involved, either to help me or to say, 'You take these three songs, I'll take these three songs,'" Bennett explains. "He was gracious and said, 'Hey, this is your baby.'"

While all this was going on, Brian got hooked on the African-American spiritual "That Lucky Old Sun," written by Beasley Smith and Haven Gillespie. A folkie orchestral arrangement sung by Frankie Laine topped the charts in 1949, but it was Louis Armstrong's more soulful interpretation that Brian picked up at a CD shop. He played around with the chords and when he was done had an overture and title track for the evolving piece.

As writing and recording heated up, Bennett, Brian and Melinda agreed that any new conceptual work with the names Wilson and Parks attached would inevitably draw comparisons to *Smile*. And if it was going to hold up, a heavy number or two along the lines of "Surf's Up" would be needed. "Unfortunately Brian wasn't in that headspace at the time. He was in this real fun, nostalgic, '60s place," Bennett says. So it wasn't surprising that the song Brian returned with was not at all moody, but rather an old-timey number called "Beatle Man" that includes the lines "Beatle Man, what's your plan/Elton boy, whatchya got cooking?"

"It was all about his contemporaries. He was calling them out, like, 'What are you guys up to these days?'" Bennett explains. "I remember Brian's review of McCartney's then-recent album. He said, 'Paul can do better.'" Although the song wasn't what they were looking for, Bennett felt the strong melody could form the basis of something else and suggested adding a minor chord and slowing the tempo. "It became the first song where, instead of my just writing the lyrics, we were kicking each other off the piano bench and trading ideas of where the song could go. It was thrilling."

The piano intro — a sudden burst of emotion, then a catching of breath — was something Bennett already had kicking around, and then Brian took up the key a half-step to D-flat, which was a very unorthodox choice leading into the verse, which starts in A. "That was the first of his suggestions where I was like, 'Are you sure?'" Bennett recalls. "It didn't make any sense to me, but somehow it works."

Brian left the song's new lyrics up to Bennett, who was briefly tempted to emulate Parks' epic, abstract *Smile* approach. "But that was the 24-year-old Brian Wilson smoking dope," he says. "Now he was 64, so it had to make sense for him and his age group. It was a really tough path, because we already had a syllable pattern. It's not like I could just sit down and write poetry. I had to make it all fit. I also wanted to try to keep to Brian's lyrical instincts."

Based on lyrics Brian devised for a number called "Oxygen to the Brain" that address his wasted years, Bennett felt he could help Brian craft another semi-autobiographical song. At the same time, he wasn't sure how Brian would respond to lines about feeling lost and alone. Bennett's wife, Jenny, a Brit he met on the *Smile* tour, came up with the title "Midnight's Another Day" for the song "Beatle Man" had now become and assisted

Bennett's writing throughout the album. "She would say, 'Brian won't be comfortable singing that.' She helped me keep it real and more emotional," he says.

The metaphoric finished lyrics support Brian's most complex composition in years. The same could be said for the production, with the eventual recording bolstered by Paul Von Mertens' arrangement of a five-piece string section. Bennett suggested incorporating a French horn à la "Surf's Up," while Brian came up with three countermelody lines that he sang to Bennett over the phone. Bennett calls the song his "proudest moment" of the project.

He and Brian also came up with the equally moving ballad "Southern California," which recaps Brian's life from a positive perspective. "Instead of making it 'Oh, poor Brian, he's had a rough time of it,' I thought, at the end of the day, he conquered the world with his music and he did it with family and friends. It's not so bad," Bennett says. The two cuts bring the necessary gravitas to the song cycle's fifth and final movement.

Bennett roughed out a song order and asked Darian Sahanaja to thread the album with recurring snippets and variations of the theme of "That Lucky Old Sun," similar to how Sahanaja helped the flow of *Brian Wilson Presents Smile*. Sahanaja also came up with the masterstroke of rerecording the vocal intro of "Can't Wait Too Long" — Brian's great, unfinished multipart song from the *Wild Honey* era — to smooth over the transition between the military march of "Oxygen to the Brain" and "Midnight's Another Day." He also edited down some of the songs for live performance.

"Midnight's Another Day" was previewed on Brian's website ahead of the debut of the complete work — officially titled *That Lucky Old Sun (A Narrative)* — in London on September 10, 2007, on the first night of another six-night stand. It was another home run. NME.com reported, "Wilson's new music was received warmly by the capacity crowd, who gave their hero a standing ovation."[1]

The tour moved to Australia in the New Year before the band hunkered down in L.A. in April to record the new piece. As with *Smile*, they had already honed the material on the road. There were more personnel changes, with drummer Jim Hines leaving the band and Todd Sucherman returning. Longtime bassist Bob Lizik appears on the record, but also would be gone soon afterwards. As befitting music that mined Brian's history, *That Lucky*

Old Sun was released by Capitol, where the initial recording sessions were also held, making it Brian's first LP made at "the tower" since *Surfin' U.S.A.*

Smile aside, it proved to be Brian's most consistent solo record — a musical extravaganza that effectively balances rock 'n' roll, chamber pop, epic balladry and Tin Pan Alley. The songs are irresistibly hooky and Brian sings them with gusto. That he could finish off *Smile* at that point in his life came as a major surprise, but following up with such a strong album of new material was arguably an even bigger revelation.

Released on September 2, the album, on which Bennett is credited with "additional production," drew a few negative and tepid reviews, notably from the *Guardian* and the *New York Times*, but appraisals were generally strong and often rapturous. "You have to go back to *Surf's Up* . . . to hear a Beach Boys long-player as good," raved *Mojo*.[2] It peaked at #21 in the U.S., the highest placement for an album of new Brian or Beach Boys songs in more than 30 years, and reached #37 in the U.K.

For Bennett, his relationship with Brian had evolved significantly since he first showed up in the studio with his guitar a decade earlier. Along the way, he saw how Brian's stable family life and supportive new band allowed him to get healthier and happier and reach artistic heights few would have thought possible. "The most rewarding part of having this gig," he says, "has been witnessing a human being's life improve."

BRIAN WILSON ON...
RHAPSODY IN BLUE

Written by: George Gershwin
Lead vocal: Brian Wilson
Produced by: Brian Wilson
Recorded: early 2010
Released: August 17, 2010,
on *Brian Wilson Reimagines Gershwin*

Brian had long dreamed about making a record of songs by George Gershwin and his lyricist-brother, Ira. In 2010, that dream became reality.

As it turned out, Walt Disney Records had its own project in mind for Brian. The label wanted him to "Brian-ize" a collection of famous tunes from Disney films. He took on that assignment and made his Gershwin concept part of the deal. Disney execs came up with a pool of 25 suitable Gershwin compositions, from which he selected 11, including "They Can't Take That Away from Me" and "Someone to Watch Over Me" — standards best known from versions by the likes of Billie Holiday and Ella Fitzgerald. Brian's band member Paul Von Mertens, who would provide the orchestral arrangements, helped Brian determine which songs he could sing well in his register.[1]

Things got even more interesting when Warner/Chappell Music and the Gershwin estate granted Brian access to more than 100 unfinished Gershwin compositions for the undertaking. He chose "Will You Remember Me?" — an outtake from the 1924 musical *Lady, Be Good!* — and a fragment dating from 1929. Guided by piano demos, he had

Scott Bennett supply new words, continuing where their collaboration left off on *That Lucky Old Sun*. Together they crafted the original songs "The Like in I Love You" and "Nothing but Love."

"I felt so thrilled to think I was going to 'work' with George Gershwin. I blew a gasket in my head. I couldn't believe it," Brian told this author in an interview for *Maclean's*. The album brought Brian's musical history full circle. After all, it was Gershwin's symphonic jazz masterwork "Rhapsody in Blue" that triggered his musical awakening. As the story goes, he was two when he heard it at his grandmother's house and asked for it to be played over and over. "'Rhapsody in Blue' is the song of my life," he said.[2]

Some historians hear Gershwin even in Brian's melodies and piano on the early Beach Boys surf LPs, and he produced a version of Gershwin's "Summertime" for singer Sharon Marie back in 1963. He also acknowledges Gershwin as an influence on *Smile*. Like "Rhapsody in Blue," *Smile* brings orchestral arrangements to pop music and incorporates a multipart structure usually associated with classical composition. In the early 1970s, Brian became determined to really deconstruct "Rhapsody." "I learned how to play the pretty part — the violin part — when I was 28," he recalled. "I had a copy of Leonard Bernstein's version. I went from the record to my piano — back and forth. I learned two bars at a time until I had that whole centerpiece down."[3] The Gershwin influence on Brian's writing has become more pronounced over the years, showing up in songs from "This Isn't Love" on *Live at the Roxy Theatre* to the Tin Pan Alley moments of *That Lucky Old Sun*.

What makes *Brian Wilson Reimagines Gershwin* unique among modern interpretations of the Great American Songbook is Brian's trademark group vocal arrangements applied to numbers traditionally sung solo — or not sung at all. That's apparent right from the album's opening segment — "the pretty part" of "Rhapsody," delivered not by violins but by Brian's wordless vocals, stacked as high as the Chrysler Building. "I did that so I could show off my voice. I have a very good harmonic voice," he felt required to mention. The track brings to fruition a mid-'90s effort by him and Van Dyke Parks to adapt the song to harmonies.[4]

The album features a four-song suite from the classic 1935 African-American opera

*Porgy and Be*ss, Brian's favorite section being "I Loves You, Porgy," which he performs with particular passion. Mertens' instrumentation, meanwhile, downplays the sly humor and brings out the sinister in "It Ain't Necessarily So," while "Summertime" has a similarly foreboding tone. Elsewhere, "I Got Plenty o' Nuttin'" is transformed into an instrumental evoking Mark Twain's America with a bass harmonica right out of *Pet Sounds*' "I Know There's an Answer."

"Isn't it a nice album?" Brian gushed. "It's very simple but direct."[5] He wanted to know the author's favorite number on the album ("I Got Plenty o' Nuttin'") and thoughts on specific tracks. He has always fed on outside opinion. It has propelled him when it's good and cut deeply when it's not. He should have felt buoyed, then, by the LP's reception. Released through Disney's Pearl Series imprint, it entered the Billboard 200 at #26 and climbed to the top of *Billboard*'s Jazz Albums chart. While some found the arrangements short of Brian at his most inventive, most reviews were positive. His link to the Gershwins was further underlined in March 2011 when he was announced as the recipient of the UCLA Alumni's annual George and Ira Gershwin Award for Lifetime Musical Achievement.

Things were equally productive on the home front, where Brian's family expanded to five children after he and Melinda adopted Dash and Dakota Rose. None of these personal and professional highlights would have been possible without the dramatic improvement of Brian's mental and physical health. He admitted he had to keep working on the physical part. "I walk at a park down about a mile from my house almost every day," he said. "But I gained 25 pounds over two months. I have to get on a good diet."[6] And that's no easy task for a man who's always loved to eat.

The Gershwin album appeared just a couple of days before his old friend Paul McCartney wrapped a tour that sold out arenas throughout North America. It was fitting that Brian should again share the spotlight with the Beatle with whom he has been most closely identified, both being bass players — born two days apart — and both revered for their timeless melodies. He acknowledged he was genuinely shaken by the Fab Four. "I was envious as hell," he recalled, "because they eclipsed everybody. Paul and John's voices really do a good thing, and their songs are very creative and unique. 'I Want to Hold Your Hand,' 'Tell

Me Why,' 'Ob-La-Di, Ob-La-Da' — I love all their stuff." He saw The Beach Boys and The Beatles not as rivals but as mutual admirers. "I hoped they liked *Pet Sounds* as much as I liked *Rubber Soul*," he said.[7]

He could be just as proud of The Beach Boys' legacy. As TPMCafé blogger Amanda Marcotte wrote, "No one would have guessed in 1963 that The Beach Boys would be the single biggest influence on indie rock in 2009."[8] Tributes to Brian and his group are common among musicians young enough to be his grandchildren. Usually the influence is heard in the music, while sometimes the reference is more direct, as in "On the Beach Boys Bus" by Bill Wells & Maher Shalal Hash Baz, "How the Beach Boys Sound to Those with No Feelings" by Extra Happy Ghost!!, Rich Aucoin's "Brian Wilson Is A.L.I.V.E." and Pete Yorn's "Murray" (*sic*) about Brian's larger-than-life father. The fact Brian was so widely admired by modern acts was not lost on him. "I know," he said. "I know that. My band used to be amongst those groups." He didn't listen to these younger artists, however. "I know I should, but I don't," he said, adding that he didn't own an iPod and was happy to tune his radio to L.A. oldies station K-EARTH

101 for his daily dose of The Rolling Stones, Diana Ross, Marvin Gaye and The Doors — artists whose great years coincided with The Beach Boys'.

In spring 2011, he played several dates on the U.S. East Coast, followed that summer by his first substantial Canadian tour, in which he performed the entire Gershwin album to enthusiastic crowds. It was bold enough for a 69-year-old artist to continue presenting complete new works live, but for notoriously stage-shy Brian, just getting up there every night was an act of bravery. "For about an hour before I go onstage I feel all nervous as hell, then as soon as I hear the first note the band plays, I'm okay," he said.[9]

It was no different when he and The Beach Boys were young, fresh-faced pop stars in striped shirts rocking concert halls and national TV shows. "I always felt the nerves," he continued. "I would always tell Carl, 'I'm nervous, Carl, I'm nervous.' He would go, 'Don't worry, it will go okay.' He was the stabilizer." All of a sudden Brian was rolling with memories of the old days. "Mike was the joker," he said. "I was busy trying to produce our records and sometimes Mike would not stop talking, and Carl would say, 'Mike — come on, let's get recording.'" But Brian would be happy once he got Mike's vocals down, and he credited his cousin's lead on "California Girls" as one reason it's his favorite Beach Boys record.

As the band's 50th anniversary drew nearer, various initiatives kept the group and its members front and center. Capitol/EMI released *The Smile Sessions* boxed set and two-CD version on November 1 to the expected euphoric reviews and later "re-issue of the year" honors from *Rolling Stone*. It charted at #27 in the U.S. and #25 in the U.K. Curiously, its appearance followed that of Brian's *In the Key of Disney* by only one week, burying interest in that album. That was unfortunate, as the loose, straightforward approach given the Disney tunes does right by 70-plus years of great songwriting, from the Sherman Brothers to Randy Newman. The LP had a cup of coffee on the U.S. charts, peaking at #83.

In December, The Beach Boys' home state returned the favor of half a century of good PR by inducting the group into the California Hall of Fame. Meanwhile, Hollywood looked to get in on the act, with no fewer than three feature films in the pipeline. Aaron Eckhart was announced to play Dennis in *The Drummer*, a drama from husband-and-wife filmmakers Randall Miller and Jody Savin (collaborators on *Bottle Shock*) that was to chronicle the last six years of Dennis' life, beginning with his artistic triumph on *Pacific Ocean Blue*. Meanwhile, producer Bill Pohlad (*The Tree of Life*) and John Wells Productions revealed they had Oscar nominee Oren Moverman — who co-wrote the experimental Bob Dylan biopic *I'm Not There* — working on a script about Brian's life. In a totally different vein was an untitled musical that would use Beach Boys' songs as the backdrop for a teenage love story, as *Mamma Mia!* did with Abba hits. Fox 2000 reportedly paid more than $2 million for the rights to the untitled project, which was to be produced by John Stamos, Craig Zadan and Neil Meron, who collaborated on the miniseries *The Beach Boys: An American Family*. The screenplay for the musical was written by Oscar Nominee Susannah Grant (*Erin Brockovich*) and Emmy Award–winner Michael Sucsy (*The Vow*) was to direct.

But nothing excited fans more than the announcement that most of the surviving members would reunite for the band's 50th anniversary. As a trial run, Brian, Mike, Alan and Bruce had entered Capitol Studios in

After 50 years, the group kicked off its anniversary festivities with a performance at the 2012 Grammy Awards. From left: Bruce, David, Brian, Mike and Alan. [© AP Photo/Mark J. Terrill]

summer 2011 to record — what else? — "Do It Again." The track was intended for a new Beach Boys album — the first since 1996's *Stars and Stripes Vol. 1* — to be produced by Brian and executive produced by Mike. Even more surprising was word of a 2012 international tour with 50 or so dates featuring those four members and David Marks. It kicked off with an appearance on the Grammy Awards broadcast in which the band performed "Good Vibrations" after young admirers Maroon 5 sang "Surfer Girl" and Foster the People covered "Wouldn't It Be Nice." Capitol/EMI looked to fuel interest with the promise of catalog releases including yet another hits collection and career-spanning boxed set.

Yes, surf's up again for "America's band." Through its history, the group has soared to the top, withstood the British Invasion and repeatedly fallen in and out of favor. There've been creative differences, dustups, breakups and lawsuits. The lowest points have been the tragic loss of two core members. But the spirits of Dennis and Carl will live on as long as the music does, and it's not going anywhere. As they readied to embark on the Celebration tour, the surviving members were past or near retirement age yet were goin' on because hundreds of thousands of fans around the world wanted them to.

Most incredible of all has been Brian's resurgence. It's understandable that he would have been burned out by the '60s. In that decade, The Beach Boys released 20 albums in eight years, and he produced most every track and wrote the lion's share. Does he ever reflect on what an amazing accomplishment that is? "Yeah, I do think that sometimes. I wonder how I did it. I was young and creative," he said, adding, "Songs don't come as quick these days."

Many of The Beach Boys' contemporaries and collaborators were long gone by 2012, while Brian was not only here but also in his most productive period since the 1960s. He knew better than anyone that, along with his happy family life, serving his genius was keeping him afloat in the deep waters that had taken him down before.

"I don't plan on retiring," he said. "If I retire, it's kind of like saying I'm getting lazy. And I don't think I want to be lazy."

ENDNOTES

Intro — The Hawthorne Hotshots

1 Timothy White, *The Nearest Faraway Place* (New York: Henry Holt, 1994).

2 City of Hawthorne, CA <http://cityofhawthorne.com/about/history.asp>.

3 White, 78.

4 David Leaf, *The Beach Boys and the California Myth* (New York: Grosset & Dunlap, 1978), 19.

5 Steven Gaines, *Heroes and Villains: The True Story of The Beach Boys* (Toronto: Signet, 1987), 48.

6 Gaines, 57.

7 White, 120.

8 Sunny Watson's West Coast Swing Dance <http://www.streetswing.com/histburl/a2jennielee.htm>.

9 Keith Badman, *The Beach Boys: The Definitive Diary of America's Greatest Band Onstage and in the Studio* (San Francisco: Backbeat Books, 2004), 17.

"Surfin' U.S.A."

1 Ken Sharp, "Riding the Waves: My Life as a Beach Boy by Al Jardine," *Record Collector*, August 2009: 60.

2 Jon Stebbins, *The Lost Beach Boy* (London: Virgin Brooks, 2007), 78.

3 Dave Marsh and Kevin Stein, *The Book of Rock Lists* (New York: Dell Publishing, 1984), 596.

4 Stebbins, 97.

5 Stebbins, 104.

6 White, 170.

7 Stebbins, 168.

8 Stebbins, 221.

"Surfer Girl"

1 Brian Wilson with Todd Gold, *Wouldn't It Be Nice: My Own Story* (New York: HarperCollins Publishers, 1991), 79.

2 Jim Fusilli, *33 1/3: Pet Sounds* (New York: Continuum International Publishing Group, 2005), 23.

"In My Room"
1 Wilson with Gold, 58.
2 David Leaf, *Surfer Girl/Shut Down Volume 2*, CD booklet (Toronto: EMI Music Canada, 1990), 8.
3 Alan Boyd and Steven R. Monroe, *Nashville Sounds: The Making of Stars and Stripes*, DVD (Delilah Films, Disney Channel, 1996).
4 Wilson with Gold, 34.
5 Gaines, 82.
6 Brad Elliott, *The Beach Boys Rarities,* liner notes (London: EMI Records Limited, 1983).
7 Bellagio 10452, ed. Andrew G. Doe <http://www.btinternet.com/~bellagio/gigs64.html>.

"Fun, Fun, Fun"
1 Stebbins, 98.
2 Gaines, 113.
3 Badman, 63.
4 Badman, 48.

"Don't Worry Baby"
1 Wilson with Gold, 82.
2 Gaines, 126.
3 Wilson with Gold, 104.

"I Get Around"
1 Badman, 55.
2 Gaines, 115.
3 Badman, 54.
4 Gaines, 205.
5 Ellis Amburn, *Dark Star: The Roy Orbison Story* (New York: Carol Publishing Group, 1990), 164.

"Kiss Me, Baby"
1 Wilson with Gold, 98.
2 Bellagio 10452 < http://www.btinternet.com/~bellagio/gigs64.html>.
3 Badman, 73.

4 Craig Slowinski, "The Beach Boys Today! LP," beachboysarchives.com <http://www.tiptopwebsite.com/custommusic2/craigslowinskicom.pdf#page=1>.
5 Alan Boyd, *Endless Harmony: The Beach Boys Story*, DVD (Delilah Films, 2000).
6 Slowinski.

"Do You Wanna Dance?"
1 Slowinski.
2 Badman, 82.

"Help Me, Rhonda"
1 Wilson with Gold, 111.
2 *Brian Wilson: Songwriter 1962–1969*, DVD (Sexy Intellectual, 2010).
3 Jon Stebbins, *The Beach Boys FAQ: All That's Left to Know About America's Band* (Milwaukee: Backbeat Books, 2011), 167.
4 Badman, 82.
5 "Hot 100," *Billboard.com* <http://www.billboard.com/#/charts/hot-100?chartDate=1965-05-29>.

"I'm Bugged at My Ol' Man"
1 Hard Rock Memorabilia <http://memorabilia.hardrock.com>.
2 Hard Rock Memorabilia.
3 Leaf, *The Beach Boys and the California Myth*, 159.
4 Wilson with Gold, 93.
5 Peter Ames Carlin, *Catch a Wave: The Rise, Fall & Redemption of The Beach Boys' Brian Wilson* (Emmaus, PA: Rodale, 2006), 73.
6 Hard Rock Memorabilia.
7 Hard Rock Memorabilia.
8 Hard Rock Memorabilia.
9 Hard Rock Memorabilia.
10 Wilson with Gold, 97.
11 Carlin, 34.

12 White, 209.

13 Tom Nolan with David Felton, "The Beach Boys: A California Saga," *Rolling Stone*, November 11, 1971: 50.

"Girl Don't Tell Me"

1 John Milward, *The Beach Boys: Silver Anniversary* (New York: Doubleday & Company, 1985), 97.

2 Carlin, 66.

3 Badman, 89.

4 Craig Slowinski, "*Summer Days (And Summer Nights!!)* sessions continued from the Summer 2009 edition of *Endless Summer Quarterly . . .*" <http:// www.tiptopwebsite.com/custommusic2 /craigslowinskicom3.pdf>.

"California Girls"

1 David Leaf, *Beautiful Dreamer: Brian Wilson and the Story of Smile*, DVD (BriMel, 2004).

2 David Leaf, "The Making of *Pet Sounds*," *The Pet Sounds Sessions*, CD booklet (Hollywood: Capitol Records, 1996), 13.

3 Slowinski.

4 Badman, 93.

5 "Hot 100," *Billboard.com* <http://www.billboard .com/#/charts/hot-100?chartDate=1965-08-28>.

"The Little Girl I Once Knew"

1 Alan Boyd, *Hawthorne, CA*, CD booklet (Hollywood: Capitol Records, 2001).

2 Badman, 104.

3 John Lennon, "Blind Date," *Melody Maker,* December 11, 1965: 10.

4 WorthPoint <http://www.worthpoint.com/ worthopedia/beatles-monthly-magazine-special- big-143224726>.

5 *Back to the Beach: A Brian Wilson and The Beach Boys Reader*, ed. Kingsley Abbott (London: Helter Skelter Publishing, 1999), 26.

"Barbara Ann"

1 Bellagio 10452 <http://www.btinternet .com/~bellagio/gigs65.html>.

2 Stebbins, *The Lost Beach Boy*, 50.

3 Badman, 34.

4 White, 174.

5 David Leaf, *Beach Boys' Party!/Stack-O-Tracks*, CD booklet (Toronto: Capitol Records, 2001), 7.

6 Mikal Gilmore, "Jan and Dean's brief encounter," *Rolling Stone*, November 2, 1978: 18.

"Sloop John B"

1 Carlin, 80.

2 Wilson with Gold, 46.

3 Leaf, "The Making of *Pet Sounds*," 25–26.

4 Bellagio 10452 <http://www.btinternet .com/~bellagio/gigs65.html>.

5 Brad Elliott, "Pet Sounds Sessionography," Brad Elliott <http://www.bradelliott.com/writings/ps3 .html>.

6 Elliott.

7 "Hot 100," *Billboard.com* <http://www.billboard. com/#/charts/hot 100?chartDate=1966-05-07>.

8 "1966-05-21 Top 40 Official UK Singles Archive," Official Charts <http://www.theofficialcharts.com/ archive-chart/_/1/1966-05-21/>.

9 Stebbins, *The Beach Boys FAQ: All That's Left to Know about America's Band*, 298–299.

10 Patrick Doyle, "Mike Love 'Looking Forward' to Beach Boys 50th Anniversary Tour," *Rolling Stone*, December 19, 2011 <http://www.rollingstone.com/ music/news/exclusive-mike-love-talks-beach-boys- 50th-anniversary-tour-20111219>.

"I Just Wasn't Made for These Times"
1 Fusilli, 78.
2 Elliott.
3 Badman, 126.
4 Charles L. Granata, *Wouldn't It Be Nice: Brian Wilson and the Making of the Beach Boys' Pet Sounds* (Chicago: A Cappella Books, 2003), 173.

"Caroline, No"
1 Carlin, 17.
2 Leaf, *The Beach Boys and the California Myth*, 86.
3 Jules Siegel, "Goodbye Surfing, Hello God!" *Cheetah*, October 1967.
4 Elliott.
5 Leaf, 157.
6 Leaf, 85.

"Let's Go Away for Awhile"
1 David Leaf, *The Pet Sounds Sessions*, CD booklet (Hollywood: Capitol Records, 1996), 15.
2 DJ M, "Brian Wilson/Andy Paley/Sean O'Hagan," Uncanny, May 13, 2005 <http://uncanny1.blogspot.com/2005/05/brian-wilsonandy-paleysean-ohagan.html>.
3 Bellagio 10452 <http://www.btinternet.com/~bellagio/gigs96.html>.

"Wouldn't It Be Nice"
1 Wilson with Gold, 135, 157.
2 Wilson with Gold, 135.
3 Granata, 173.
4 Mark Linett, *The Pet Sounds Sessions*, CD booklet (Hollywood: Capitol Records, 1996), 27.
5 "Taylor Swift Reveals Newfound Obsession with American History," *Rolling Stone*, August 4, 2011 < http://www.rollingstone.com/music/news/taylor-swift-reveals-newfound-obsession-with-american-history-20110804>.
6 Chris Kimek, "In concert: She & Him at 9:30 Club," *The Washington Post*, Click Track, July 8, 2010 <http://blog.washingtonpost.com/clicktrack/2010/07/in_concert_she_him_at_930_club.html >.

"God Only Knows"
1 Wilson with Gold, 138.
2 Leaf, "The Making of *Pet Sounds*," 11.
3 Leaf, 32.
4 Leaf, 125.
5 Scott Mervis, "Wilson all smiles about recent honor, resurrected career," *Pittsburgh Post-Gazette*, December 26, 2007 < http://www.post-gazette.com/pg/07360/844253-42.stm>.

"Here Today"
1 Leaf, 45.
2 Leaf, 11.
3 Granata, 134.
4 Leaf, *The Pet Sounds Sessions*, CD booklet, 16.
5 Al Kooper, "100 Greatest Recordings of All Time," Al Kooper <http://www.alkooper.com/hot100.html>.
6 Al Kooper, "There's No Denyin' Brian Survivin'," Al Kooper, August 1999 <http://www.alkooper.com/oldcolumns03.html>.

"Good Vibrations"
1 Gary Weis, NBC, *The Beach Boys*, August 5, 1976.
2 Ben Edmonds, *Beach Boys '69*, album liner notes (Toronto: Capitol Records, 1976).
3 Craig Slowinski and Alan Boyd, "The Beach Boys – Smile Sessionography," *The Smile Sessions,* CD booklet (Hollywood: Capitol Records, 2011) np.
4 Leaf, *The Beach Boys and the California Myth*, 90.
5 Badman, 150.

"Heroes and Villains"

1 Domenic Priore, *Smile: The Story of Brian Wilson's Lost Masterpiece* (New York: Bobcat Books, 2007), 34.
2 White, 271.
3 David Dalton, "Let's go trippin!'" *Mojo*, June 1998: 92.
4 Badman, 132.
5 David Leaf, *Smiley Smile/Wild Honey*, CD booklet (Toronto: EMI Music Canada, 1990) 14.
6 Badman, 178.
7 Carlin, 119.

"Our Prayer"

1 Badman, 231.

"Surf's Up"

1 Priore, 89.
2 Siegel.
3 Slowinski and Boyd.
4 CBS, *Inside Pop: The Rock Revolution*, April 25, 1967.
5 Carlin, 163.
6 Slowinski and Boyd.
7 Slowinski and Boyd.
8 Arthur Schmidt, "Surf's Up, The Beach Boys," *Rolling Stone*, October 14, 1971: 48.

"Wonderful"

1 Badman, 195.
2 Slowinski and Boyd.
3 Morgan Neville, *Brian Wilson: A Beach Boy's Tale*, TV special (Peter Jones Productions, A&E, 1999).

"Darlin'"

1 Wilson with Gold, 171.
2 Brad Elliott, *Surf's Up! The Beach Boys on Record 1961–1981* (London: Helter Skelter Publishing, 2003), 278.

3 Elliott, 279.
4 Ken Sharp, "Brian Wilson: Surf's up again," *Goldmine*, Sept. 8, 2000: 50.
5 Wilson with Gold, 192.
6 Gaines, 263.

"Little Bird"

1 Jon Stebbins, *The Real Beach Boy* (Toronto: ECW Press, 2000), 92.

"Meant for You"

1 Badman, 219.
2 Timothy Ferris, "The Fillmore East closes. More. More," *Rolling Stone*, July 22, 1971: 10.

"Do It Again"

1 Brad Elliott, *Endless Harmony Soundtrack*, CD booklet (Toronto: Capitol Records, 1998), 11.
2 Badman, 221.
3 Stephen W. Desper, "More Desper Archives," Cabin Essence, November 23, 2002 <http://www.surfermoon.com/essays/desperarchive2.html>.
4 Badman, 89.
5 Bellagio 10452 <http://www.btinternet.com/~bellagio/gigs68.html>.
6 Badman, 235.

"Forever"

1 Vincent Bugliosi with Curt Gentry, *Helter Skelter: The True Story of the Manson Murders* (W.W. Norton & Company, 1994), 250.
2 Keith Altham, "The Rave Interview," *Rave*, May 1969.
3 Tom Nolan, "Surf's Up! Melcher's Nightmare Is Over," *Rolling Stone*, May 9, 1974: 22.
4 Gaines, 209.
5 Nolan with Felton, 52.
6 Bugliosi with Gentry, 250.

7 Nolan with Felton, 52.

8 Andrew Doe and John Tobler, *The Complete Guide to the Music of The Beach Boys* (London: Omnibus Press, 1997), 76.

9 Peter Reum, "This Whole World," *Endless Summer Quarterly*, Winter 2010/2011: 15.

10 Badman, 241.

11 David M. Beard, "Slip on Through," *Endless Summer Quarterly*, Winter 2010/2011: 10.

12 Bugliosi with Gentry, 336.

13 Leaf, *The Beach Boys and the California Myth*, 137.

14 Leaf, 137.

15 Adam Webb, *Dumb Angel: The Life and Music of Dennis Wilson* (Creation Books, 2001), 86.

16 Bugliosi with Gentry.

"This Whole World"

1 Badman, 258.

2 Timothy White, "The Beach Boys — Brothers-in-Arms: The Pioneering Road to *Sunflower* and *Surf's Up*," *Sunflower/Surf's Up*, CD booklet (Toronto: Capitol Records, 2000).

3 Wilson with Gold, 192.

4 Badman, 257.

5 Badman, 257.

6 Bellagio 10452 <http://www.btinternet.com/~bellagio/gigs73.html>.

7 Jim Miller, "Records: Sunflower," *Rolling Stone*, October 1, 1970: 42.

"Long Promised Road"

1 Gaines, 234.

2 Stephen W. Desper, "Recording Long Promised Road," Uncanny, June 27, 2005 <http://uncanny1.blogspot.com/2005/06/recording-long-promised-road.html>.

"Feel Flows"

1 Robert Christgau, "The Beach Boys," Robert Christgau <http://www.robertchristgau.com/get_artist.php?name=beach+boys>.

2 Nolan with Felton, 50.

3 Billy Hinsche, *1974: On the Road with The Beach Boys, Disc 2: The Interviews*, DVD (MFM Productions, 2011).

4 Maura Kelly, "Nancy Wilson," *The Believer*, August 2007 <http://www.believermag.com/issues/200708/?read=interview_wilson>.

"'Til I Die"

1 Badman, 257.

2 Leaf, 144.

3 Carlin, 162.

"Disney Girls (1957)"

1 White.

"Sail on Sailor"

1 Badman, 250.

2 Elliott, *Surf's Up! The Beach Boys on Record 1961–1981*, 386.

3 Badman, 305.

4 Andrew G. Doe, "Brian on Carl and the Passions, Holland and the Light Album," The Smiley Smile Message Board, January 9, 2011 <http://smileysmile.net/board/index.php/topic,9773.0.html>.

5 Wilson with Gold, 193.

6 Elliott, 284.

7 Badman, 323.

8 Phil Collins, No Way Out: A Phil Collins Forum, October 25, 2006 <http://philcollins.conforums.com/index.cgi?board=music&action=print&num=1161470333>.

9 "The Grammy Picks: Theirs & Ours," *Rolling Stone*, February 14, 1974: 11.

"Good Timin'"
1 Judith Sims, "Chicago," *Rolling Stone*, July 19, 1973: 22.
2 Bellagio 10452 <http://www.btinternet .com/~bellagio/gigs73.html>.
3 Eliot Wald, "Beach Boys & Chicago: Surf's Up in K. C.," *Rolling Stone*, June 19, 1975: 86.
4 Robert Christgau, "Beach Boys at Summer's End," *Village Voice,* June 23, 1975 <http://www .robertchristgau.com/xg/music/chicago-75.php>.
5 Gaines, 267.
6 Gaines, 267.
7 John Swenson, "Beach Boys: No More Fun, Fun, Fun," *Rolling Stone,* October 20, 1977: 13.
8 Craig Slowinski, "Brian on Carl and the Passions, Holland and the Light Album," The Smiley Smile Message Board, January 9, 2011 <http://smileysmile .net/board/index.php/topic,9773.25.html>.

"It's OK"
1 Elliott, 230.
2 David Felton, "The Healing of Brother Bri," *Rolling Stone*, November 4, 1976: 40.
3 White, *The Nearest Faraway Place*, 382.
4 Wilson with Gold, 228.
5 Gaines, 288.
6 Michael deMartin, "'The Warmth of the Sun' Rises Tomorrow . . . and More . . ." The Beach Boys, May 21, 2007 <http://beachboyswarmth.blogspot.com/>.
7 Badman, 367.

"Johnny Carson"
1 Carlin, 212.
2 Carlin, 212.
3 Leaf, 181.
4 Sharp, "Riding the Waves: My Life as a Beach Boy by Al Jardine," 65.
5 Timothy White, "Johnny Carson: The *Rolling Stone*

Interview," *Rolling Stone*, March 22, 1979: 54.

"Farewell My Friend"
1 David Leaf, "Dennis Wilson: It's About Time," *Pet Sounds*, September 1977.
2 Stebbins, *The Lost Beach Boy*, 107.
3 Jon Stebbins and David Beard, "Dennis Wilson: Chronology of a Solo Artist," *Pacific Ocean Blue*, CD booklet (The EU: Sony BMG Music Entertainment, 2008).
4 Ben Edmonds, "Love Remember Me: Dennis Wilson's Dreams Delivered," *Pacific Ocean Blue*, CD booklet.
5 "Random Notes," *Rolling Stone*, November 17, 1977: 41.

"Keepin' the Summer Alive"
1 Christopher Connelly, "California Girls," *Rolling Stone*, May 2, 1991: 29.
2 Elliott, 296.
3 Gaines, 322.

"Getcha Back"
1 Wilson with Gold, 305.
2 Jim Jerome, "Death of a Beach Boy," *People*, January 16, 1984: 25.
3 Bellagio 10452 <http://www.btinternet. com/~bellagio/gigs84.html>.
4 Wilson with Gold, 318.
5 Parke Puterbaugh, "Records: The Beach Boys," *Rolling Stone*, August 15, 1985: 46.
6 White, *The Nearest Faraway Place*, 340.

"Love and Mercy"
1 Jerry McCulley, "Trouble in Mind — A Revealing Interview with Brian Wilson," *Back to the Beach: A Brian Wilson and The Beach Boys Reader*, 189.
2 Wilson with Gold, 336.

3 Kingsley Abbott, "Two Soulmates Touching in the Dark: Brian Wilson, Gary Usher and The Wilson Project," *Back to the Beach: A Brian Wilson and The Beach Boys Reader*, 184.

4 White, 344.

5 David Leaf, *Brian Wilson*, CD booklet (Los Angeles: Warner Bros. Records & Rhino Entertainment, 2000), 4.

6 Leaf, 4.

7 Bellagio 10452 <http://www.btinternet .com/~bellagio/gigs87.html>.

8 Bellagio 10452 <http://www.btinternet .com/~bellagio/gigs87.html>.

9 Michael Goldberg, "God Only Knows," *Rolling Stone*, August 11, 1988: 56.

10 Goldberg, 52.

"Kokomo"

1 Scott Brown and Michael Endelman, "Kokomo," EW.com, May 28, 2004 <http://www.ew.com/ew/article/0,,640541_3,00.html>.

2 Wilson with Gold, 349.

3 "*Cocktail* (1988)," Box Office Mojo <http://www.boxofficemojo.com/movies/?id=cocktail.htm>.

4 *Good Vibrations: Thirty Years of The Beach Boys*, CD liner notes (Hollywood: Capitol Records, 1993).

5 DJ Funktual, "100 Worst Songs of All-Time Ever" <http://dj-funktual.hubpages.com/hub/100-Worst-Songs-of-All-Time>.

6 "Kokomo (song)," Wikipedia <http://en.wikipedia.org/wiki/Kokomo_(song)>.

"Still I Dream of It"

1 White, 353.

2 Wilson with Gold, 332.

3 White, 353.

4 David Wild, "Mike Love Sues Brian Wilson," *Rolling Stone*, October 1, 1992: 21.

5 White, 353.

6 Chris Mundy, "Random Notes," *Rolling Stone*, November 14, 1991: 13.

7 "Settlement Ends Beach Boys Feud," *Los Angeles Times*, Company Town Annex, December 21, 1994 <http://articles.latimes.com/1994-12-21/business/fi-11506_1_mike-love>.

8 Carlin, 280.

9 Carlin, 271.

10 Carlin, 223.

"Mrs. O'Leary's Cow"

1 Carlin, 294.

2 Carlin, 301.

3 Verlyn Klinkenborg, "Brian Wilson and the Significance of an Abandoned Masterpiece," *The New York Times*, September 18, 2004, Editorials/Op-Ed.

4 Barry Rehfeld, "When the Voices Took Over," *Rolling Stone*, June 6, 1985: 17.

5 Eric Aniversario, ed., Eric's Beach Boys Setlist Archive <http://members.tripod.com/~fun_fun_fun/2-20-04.html>.

"Midnight's Another Day"

1 "Brian Wilson premieres new 'song cycle' in London," *NME.com*, September 10, 2007 <http://www.nme.com/news/brian-wilson/31027>.

2 "That Lucky Old Sun," Metacritic <http://www.metacritic.com/music/that-lucky-old-sun/critic-reviews>.

"Rhapsody in Blue"

1 Mikael Wood, "Brian Wilson Reaches Back for 'Gershwin' project," Billboard.com, August 6, 2010 <http://www.billboard.com/features/brian-wilson-reaches-back-for-gershwin-project-1004108050.story#/features/brian-wilson-reaches-back-for-gershwin-project-1004108050.story>.

2 Mark Dillon, "His life's song," *Maclean's*, August

30, 2010: 64.

3 Dillon, 64–65.

4 White, 360.

5 Dillon, 64–65.

6 Dillon, 66.

7 Dillon, 65.

8 Amanda Marcotte, "The Internet Is The Beach Boys in 1963," *TPMCafé*, August 12, 2009 <http://tpm cafe.talkingpointsmemo.com/2009/08/12/the_ internet_is_the_beach_boys_in_1963/>.

9 Dillon, 66.

Acknowledgments

This book would not have been possible without the previous works of the authors cited in the endnotes. Their research and insights have provided the foundation for understanding the epic story of The Beach Boys. I also would like to mention Bret D. Wheadon's website The Beach Boys: The Complete Guide (Beach Boys.com), which aggregates media mentions of the band on a daily basis, documenting its ongoing pervasiveness in popular culture.

Session and release date information was compiled from various sources, including liner notes from the group's EMI/Capitol Records CD catalog. Brad Elliott's 1981 book *Surf's Up! The Beach Boys on Record 1961–1981* was a landmark piece of research, and Mr. Elliott continued his fine work both for Capitol and on his website (BradElliott.com). Keith Badman's *The Beach Boys: The Definitive Diary of America's Greatest Band on Stage and in the Studio* arrived in 2004 offering unprecedented detail of the band's first 15 years. Building on Mr. Badman's information is Andrew G. Doe's website Bellagio 10452 (www.btinternet.com/~bellagio/), which features contributions from many, especially Ian

Rusten. U.S. chart information was sourced from *Billboard* magazine, and U.K. data from The Official Charts Company (TheOfficial Charts.com). I would like to thank historians Ian Rusten, Alan Boyd, Mike Megaffin, Peter Reum and Craig Slowinski for answering my questions. I was also helped enormously by Bruce Johnston and authors David Leaf, Jon Stebbins and Peter Ames Carlin.

This project never would have gotten off the ground without the early support of Tara Parker and Michael Levine. Special mention goes to my agent Hilary McMahon for her tireless efforts. Thanks to Mark Halperin for his feedback every step of the way and to Peter Reum for his appraisal of my manuscript. I'm grateful to my neighbor Dave Gee for his beautiful design and to Rachel Ironstone for coordinating the visuals. Thanks to the rest of the great crew at ECW Press: Jack David for acquiring the book, David Caron, Michael Holmes, Jen Hale and Jennifer Knoch for their invaluable input, and Erin Creasey and Jenna Illies for their marketing and promotional savvy.

It takes a village to write a book, and this village is inhabited by citizens who have been most gracious of time and spirit. I humbly thank those who took the time to speak with me, and for their parts in making these interviews possible, thanks go to: Jean Sievers, Elliott Lott, Jay Jones, Jennifer Ballantyne, Charlotte Thompson, Carrie Marks, Mary Ann Jardine, David Bendett, Mike Megaffin, Toby Mamis, Camilla McGuinn, James Martin, Michele Harrison, William Berrol, David M. Beard, Lauren Auslander, Katie Kramer, Jennifer Allen, Renee Pfefer, Stephanie Hardman, Daniel Efram, Terry Anzaldo, Taryn Kaufman, Laure Dunham, Nils Bernstein, Kathy Henley, James Bailey, Andrew Coles, Laura Gardner, Renée Mellow and Aaron Wilhelm.

For their help with photos, thanks to: Ed Roach, Jarrett McGehee, Steve Levine, Hal Blaine, Mark Linett, Mike Eder, Xilonen Oreshnick, Dennis Diken, Christopher Bolger, Alan Boyd, Dean Torrence, Scott Totten, Jim Fusilli, Andrei Jackamets, Jace Lasek, Richmond Lam, Robert Schneider, Roger Ferguson, Rob Bonfiglio, Taryn Kaufman, Jill Jarrett, Mike Kowalski, Gregg Jakobson, Courtney Mabeus, Adam Marsland, Danielle Dauenhauer, Greg Laney, Russ Titelman, Allen Parker, Darian Sahanaja, Amy Rodrigue, Scott Bennett, George Dougherty, Andrew Kolb, Peter Bagge, Robert S. Nicksin, Paul Perrier and Tom Martin.

For their contributions along the way, I am indebted to Natasha Daneman, Chris Jackson, Sandy Hunter, Paul Whitelaw, Marc Hendrickx, Jeff Apter, Matthew Sweet, Robert Schneider, Jon Einarson, Billy Hinsche, Paul Dash, Walt Everett, Marc Glassman, Rob Bowman, Probyn Gregory, Sandy Brokaw, Sarmishta Subramanian and George Heon. Thanks to John Spencer for going on safari with me. Thanks to my parents, Arnold and Elizabeth, my brother, Arnold Jr., and to my cousin Tracy for introducing me to The Beach Boys.

I am grateful for the generous support of the Ontario Arts Council Writers' Reserve Program.

Last but not least, thanks to members of The Beach Boys for sharing their stories with me and for five decades of great music. Long may you surf.

INDEX

A

"Add Some Music to Your Day," xii,
182, 203, 226
Adult Child (unreleased album), 272–273
All-Star Tribute to Brian Wilson, An (TV
special), 151–152, 193, 198, 276
"All Summer Long," 37, 150, 217
All Summer Long (LP), 34, 35–37, 72
"Almost Summer," 227
American Graffiti (film), 37, 150, 217
Asher, Tony, 30, 89–96, 97–100, 108,
113, 114, 119,124, 127

B

Bachman, Randy, 242–247
"Barbara Ann," 11, 62, 74, 76, 78,
79–82, 83, 103
"Be My Baby," 16, 28, 29, 270
"Be True to Your School," xii, 10, 17, 18
Beach Boys, The: after Carl's death,
53–54, 173; after Dennis' death, 249;
50th anniversary tour and album
plans, ix, 8, 88, 293–295; honors and
awards, ix, 70, 209, 265, 283, 293;
record as Pendletones, xiii, xvii, xviii;
resurgence in mid-1970s, 217–219;
sign with Capitol Records, xix; sign
with CBS Records, 220; sign with
Warner Bros. Records, 182; touring
lineup in 1968, 170, 172; touring
lineup in 1974, 216; touring lineup in
new millennium, 88. *See also names
of albums, songs and band members*
Beach Boys, The (LP), 248–254, 255,
257
Beach Boys: An American Family, The
(miniseries), 58, 293
Beach Boys' Christmas Album, The, 39,
49, 71, 76, 234, 284
Beach Boys Concert (1964 LP), 39, 45,
76
Beach Boys in Concert, The (1973 LP),
53, 110, 173, 193, 213, 237
Beach Boys Love You, The, 32, 82,
229–234, 272
Beach Boys' Party!, 76, 79–81, 150, 236
Beach Boys '69. See *Live in London*
Beach Boys Today, The, 39, 42–43,
44–46, 49, 62, 74, 93, 105
Beach Boys: 25 Years Together, The (TV
special), 156, 198, 213
Beatles, The, ix, 12, 18, 30, 36, 40,
46, 64, 73, 157, 165, 179, 256;
admiration for Beach Boys, 73; Beach
Boys' admiration of, 16, 291–292;
Beach Boys influenced by, 20, 62–63,
79, 90–91, 187; Beach Boys' influence
on, 95, 101; rivalry with Beach Boys,
24, 34, 35, 37, 51, 70, 81, 117, 131,
133
Bennett, Scott, 275, 276, 283–288, 290
Berry, Chuck, xvi, 1–3, 11–12, 14, 23,
32, 40, 154, 170, 227, 243
Best of The Beach Boys, 43, 95
Best of The Beach Boys Vol. 2, x
Best of The Beach Boys Vol. 3, 71, 74,
181
Blaine, Hal, 16, 23–29, 31, 41, 46, 67,
69, 78, 80–81, 85, 94, 99, 109, 114,
226, 278
Boyd, Alan, 40, 42, 43, 132, 145, 190,
198, 243

"Break Away," xii, 177, 182
Brian Wilson (LP), 256–260
Brian Wilson Presents Pet Sounds Live,
122, 276
Brian Wilson Presents Smile, 127,
137–138, 140, 145, 147, 198–199,
275–283, 287
Brian Wilson Reimagines Gershwin,
289–292
Britz, Chuck, 13, 51, 68, 109, 131–132,
145
Brother Records, 40, 121, 134, 136, 154,
155, 160, 163, 176, 182, 207, 231
Brother Studio, 140, 222, 224, 228,
229, 240

C

"California Dreamin'," 32, 261
"California Girls," x, 12, 43, 62, 66–71,
73, 95, 127, 219, 246, 271, 293
"California Saga: California," 210, 212
Campbell, Glen, 42, 49, 63, 78, 94, 99,
117, 256
Candix, xviii–xix
Capitol Records, xix, 19–20, 39, 60,
130, 288; Beach Boys' relationship
with, 13, 53, 78, 81, 121, 179, 181–
182; handling of Beach Boys' catalog,
8, 43, 124, 147, 198, 217, 218, 269,
284, 293–295; promotion of Beach
Boys, 34, 57, 127, 131; reaction
to *Pet Sounds*, 95; release of Beach
Boys' records, 9, 14, 53, 62, 74, 76,
81, 100, 115, 182; sued by Beach
Boys, 132, 134, 182
Capp, Frank, 27, 72, 85, 94, 99, 109,
145
Caribou Ranch, 216–218, 220, 243

Caribou Records, 216, 220, 254

Carl & the Passions — "So Tough," xii, 208–209

Carl Wilson (LP), 220

"Caroline, No," 74, 91, 97–101, 122, 172, 193–194

Carter, Ed, 54, 169–170, 172, 191, 201, 216

CBS Records, 220, 231

Chaplin, Terence William "Blondie," 204, 206–214, 216

Chicago (band), 156, 215, 216, 218–219

"Child of Winter (Christmas Song)," 162, 213, 218

Christian, Roger, 9–10, 28–29

Classics: Selected by Brian Wilson, 151

Cocktail (film soundtrack), 261, 264, 266

Cole, Jerry, 67, 85, 109, 183

Columbia (recording studio), 69, 93, 115, 120, 125, 151

"Cool, Cool Water," 174, 179, 184, 185, 203

"Cotton Fields," xii, 166, 182, 212

Cowsill, John, 88, 173

D

Dale, Dick, xviii, 3, 4, 5, 85

"Dance, Dance, Dance," xii, 40, 46, 141, 148

"Darlin'," 119, 155–157

Desper, Stephen, 146, 169, 184, 188, 198, 201, 212

"Disney Girls (1957)," 201–203

"Do It Again," 168–173

"Do You Wanna Dance?," 44–47

"Don't Let the Sun Go Down on Me," 205, 217, 237

"Don't Worry Baby," x, 25, 28–32, 38, 45, 53, 243

Douglas, Steve, 25, 41, 46, 68, 85, 94, 100, 109, 119, 226

Dragon, Daryl, 170, 172, 178, 179, 202

Dragon, Dennis, 170, 173, 183, 201

Dragon, Doug, 169, 170

Dragon, Kathy, 170, 201

Dylan, Bob, ix, 4, 15, 31, 36, 70, 89, 120, 157, 258, 269, 293

E

Ed Sullivan Show, The, 34, 40, 170

EMI, 134, 293, 294

Endless Harmony Soundtrack, 43, 130, 198, 243

Endless Summer, 43, 63, 150, 213, 217, 218, 225, 284

F

"Farewell My Friend," 235, 240

Fataar, Ricky, xii, 172, 204, 206, 214

"Feel Flows," 191–194

15 Big Ones, 82, 222, 225–227, 229–231, 235, 254

Figueroa, Bobby, 54, 173, 216, 220

Flame, The, 172, 206–208, 211

"Forever," 174, 176, 177, 179–180, 184

Foskett, Jeffrey, 262, 275

Four Freshmen, The, xv, 1, 16, 93, 202

"409," xviii, xix, 9, 50

Four Seasons, The, 1, 18, 24, 120

"Friends," xii, 159, 168, 170

Friends (LP) 140–141, 161, 164–168, 184, 284

"Fun, Fun, Fun," 11, 23–25, 27, 83, 89, 219, 237

G

"Getcha Back," 251–254

Gettin' in Over My Head, 162, 276, 281

"Girl Don't Tell Me," 62–65, 183

Girls on the Beach, The (film), 35

"God Only Knows," 29, 91, 111, 113–118, 126, 167, 271

"Goin' On," 242–243

Going Public, 203

Gold Star (recording studio), 93, 109, 125, 130, 154, 178, 280

"Good Timin'," 218, 220, 221, 234

Good Timin': Live at Knebworth England 1980, 239, 244

"Good Vibrations," 102, 119, 121, 123–128, 130–132, 135, 140, 155, 166, 167, 170, 194, 227, 264, 294

Good Vibrations: Thirty Years of The Beach Boys (boxed set), 132, 140, 147, 151, 198, 273

Gordon, Jim, 27, 114, 278–279

Grammy Awards, ix, 127, 147, 193, 198, 205, 265, 282, 283, 294

Guercio, James "Jim," 215–221

H

Hawthorne, CA (LP), 43, 162, 178

"Help Me, Rhonda," x, 39, 48–55, 62, 71, 74, 122

"Here Today," 91, 119–120, 122

"Heroes and Villains," 53, 129–132, 134–137, 148, 208, 256, 276, 277

Hinsche, Billy, 54, 135, 212, 214, 216, 217, 230, 235–241

Hinsche, Otto "Pop," 235–237, 239–240

Holland, 105, 173, 184, 206, 209–214, 215, 222, 237

Honeys, The, xii, 4, 13, 24, 141
"Honkin' Down the Highway," 230, 231–232
Hutton, Danny, 21, 130, 153–158, 279–280

I

"I Can Hear Music," xii, 186
"I Get Around," x, 12, 28, 29, 34–38, 39, 40, 45, 95, 148, 246
"I Just Wasn't Made for These Times," 89, 91–95, 109
I Just Wasn't Made for These Times (soundtrack LP), 167, 260, 268
"I'm Bugged at My Ol' Man," 60–61
Imagination, 106, 275, 284
"In My Room," 14, 17–22, 45, 141, 197, 216, 271
Inside Pop: The Rock Revolution (TV special), 145–146
In the Key of Disney, 14, 289, 293
"It's Getting Late," 254
"It's OK," 222–224, 227

J

Jakobson, Gregg, 174–177, 179, 180, 235, 238
Jan & Dean, xvii, 8, 13, 24, 30, 40, 76–80, 82–83, 156
Jardine, Alan Charles "Al": compositions, 189, 209, 210, 226, 230, 234, 243, 250, 252; goes solo in 1998, 53–54; leaves Beach Boys in 1962, xviii; rejoins group in 1963, 4, 54; reunites with group in 2011–2012, 54, 293–294; upbringing, xvi; vocals, 48–50, 53, 146, 253, 263
"Johnny Carson" (song), 229, 232–233

Johnson, Plas, 46, 94, 99, 109, 124
Johnston, Bruce: career outside Beach Boys, 31, 32, 76, 203, 204–205, 249; compositions, 184, 200–202, 205, 243, 253; influence on band, 104, 169–170, 249; joins Beach Boys, 63; leaves group and returns, 204–205; productions, 215, 220, 234, 242; vocals, 69, 72–73, 88, 113, 115, 140, 180, 200, 217, 220, 237, 253, 263

K

Kalinich, Stephen, 159–163
Kaye, Carol, 41, 49, 66–70, 71–72, 85, 99, 114, 124, 145, 278
"Keepin' the Summer Alive," 242–246
Keepin' the Summer Alive (LP), 242–246
"Kiss Me, Baby," 39–43
"Kokomo," 261–267
Kowalski, Mike, 169–170, 172, 173, 207

L

L.A. (Light Album), 205, 215, 220, 234
Landy, Dr. Eugene, 230, 268; Brian's reaction to death of, 284; ends treatment of and relationship with Brian, 259, 270; influence on Brian's solo career, 255, 257–259, 268, 269; interference on Beach Boys recordings, 230, 250, 264, 266; therapeutic treatment of Brian, 224–225, 229, 233, 248–249, 269, 271;
Leaf, David, x–xi, xv, 66, 98, 100, 125, 147, 195–199, 235
Lennon, John, 21, 58, 63, 73, 89, 165, 217, 291
"Let's Go Away for Awhile," 87, 102–104

Levine, Steve, 248–254, 257
Linett, Mark, 43, 109, 110, 132, 144–148, 190, 198, 282
"Little Bird," 159–161, 163
"Little Deuce Coupe," xii, 14, 29, 216
Little Deuce Coupe (LP), 5, 9, 10
"Little Girl I Once Knew, The," 71–75, 81, 86, 125
"Little Honda," 35, 36, 143, 165
"Little Saint Nick," 39
Live Aid, 254
Live 8, 283
Live at the Roxy Theatre (Brian Wilson LP), 43, 75, 157, 198, 290
Live in London, x, 110, 157, 172, 182
"Long Promised Road," 186–190, 191, 195
"Love and Mercy," 255, 256, 258, 259–260, 264
Love, Michael Edward "Mike": as front man, 12, 213, 245, 267; Dennis and, 83, 226–227, 248; issues with Brian's songs, 94–95, 131, 262–263, 272; lyrics, 23–24, 34, 36, 39–40, 48, 69, 72, 108, 126, 155, 164, 165, 168, 210, 223, 225, 242, 251, 262; sues Brian, 270; Transcendental Meditation and, 160, 165, 184, 209, 210, 240, 263; upbringing, xvi; vocals, 2, 9, 12, 23, 36, 42, 69, 72, 80, 84, 108, 110, 120, 126, 129, 149, 166, 168, 227, 232, 243–244, 252, 263, 293
Love, Stan, 233, 270, 272
Love, Stephen, 213–214, 216, 228, 250

M

Maharishi Mahesh Yogi, 160, 165, 168,

175, 226, 263

Mamas & the Papas, The, 27, 46, 86, 140, 142, 261, 262

Mankey, Earle, 190, 222–228, 229

Manson, Charles, 174–179

"Marcella," 173, 208, 245

Marks, David Lee: as guitarist, xv, xviii, 1–2, 4; health issues, 8; joins Beach Boys, xviii; post–Beach Boys career, 6–8, 83; quits group, 4–6; reunites for 50th anniversary, 8, 294; second stint with group, 8

McCartney, Paul, 22, 34, 73, 89, 95, 133, 162, 165, 207, 230, 286, 291

McGuinn, Roger, 29–33, 230

"Meant for You," 164, 166–167

Melcher, Terry, 31; Beach Boys and, 32, 115, 120, 248, 251, 252, 261, 262, 264, 270; Bruce Johnston and, 174, 203, 204, 205; Charles Manson and, 176, 178

Mertens, Paul Von, 275, 287, 289, 291

"Midnight's Another Day," 286–287

Migliori, Jay, 25, 41, 46, 68, 94, 99, 109, 226

M.I.U. Album, 173, 234

Moffitt, Steve, 209, 223

Monterey International Pop Music Festival, 121–122

Morgan, Hite and Dorinda, xvi–xix, 14, 85

"Mount Vernon and Fairway (A Fairy Tale)," 210

"Mrs. O'Leary's Cow," 275, 278–282

N

Nonesuch Records, 282

O

O'Hagan, Sean, 103–107

"Our Prayer," 139–142, 276, 281

P

Pacific Ocean Blue, xii, 82, 163, 174, 220, 235, 238, 239–241, 293

Paley, Andy, 147, 198, 256, 273

Parks, Van Dyke: involvement on *Brian Wilson Presents Smile*, 147, 151, 278; involvement on "Sail on Sailor," 206, 211, 212; later collaborations with Brian, 285–286, 290; leaves *Smile* project, 132; Mike Love's thoughts on, 131, 262–263; writing lyrics for *Smile*, 124–125, 129–131, 133, 138, 143, 144, 149, 151, 196, 278, 286

Pet Sounds: acclaim for, xii, 95, 103–105, 121, 122, 131, 150, 185, 193; Capitol Records' handling of, 95, 115, 181; commercial reception, 10, 62, 126; lyrical themes, 74, 86, 91, 99, 101, 108–109, 114, 119, 187–188, 272; Mike Love's feelings about, 94–95, 100; recording of, 25, 71, 86, 93–94, 99–100, 102, 109, 110, 114–115, 119–120, 147, 259; writing of, 89–93, 97–99, 103, 108, 113, 119, 123

Pet Sounds Sessions, The (boxed set), 86, 99, 100, 109, 110, 115, 121, 125, 147, 148, 198

Phillips, John, 140, 261, 262

Pohlman, Ray, 25, 41, 67, 94, 119, 124, 183, 226

Postcard from California, A, 54

R

Randi, Don, 71–72, 94, 115, 120

Redwood, 155–157

"Rhapsody in Blue," xiv, 28, 270, 289–290

Rieley, Jack, 147, 186–187, 191, 204, 206, 208, 209, 210, 212, 213

Rock and Roll Hall of Fame, ix, 255

"Rock and Roll Music," 32, 227, 264

Rolling Stones, The, 38, 40, 95, 120, 157, 165, 193, 209, 213, 269, 292

Roth, David Lee, 70, 254

Rovell, Diane, 13, 26, 108, 115, 155, 183, 184, 206

Royal Festival Hall, 276, 281, 285

S

Sahanaja, Darian, xi, 275–282, 287

"Sail on Sailor," 106, 151, 206, 211–214, 239

Sgt. Pepper's Lonely Hearts Club Band, 95, 101, 133

"Shut Down," 3, 5, 9–12, 29, 165

Shut Down Volume 2, 23, 28, 29, 34, 35, 244

"Slip on Through," 47, 181, 183, 184, 185

"Sloop John B," 76, 84–88, 99, 100, 129

Smile, xi, xii, 125, 127, 135–137, 145, 172, 276, 281; abandoned, 132, 134, 145, 150, 280; bootlegs, 137, 147, 269; Brian's later aversion to, 137, 140, 146, 276; Brian's paranoid behavior during recording, 132–134; group revisits songs, 140, 146–147; lyrical themes, 129–132, 139, 143, 144, 151, 232, 277–278, 286, 290;

recording of, 25, 130, 131, 133, 134, 154, 160

Smile Sessions, The (boxed set), 125, 132, 134, 136–138, 145, 147, 148, 293

Smiley Smile, 81, 121, 123–125, 127, 129, 131, 134, 135, 149–151, 153, 154, 157, 273, 280

Sounds of Summer, 193, 284

Spector, Phil, 13, 16, 24, 25, 27–29, 53, 67, 78, 81, 102, 132, 135, 155, 183, 251

Spirit of America (LP), 74, 218

Spring (group), xii, 141, 162

Spring (LP), 155, 179, 184, 206

Stamos, John, 58, 88, 180, 264, 266, 270, 293

Stars and Stripes Vol. 1, 21, 100, 104, 294

Still Cruisin', 261, 266

"Still I Dream of It," 268, 272–273

Summer Days (And Summer Nights!!), 48, 51–53, 55, 60, 62–63, 66

Summer Dreams: The Story of The Beach Boys (TV movie), 58, 269

Summer in Paradise, 32, 180, 270

Sunflower, 105, 146, 174, 179, 181, 184, 185, 189, 203, 230, 234, 254

"Surf City," 13, 14, 27, 78

"Surf's Up," x, 140, 143–147, 196–199, 208, 276, 282, 286, 287

Surf's Up (LP), xii, 172, 186, 189–191, 193, 195, 196, 198, 200, 202–204, 206, 209, 288

"Surfer Girl," 13–16, 18, 53, 89, 218, 294

Surfer Girl (LP), 13, 14, 17, 20, 50

"Surfin'," xvii–xix, 44, 77

"Surfin' Safari," xviii–xix, 20, 77, 95, 217

Surfin' Safari (LP), xix, 4, 7, 35, 45, 232

"Surfin' U.S.A.," xi, 1–3, 5, 8–10, 14, 62, 77–78, 237

Surfin' U.S.A. (LP), 2–4, 9, 10, 13, 17, 288

Sweet Insanity (unreleased Brian album), 269

T

T.A.M.I. Show, The (film), 40

Tanner, Paul, 94, 124, 153

That Lucky Old Sun (LP), 283–288, 290

"This Whole World," 181, 183–184

Thomas, Joe, 106–107, 275

Three Dog Night, 157–158

"'Til I Die," 195–199, 204

Titelman, Russ, 255–260

Torrence, Dean, 8, 76–83, 173, 231

Totten, Scott, 85–88

20/20, 139, 140, 157, 168, 171, 177, 182

Two Lane Blacktop, 162–163

U

Usher, Gary, 4, 9, 17, 20, 31, 57, 60, 255, 258

V

Venet, Nick, xix, 1, 2, 9, 20

W

Walt Disney Records, 289, 291

Warmth of the Sun, The (LP), 193, 227

Warner Bros. Records, 20, 179, 182–184, 189, 198, 210–212, 220, 231–232, 256, 259

Was, Don, 269, 271–274

Western Studio, xviii, 13, 25, 29, 41, 42, 66, 71, 79, 89, 93, 109, 114, 125, 145, 151, 154

What I Really Want for Christmas, 283–284

"When I Grow Up (To Be a Man)," xii, 25, 39–40, 170

"Wild Honey," xii, 153–154, 208

Wild Honey (LP), 153–157, 161, 168, 189, 234

Wilson, Audree Korthof, xiv, xv, xvii, 17, 41, 59, 51, 55–56, 123, 185, 270, 271

Wilson, Brian Douglas: awards, 114, 282, 283, 291; becomes Beach Boys' official producer, 13; childhood, xiv–xvi, 92; drug use, 30, 32, 68, 91, 98, 130, 132, 139, 158, 225, 242; lawsuit against A&M Records, 269, 270; musical influences, xiv–xvii, 1, 2, 13, 18, 28, 48, 62–63, 66, 93, 102, 113, 142, 154, 256, 290; psychological issues, xv, 20–21, 41–42, 132–134, 158, 210, 222, 224–225, 242, 248, 269–271, 280, 284; pulls away from group, 16, 20–21, 146, 157, 185, 186, 209, 233–234, 242, 243; quits touring with Beach Boys, 4–5, 41; rehabilitation, 224–225, 229, 248–249, 255, 270–271, 295; returns to active Beach Boys duty, 225–228, 249–250; solo career, 255–260, 268–269, 271–272, 275–282, 283–288, 289–293; women and, 2, 13, 29, 40–41, 48, 97–98, 108, 268, 271, 272

Wilson, Carl Dean: as band leader,

42, 88, 186, 190, 192, 204, 208,
213, 292; cancer and death of, 8,
173, 271, 273; childhood, xv–xvi;
compositions and productions, 63,
169, 176, 186–190, 191–194, 195,
207, 210, 212, 218, 242–245,
253, 254; guitar playing, xv, xvi,
xviii, 1–2, 4, 5, 20, 23, 40, 46, 49,
63, 67, 124, 170, 186, 191, 208,
236; marriages, 135, 236, 240, 262;
spirituality, 115, 121, 126, 191, 247;
vocals, 64, 86–87, 115, 126, 146,
149, 156, 183, 186, 191, 220, 242,
254, 262
Wilson, Carnie, 54, 140–142, 163, 268,
272, 284
Wilson, Dennis Carl: Charles Manson
and, 174–179; childhood, xv;
compositions and productions, 47,
159–163, 174–180, 183–185, 186,
235, 239–241; death, 249; drug and
alcohol problems, 83, 161, 163, 175,
179, 240, 248–249; drumming, xvii,
xviii, 3, 11, 15–16, 24, 25, 46, 63,
169, 218, 246, 248; vocals, 44–47,
126, 161, 178, 212, 227, 239, 240;
wives and girlfriends, 176, 177–178,
219, 240, 246, 248; womanizing, xv,
16, 161, 175, 177, 238
Wilson, Melinda (Ledbetter), 106, 118,
137, 268, 271, 275, 276, 282, 285,
291
Wilson, Murry Gage: as Beach Boys'
publisher, 55–57, 69, 162, 269–270;
at "Help Me, Rhonda" session,
49–51; beating of sons, xv, 56;
death, 61, 215, 235; helping launch
sons' careers, xvi, xviii, xix, 20, 57;
marriage, xiv, 55–56; power struggle
with Brian, 5, 23, 26, 35, 51, 57, 60,
78; upbringing, xiii–xiv
Wilson, Wendy, 54, 140–141, 163, 268,
270, 272
Wilson–Rutherford, Marilyn (Rovell), xii
as Brian's muse, 29, 72, 98, 151
concern over Brian's behavior, 30, 42,
158, 224–225, 242, 248; marriage to
Brian, 21, 40, 41, 242, 272; singing
career, 13, 115, 141, 147, 155, 183,
184, 206
"Wipe Out," 266
Wonder, Stevie, 153–154, 252, 272
"Wonderful," 135, 149–151
"Wouldn't It Be Nice," 53, 91, 99, 108–
112, 113, 115, 132

Y

"You Are So Beautiful," 239

Mark Dillon is a Toronto-based freelance journalist and writer. He is the former editor of *Playback*, the business publication of the Canadian film and TV industries. His articles have also appeared in *Maclean's*, the *Globe and Mail*, the *Hollywood Reporter*, and *American Cinematographer*.

At ECW Press, we want you to enjoy this book in whatever format you like, whenever you like. Leave your print book at home and take the eBook to go! Purchase the print edition and receive the eBook free. Just send an email to ebook@ecwpress.com and include:

• the book title
• the name of the store where you purchased it
• your receipt number
• your preference of file type: PDF or ePub?

A real person will respond to your email with your eBook attached. Thank you for supporting an independently owned Canadian publisher with your purchase!